T4-ADA-410

Intersecting Diasporas

SUNY series in Italian/American Culture

Fred L. Gardaphé, editor

Intersecting Diasporas

Italian Americans and Allyship in US Fiction

SUZANNE MANIZZA ROSZAK

SUNY PRESS

Cover: James McNeill Whistler, *Variations in Violet and Grey—Market Place, Dieppe* (1885). Metropolitan Museum of Art.

Published by State University of New York Press, Albany

© 2021 State University of New York

All rights reserved

Printed in the United States of America

No part of this book may be used or reproduced in any manner whatsoever without written permission. No part of this book may be stored in a retrieval system or transmitted in any form or by any means including electronic, electrostatic, magnetic tape, mechanical, photocopying, recording, or otherwise without the prior permission in writing of the publisher.

For information, contact State University of New York Press, Albany, NY
www.sunypress.edu

Library of Congress Cataloging-in-Publication Data

Name: Manizza Roszak, Suzanne, 1985– author.
Title: Intersecting diasporas : Italian Americans and allyship in US fiction / Suzanne Manizza Roszak.
Description: Albany : State University of New York, [2021] | Series: SUNY series in Italian/American culture | Includes bibliographical references.
Identifiers: LCCN 2020039943 (print) | LCCN 2020039944 (ebook) | ISBN 9781438481616 (hardcover : alk. paper) | ISBN 9781438481630 (ebook)
Subjects: LCSH: American fiction—Italian American authors—History and criticism. | American fiction—Minority authors—History and criticism. | American fiction—20th century—History and criticism. | Italian Americans in literature. | Ethnic groups in literature. | Social justice in literature. | Whites—Race identity—United States. | United States—Ethnic relations—20th century.
Classification: LCC PS153.I8 M35 2021 (print) | LCC PS153.I8 (ebook) | DDC 813/.509352951—dc23
LC record available at https://lccn.loc.gov/2020039943
LC ebook record available at https://lccn.loc.gov/2020039944

10 9 8 7 6 5 4 3 2 1

To Jonny and Sander

Contents

ACKNOWLEDGMENTS ix

INTRODUCTION 1

Part I. Representational Roots

CHAPTER 1
Romance, Liberation, and Peril: Representing Italian Identities
from Outside the Diaspora(s) 19

Part II. Diasporic Writers on Italian America

CHAPTER 2
Sex and Diaspora in the New "Italian Novel": James Baldwin
and Bernard Malamud 49

CHAPTER 3
Privileged Italians, Poor Italians: Carolina De Robertis,
Chang-rae Lee, and Italy in the Americas 75

Part III. Returning the Favor: Italian Americans Write Back

CHAPTER 4
"Mayan Queens," Secondhand Suits, and Toxic White
Masculinity: Fante and DeLillo 109

CHAPTER 5
Off-White Allies: Writing Irish and Romani Women's Lives
from Puzo to De Rosa   145

CONCLUSION
The Limits of Allyship: Returning to Italy with *A Ciambra*   177

NOTES   183

BIBLIOGRAPHY   197

INDEX   211

Acknowledgments

So many people participated in the creation process for this book. I am deeply grateful for the support of the many mentors who saw me through graduate school and beyond, especially Wai Chee Dimock, Arlene R. Keizer, Julia H. Lee, and Katie Trumpener. At the Italian American Studies Association, Fred Gardaphé and Alan Gravano encouraged my research and writing when I was still working as an adjunct, teaching all across Southern California while developing new parts of this manuscript. I am indebted to Stephen Cooper and Clorinda Donato for their wisdom about Fante and for their confidence in me. To Edvige Giunta and Dennis Barone: you may not remember our brief conversations, but your work has been formative in shaping my perspective in this book. The same is true of Mary Jo Bona, Joseph P. Cosco, and Samuele F. S. Pardini, though we haven't yet met in person. Perhaps most importantly, thanks are due to my brilliant friends and collaborators, Dana Murphy and K. Adele Okoli, whose scholarship is perennially inspiring.

My readings of so many of the texts that have a place in this book have been indelibly shaped by my teaching. My heartfelt thanks go out to my students at California State University, San Bernardino; Occidental College; and Scripps College, whose fresh readings of Henry James, James Baldwin, John Fante, and others have all been inspirational. I am equally indebted to the generous department chairs and program directors at those colleges and universities who were willing to take a chance on a new and eager teacher: Kimberly Drake, Sunny Hyon, and John Swift.

The faculty of the English department at East Carolina University played an essential role in helping me see this project through to its completion. Thanks especially to Su-ching Huang, Gera Miles, Marianne Montgomery, Carla Pastor, and Rick Taylor, as well as to the Thomas

Harriot College of Arts and Sciences for its financial support of this project in its final stages. To my students at ECU: thank you for your brilliant readings of multiethnic American literature.

A brief excerpt from chapter 1 appears in my book chapter in *Rethinking Empathy through Literature*. A previous version of chapter 2 was published in *Arizona Quarterly*, together with another short passage from chapter 1, and a previous version of part of chapter 4 appeared in *Studies in the Novel*.

This book simply would not exist without the faith and encouragement of my husband, Jonny. To Sander, my wonderful toddler son—you should know that this manuscript might have languished unpublished if it weren't for the inspiration and energy generated by your birth. I am unspeakably lucky and am so grateful to you both.

Introduction

The spring of 2019 would bring a formal Proclamation of Apology from the city of New Orleans for an infamous act of violence that had occurred there more than a century before: the March 14, 1891 murder of eleven Italian Americans by an angry mob at the city jail. As those who are familiar with this event know well, the victims had been accused of killing the city's police chief. None had been convicted, however; in fact, some had been acquitted and should already have been released. It was particularly significant that the individual who shouldered the burden of apologizing for these crimes was Mayor LaToya Cantrell, the first African American woman to hold the position. Given the much more widespread history of racial violence against African Americans in that same period in the history of Louisiana and the United States more broadly, the apology had fraught implications that both complicated and deepened the significance of this moment of reconciliation. Read in this context, Cantrell's statement about the attack—which she described as "an act of anti-immigrant violence" from one of the "serious and dark chapters" in the city's history—can be understood as a painful and complex act of solidarity across two diasporic communities whose American identities have been diversely shaped by experiences of displacement, alienation, accommodation, and resistance (qtd. in Katz).

This book traces reciprocal expressions of this sort of allyship across modern and contemporary American literature, where writers from the Italian diasporic community in the United States have joined with writers from other diasporas in the work of telling one another's stories: deconstructing stereotypes, testifying to injustices that have been perpetrated against them, and guarding against identity loss in an assimilationist America. In the process, this book addresses a series of questions. How have authors from other diasporas written in solidarity with Italian America, with writers from James Baldwin and Bernard Malamud to Carolina De Robertis and Chang-rae Lee disrupting stereotypical visions of Italian and Italian American identity even as they confront Italians' own complicity with white racism? In turn, how have Italian American writers like John Fante and Tina De Rosa written in solidarity with Black, Chicanx, Jewish, Romani, and other diasporic communities on US shores, unsettling stereotypes and dissecting Italian America's history of flawed allyship across diasporas? And how do these gestures of literary solidarity dovetail with other forms of social protest: moments in each text when the writers' critiques of toxic masculinity, antiqueerness, and socioeconomic injustice come to the fore? In examining these questions, *Intersecting Diasporas* traces the tenuous gestures of allyship that emerge between Italian Americans and these other groups in modern and contemporary US fiction as they represent one another's struggles to carve out a life in the United States.

Defining Terms: From Diaspora to *Italianità*

In his 1991 article "Diasporas in Modern Societies: Myths of Homeland and Return," William Safran argued that only the Jewish diaspora could genuinely qualify as "the ideal type" or could fit the most traditional pattern of diasporic experience—although he also suggested that the "Armenian, Maghrebi, Turkish, Palestinian, Cuban, Greek, and perhaps Chinese diasporas" could be "legitimately" understood as diasporic based on a typology of six features of diaspora (84). Before more than a few years had passed, other theorists such as James Clifford began to actively assert the need for a more inclusive definition of the term, arguing that "we should be wary of constructing our working definition of a term like *diaspora* by recourse to an 'ideal type,' with the consequence that groups become identified as more or less diasporic. . . . Even the 'pure' forms [e.g., the Jewish diaspora]," Clifford suggested, "are ambivalent, even embattled, over basic features" (306). This more variegated vision of what a diasporic community might look like or how its traits might be expressed has fueled a diasporic turn in Italian American studies, as in so many other fields of ethnic history, literature, and culture. In a sense, it is what has made this book possible.

Still, there are individual ideas from Safran as well as from Clifford and others that are profoundly relevant to the interdiasporic conversations that are scrutinized in these pages. Despite their diversity, experiences of diaspora include central elements that distinguish them from other paradigms of migration. As Clifford testifies, these include multigenerational histories of traumatic, violent dislocation and scattering and half-measures of "selective accommodation" to new environments (307). As Safran has noted, they include the experience of group identification across geographically isolated spaces based on collective histories, as well as challenging encounters with social alienation and estrangement from those in their adopted homes who do not share these histories, and a desire to return home "when conditions are appropriate" (83–84). These experiences are often equally punctuated or heightened by the difficulty or even the impossibility of return, which Stuart Hall famously describes in his essay "Cultural Identity and Diaspora." As diaspora theory has matured beyond a restrictive definitional approach—its earlier obsession with limiting what counts as a diaspora to preserve the purity of the concept—understanding this particular combination of complexities has become more and more essential. It is especially important to understanding the narratives in this book and to grasping the work that they do across diasporas.

At the same time, the term *allyship*, as it has emerged in social justice circles, is itself fraught with controversy. For some, this term has become synonymous with temporary, superficially performative, overly conciliatory, exploitative, or otherwise empty and ineffective forms of support for marginalized communities. In contrast, in using this word, this book draws on the work of activists like Jamaican American blogger Amélie Lamont, whose online *Guide to Allyship* reminds readers that "[a] marginalized individual cannot easily cast away the weight of their identity through oppression on a whim. They must carry that weight every single day. . . . An ally understands that this is a weight that they too must be willing to carry and never put down." For the writers in this book, allyship is a true expression and embodiment of solidarity rather than a weaker alternative to it. It is essentially what Indigenous Action Media, in its article "Accomplices Not Allies: Abolishing the Ally Industrial Complex," calls being an "accomplice" in suggesting that the "work of an accomplice in anti-colonial struggle is to attack colonial structures & ideas." This is precisely what authors from James Baldwin to Tina De Rosa do with the structures of racism as they work to deconstruct ideologies and institutions that have had intensely negative, sometimes deadly reverberations across diasporic communities outside their own.

Allyship in the forms explored here is clearly far from being the sole province of white people, as it is sometimes treated in its less radical permutations. It is also subversively reciprocal rather than condescendingly one-directional, demanding a degree of real cohesion and collaboration—no matter how diffusely both of these may occur as books are written, published, and read across diasporas—as well as the recognition of crucial differences in each community's experiences of struggle and the rejection of false equivalences across diasporic boundaries. When understood in this more radical way, allyship is a deeply rooted condition or state of being, as the etymology of the word suggests. Talking about both alliances and allyship, as I do in the chapters that follow, makes it possible to emphasize not just the shared product of these writers' reciprocal representations (the alliances themselves), but also the individual condition that each writer inhabits (the spirit of allyship that the author embodies and shows to others, even if sometimes unwittingly, through their work). Finally, it is worth noting that the reciprocal approach to allyship displayed by diasporic writers of color toward Italian Americans sometimes takes the form of a sort of calling to account or "tough love." In the hands of contemporary novelists like Chang-rae Lee and even sometimes in the earlier texts, allyship manifests less as a vindication of *italianità* or an exploration of anti-Italian sentiment than as an exhortation to remember the history of these things before their disappearance from memory makes the Italian diasporic community into the oppressors themselves, giving them a role that some Italian Americans have already long embraced in an attempt to assert themselves as less ambiguously white. What support and solidarity look like in narratives written across intersecting diasporas can therefore vary widely according to the communities' evolving positions in the adopted homeland they all share—though what remains constant is the literary work of "carry[ing] that weight."

Even the concept of *italianità* is somewhat embattled, complicated as it is by the uneasy sense that a clearly Italian national identity had not quite been established before so many Italian immigrants began to arrive in the United States, given the timing of Italy's unification and the marginalization of the southern Italians who made up such a large portion of those displaced from Italy after a certain point. In the introduction to their book *From the Margin: Writings in Italian Americana*, Tamburri,

Giordano, and Gardaphé propose a way of defining Italianness that may be especially useful here:

> *Italianità* is indeed a term expressive of many notions, ideas, feelings, and sentiments. To be sure, it is any and all of these things that lead young Italian Americans back to their real and mythical images of the land, the way of life, the values, and the cultural trappings of their ancestors. It could be language, food, a way of determining life values, a familial structure, a sense of religion; it could be all of these and certainly much more. (6)

This willingness to recognize the "mythical" in self-constructions of *italianità* within the diaspora is critical, as it makes possible some modes of reading that might otherwise escape us: especially readings that privilege diasporic longing for a lost and imagined homeland among later generations of immigrants rather than treating that longing impulse as suspect because it seems less grounded in the "real." Simultaneously, an important question is how externally imposed constructions of *italianità*, as it was differently imagined by Anglo-American observers and imaginers of Italian culture, were reflected in and shaped American literary and social history.

Recalling Histories

When Italian America is included in comparative diaspora studies as I have suggested above, it becomes important to acknowledge the historically tenuous position of Italian Americans between the realm of the marginalized and that of the oppressor: something that scholars in ethnic studies and Italian American studies in particular have been thinking about for decades. Italian American identity has continued to exist uncomfortably between census categories long after what A. Robert Lee calls the "figural transformation . . . of imputed Mediterranean darkness into American whiteness" (247). Thomas A. Guglielmo and others have at length considered the contributions of white privilege to the experiences of Italians in the United States, beginning with the privilege of citizenship itself as a benefit of whiteness. As Guglielmo notes, those Italian Americans who claim that they or their ancestors in the US pulled themselves up by their bootstraps as immigrants without government assistance are missing the fact that their "whiteness—conferred more powerfully by the federal government than by any other institution" through the benefit of citizenship and their legal status as white people—"was their single most powerful asset in the 'New World': it gave them countless advantages over 'nonwhites' in housing, jobs, schools, politics, and virtually every other meaningful area of life" (42–43). To put it another way, "the new [Italian] immigrant could claim whiteness via naturalization and naturalization via whiteness" (*Working Toward Whiteness* 121).

This is not to say that the social understanding of Italians on American soil as white did not shift and develop as time went on. In *Whiteness of a Different Color*, Matthew Frye Jacobson recalls how in a "period of volatile racial meanings" beginning in the last few decades of the nineteenth century, "people such as Celts, Italians, Hebrews and Slavs" became "less and less white in debates over who should be allowed to disembark on American shores, and yet were becoming whiter and whiter in debates over who should be granted the full rights of citizenship" (75). Yet even here we can see how a linear narrative of Italians moving from nonwhite status to the benefits of whiteness is too simplifying to capture the full complexities of Italian Americans' position in their adopted homeland. In some ways, we can argue that Italians in the United States were what Guglielmo has termed "white on arrival," or WOA (qtd. in *Working Toward Whiteness* 110). In other ways, that designation ebbed and flowed as the decades went on, and many recognized that there was something different about Italian American culture, a set of "ways of being and acting both publicly and in the private sphere" that made *italianità* "a hybrid body" (Pardini 82).

A strong current of racial prejudice did influence these developments, which coincided not just with the rise of social Darwinism in general but with specifically Italian ideas about the racial identities of the southern Italians who became so central within the Italian diasporic community in the US. In Italy, the process of unification had been accompanied by an elitist impulse that had emphasized the contributions of classical Italian civilization to the cultural makeup of the Western world while denying the rightful membership of working-class laborers and essentially anyone from the south of the country in this new state. If Italy's "earliest nationalists were romantics who imagined the Italian nation as the descendants and reproducers of a distinctive Italian culture or civilization (*civiltà*) that included medieval and Renaissance art, literature, urbanity, technology, and philosophy," it is perhaps unsurprising that these "romantic nationalists viewed Italy's vast population of peasants as firmly outside the nation" (Gabaccia 50). Meanwhile, the postunification atmosphere of the late nineteenth century became marked by a heightened awareness of the geographic, cultural, and class distinctions between north and south as positivist anthropologists peddled racist ideas about the supposedly distinct racial composition of each region, including "scientific 'proof' that southern Italians were racially distinct from and hopelessly inferior to their northern compatriots," in no small part because of their supposedly "inferior African blood" (T. Guglielmo 33).

Fleeing the proliferation of such attitudes, members of the Italian diaspora in the United States met with similarly pseudoscientific attitudes on the part of Americans who objected to their presence on primarily racial grounds. David R. Roediger reminds us that in the late nineteenth century, Ivy League professor Francis Amasa Walker referred to "southern and eastern European immigrants [as] 'beaten men of beaten races,'" while the question of "whether Italians were 'full-blooded Caucasians'" shaped the 1912 congressional hearings on immigration, and Italians were looked on with suspicion for their supposed "biological powers . . . to effect a kind of conquest by procreation" in their newly chosen home (*Working Toward Whiteness* 66–67, 80). In American popular culture and daily life, these ways of racializing Italianness translated into acts of violence like the one referenced at the start of this introduction, which, as Jacobson notes, the *New York Times* flatly refused to admit had been racially motivated. They also led to discrimination against Italians in employment contexts, where a white foreman in a Pennsylvanian mining town might beckon an Italian laborer by saying, "Hey Dago, come here," spurring "sharp resentment," or where an Italian might not be able to find employment at all on the waterfront in Boston due to "the erection of color bars against 'blacks,' meaning both African American and Italian American workers" (*Working toward Whiteness* 75, 87).

Jennifer Guglielmo enumerates a range of additional contexts where the Othering of Italian Americans was historically visible, including

> the refusal of some native-born Americans to ride streetcars with or live alongside "lousy dagoes"; the exclusion of Italian children from certain schools and movie theaters, and their parents from social groups and labor unions; segregated seating

in some churches; and the barrage of popular magazines, books, movies, and newspapers that bombarded Americans with images of Italians as racially suspect. (11)

While recognizing this history is critical, it is simultaneously essential to understand how these challenges of racialization and discrimination paled in comparison with those experienced by people of color in the United States—and to what extent individuals of Italian descent not only benefited from but actively participated in upholding the structures of white supremacy during this time. The instances cataloged by Guglielmo were occasional rather than systemic and socially grounded rather than legally codified, two important distinctions that changed the tenor of Italian Americans' experiences in their adopted homeland. It also appears that the temptation to consolidate or deepen their status as white people may have been too great for some members of the diasporic community, who would ultimately use their participation in white racism to more fully assert their white identities.

Historically, many Italian Americans sought to identify with a white supremacist culture that seemed better poised to provide them with social power in their adopted home, although that culture had historically questioned the validity of Italians' own claims to whiteness. Into the latter decades of the twentieth century and beyond, Italian Americans repeatedly perpetrated acts of physical, social, and political violence against people of color and perpetuated dysfunctional fictions of white superiority that served to consolidate institutional structures of racism in this country. In the 1919 Chicago race riots, while Italian Americans had been "apparently underrepresented" among the white perpetrators, they nevertheless represented a substantial portion of those involved (*Working Toward Whiteness* 128). In 1942, the Italian American mayor of New York City allowed the exclusion of Japanese Americans from the New York at War procession, showing a clear breach of solidarity at a time when Italians were receiving vastly preferential treatment from the US government relative to Japanese Americans despite both groups' connections "by ancestry" to the Axis powers (241). Around the same time, one issue of a Fisk University–sponsored journal titled *A Monthly Summary of Events and Trends in Race Relations* noted the backlash among Italian Americans in a Chicago neighborhood where a Jewish landlord had begun renting to Black tenants, including the sentiment held by some residents that "a Jewish real estate man was attempting to cause the deterioration of an

Italian neighborhood by deliberately introducing Negro residents" (qtd. in Jacobson 114). And in 1980s and 1990s New York and Chicago, arguably little had changed since the 1910s: not only were there repeated incidents of racial violence in which perpetrators of Italian descent targeted, beat, and in some cases murdered African American children and young adults, but the attempts of both African American and Italian American protestors to bring attention to two such incidents in New York were met with harassment by Italian American onlookers who hurled "racial slurs" at those speaking out (J. Guglielmo 7).

Still, the antiracist efforts of some Italian Americans gestured toward another potential way of being and toward the possibility of allyship across diasporas. The Italian diaspora placed new bodies in American streets, a largely working-class community of protestors with a developing commitment to eradicating abuses against Black citizens of the US and other diasporic people of color. In his essay "*I Delitti della Razza Bianca* (Crimes of the White Race)," Salvatore Salerno highlights the contributions of Italian American anarchists to the antiracist discourse of the early-twentieth-century United States, where groups like L'Era Nuova published newspaper articles protesting the hypocrisy of an America that could claim itself to be the "land of the free and the home of the brave" at the same time as it was "a crime to kill a dog but an honor to lynch a Negro" (qtd. in 117). For their supposed crimes as racial traitors, Salerno reminds us, groups like L'Era Nuova were targeted by the Justice Department in addition to the racial violence that they experienced at the hands of other white people. Such sentiments on the part of those of Italian descent had transnational roots and proliferated across national boundaries, and they were often expressed in ways that addressed discrimination against people of color more broadly, as when New York City's Italian American branch of the International Ladies' Garment Workers' Union reprinted Italian antifascist Arturo Labriola's wide-ranging critique of white racism in 1934. Notably, Labriola had pointed out the actual minority status of whiteness in contrast with a transnational global community of "black, yellow, olive [and] mixed" individuals, countering discourses that have sought to disempower people of color by falsely casting them as "minorities" (qtd. in *Working Toward Whiteness* 97).

Solidarity took other forms in other contexts, as when Italian women workers helped their new African American colleagues in a Massachusetts mill community in 1913, throwing "sleeves they had sewn on the piles of neophyte black workers . . . to ensure that some piece rates were earned" (99). Such efforts continued into the latter part of the twentieth century and beyond, as further generations of protesters in the 1950s and later "sought to challenge the homogenization of mainstream, white middle-class, conformist capitalist and imperialist culture, which so infused 'white ethnic' movements" and which precipitated the Italian-led attack and murder of young Black men like Michael Griffith and Yusef Hawkins (J. Guglielmo 13). In the struggles of Italian Americans to wipe out their own prejudices as well as those of white Americans at large, tenuous bonds of allyship emerged, forming a critical social context for what I call the Italian American "ally texts" in this book, novels by writers from John Fante to Don DeLillo. At the same time, interestingly, writers like Mario Puzo would continue to reach out to these other white ethnic communities—particularly the Irish American one, where interdiasporic antagonism with Italian America had historically been a problem.

Writers and Readers Crossing Borders

This book joins the conversation about the place of Italian America in the realm of ethnic and diasporic US literature, as well as in this wider world of social protest, by examining reciprocal representations of diasporic experiences authored by Italian Americans and other diasporic writers in the United States. The problem of how to categorize literature by so-called white ethnic writers, including not just Italian Americans but also authors from the Greek, Irish, and Polish American communities, among others, has not always been a straightforward one. Instead, even today, the academic uncertainty around where to place such literatures sometimes mirrors the ambivalence with which these groups were treated upon their immigration. Nevertheless, an understanding of these racial intricacies seems in part to have been what has encouraged the field of ethnic American literary studies to accommodate and include the work of Italian American and other white ethnic writers—even if the exact terms of their inclusion have not always been certain.

In her 2005 book *Lost and Found in Translation*, Martha J. Cutter defined the category of "Anglo-Americans" as including individuals who "have forgotten an ethnic language that their parents or grandparents or great-grandparents spoke (Yiddish, Irish, Polish, Italian)" (12). Contrasting how writers including Don DeLillo and Cormac McCarthy understand the project of translation with "the way this trope is deployed in ethnic

American literature," Cutter described Italian American and Irish American authors with less explicitly bicultural identities as inhabiting a world apart from "ethnic" American writing (13). Yet with Cutter at the helm, the journal *MELUS: Multi-Ethnic Literature of the United States* also made a point of promoting scholarship on what the organization calls "ethnically specific Euro-American literary works," and their annual conference has tended to do the same. In this way, *MELUS*'s approach has been formative in encouraging a brand of inclusivity that has also long been visible in the work of organizations like the Before Columbus Foundation, where Ishmael Reed pointedly emphasized the foundation's interest in "Irish Americans and Italian Americans" as literary artists alongside "Asian Americans, African Americans, and Native Americans" (qtd. in Lee 7). At the level of individual scholarship, books like Mary Jo Bona's *By the Breath of Their Mouths* and Samuele F. S. Pardini's *In the Name of the Mother* have done essential cross-cultural work, especially with the complex interrelationships between writers or other artists from the Italian and African diasporic communities in the United States. Even where Italian America is not an explicit focus, as in Maria Antònia Oliver-Rotger's 2015 edited collection *Identity, Diaspora and Return in American Literature*, chapters on Greek and Polish American writers as well as authors with Cuban, Haitian, and Vietnamese roots remind readers that white ethnic writers have a place in the cultural fabric of multiethnic America. Such studies show that this can be done carefully and thoughtfully, without denying the racial privilege that white ethnics have inherited (and have so often endeavored to preserve) from the white supremacist culture and institutions of the United States. Instead, including Italian Americans in the conversation can be an occasion to acknowledge the existence of that white privilege, to recontest racist assumptions, and to disrupt ongoing systems of US racism.

As Oliver-Rotger's work suggests, the concept of diaspora is a unifying factor that draws together white ethnic writers and writers of color whose communities have confronted diverse experiences of displacement and their aftermath. Part of what animates this book is the idea that these often vastly different experiences create a window of opportunity for allyship: an invitation for authors to write beyond their own communities, yet into ones that are meaningfully adjacent to their own. Recent decades have seen literary theorists confront the attempts of hegemonic nation-states to disrupt and disempower transnational diasporic networks because of the potential for this type of solidarity that they seem to represent. In

Black Women, Writing and Identity, Carole Boyce Davies suggests that this potential is precisely what makes diasporic communities so threatening, arguing that "terms like 'minority,' when used to refer to people of color in the US, or 'Black,' in Great Britain, 'alien' or 'immigrant' have power only when one accepts the constraints of dominating societies or when one chooses tactical reappropriation for resistance" (14). For Boyce Davies, an alternative focus on diaspora rather than immigration creates important possibilities for solidarity not only within the African diaspora but with other oppressed peoples—other diasporic communities of color—in both American and global contexts. The narratives in this book pick up this strand of thought, suggesting that reaching across diasporas becomes an option and even an imperative for individuals driven together by similar experiences of scattering, violence, alienation, accommodation, and impossible return. These texts then ask how things change when the prospect of allyship is shaped by the power differentials and hypocritical inequalities of a country still coming to terms with its own injustice, where some diasporic communities are abused and others are afforded privileges based on their whiteness.

Despite its unearned advantages, Italian America was in need of support as it attempted to navigate and resist the complex array of stereotypes that for generations had been projected onto Italians in the United States through American literary production. The American literary community, in tandem with a group of English writers who had long been obsessed with their own ideas of Italy, had tended to produce caricatured and flattened representations of Italian people and spaces that had their own influence on how Italians on American shores were perceived more broadly. Joseph P. Cosco describes how mid-nineteenth-century American accounts of the writers' travels in Italy, "[w]hen not rhapsodizing about cultural, romantic, picturesque Italy, . . . often fixated on recurring negative images: the dirt and disorder; the oppressive Roman Catholic religion and pervasive superstition; and the stereotypical characters of the mercenary *vetturini*, the blood-thirsty *banditti*, the loafing *lazzaroni*, and the abject beggars" (7). Rather than simply reflecting anti-Italian sentiment and overexaggerated ways of imagining Italy in American popular culture, these travel narratives and so-called Italian novels influenced popular opinion in themselves, contributing to an atmosphere in which Italian Americans were sometimes romanticized and sometimes demonized but were rarely seen as more than an exotic Other—a trend that would only accelerate nearer to the end of the nineteenth century, as Italian immigration began to increase and southern Italians became more likely to be those immigrating. Such representations would continue to appear in Anglo-American fiction long after the start of the twentieth century.

Following on the heels of this history of migration and perception, fictional narratives from the 1950s and 1960s by diasporic US writers like James Baldwin and Bernard Malamud very concretely resisted received notions of Italianness, beginning work that would be interestingly reshaped and extended by contemporary novelists such as Carolina De Robertis and Chang-rae Lee. While not every one of them may have quite captured the nature of *italianità* as it tended to be variously envisioned by people of Italian descent on US soil, these writers disrupted a dominant literary and cultural narrative that had proved concretely harmful to Italian America. Oftentimes, they did this despite an astute awareness of the ways that Italian American attitudes and actions related to race, ethnicity, and religion had harmed and stood to do further harm to their own communities—an awareness that at some points would become part of the fabric of the narratives themselves and their brand of allyship.

For Italian American writers, the task was in some ways the same, but it was also different. From John Fante to Tina De Rosa and beyond, writers of the Italian diaspora in the United States have had to grapple with the overarching currents of racism against people of color in this adopted homeland that they or their ancestors have chosen, and they have written in ways that have shown resistance to prevailing stereotypes of nonwhite identity and to the falsehoods of white supremacy as they have appeared in American literature as well as popular culture. Writers like Mario Puzo have also done similar things in confronting the experiences of other diasporic groups such as the Irish in the US. At the same time, the task of these Italian American authors has more specifically been to testify to, deconstruct, and disrupt the patterns of bad allyship described earlier in this introduction, so that the fictions included in this book spotlight secondary characters and even narrator-protagonists whose blind spots offer vividly illustrative lessons for readers.

As these writers pursue complex and insistent questions of race and ethnicity, they also examine other accompanying social issues, probing their intricate, often fraught intersections and considering how they manifest in the world outside the diaspora(s). In taking on the thorny tangle of ideas that sometimes results, this book is indebted to the interdisciplinary turn in literary scholarship that is embodied by books like Michael Trask's *Cruising Modernism*, with its analysis of "status fixity" among unemployed members of the working class and individuals whose sexual identities "were likewise unsettled and roaming" (35). I am also thinking of Andreá N. Williams's study of class hierarchy and racial solidarity in representations of Black communities in the nineteenth-century US, as well as James Kyung-Jin Lee's work on interethnic urban solidarities between fictional African Americans and Asian Americans, which necessarily takes up issues of socioeconomic status as well as race and ethnicity. The diasporic narratives that I will examine here all share a similar interest in exploring how fictional collisions of diasporas and acts of literary allyship might connect with attempts to influence this array of issues both inside and outside of diasporic communities.

I begin with a chapter on four representative nondiasporic Anglo-American writers of the nineteenth and twentieth centuries—writers who, despite their engagement with these other matters of social justice, continued to draw on harmful stereotypes of Italian and Italian American spaces and people in their fiction. As narratives that probe issues from gender inequality and antiqueerness to class elitism while still reproducing tired images of Italianness, texts like Henry James's *Daisy Miller*, Edith Wharton's "Roman Fever," and Patricia Highsmith's *The Talented Mr. Ripley* become useful foils for diasporic fiction by writers addressed later in the book, who take up similar avenues for social protest while reimagining a more three-dimensional Italy. Rather than offering a comprehensive history of the Anglo-American "Italian novel," this chapter instead presents illustrative examples of some of the common distortions of *italianità* even among more progressive Anglo-American authors—examples that will help to illuminate the innovations of diasporic authors from Baldwin to Lee.

Chapter 2 puts *Giovanni's Room* in conversation with Bernard Malamud's *Pictures of Fidelman*, examining two mid-century diasporic narratives that, as quintessential works of African American and Jewish diasporic fiction, also utilize more innovative ways of imagining Italy. Representing diverse experiences of diaspora, these two texts simultaneously invoke and deconstruct long-standing Anglo-American stereotypes of Italian culture while challenging both Italian participation in white supremacy and the received wisdom of postwar 1950s and 1960s US heteronormativity. In the process, they call on genre conventions of the African American passing novel as well as recurring Jewish American literary tropes, creating complex literary currents of Black-Italian and Jewish-Italian allyship.

Carolina De Robertis has Italian immigrant relatives but identifies primarily as Latina, which puts her novel *The Gods of Tango* in a unique position in representing an Italian diasporic identity that she only distantly claims as her own. Meanwhile, Chang-rae Lee's Italian American protagonist in *Aloft* occupies a liminal position in a different sense, as the benefits of his whiteness threaten to efface his diasporic identity in a novel fueled by the racial, gendered, and class-based anxieties of contemporary US *italianità*. As chapter 3 shows, these newer Latinx and Korean American narratives embody a continuing trend of diasporic writers complexly reaching out to Italian America both inside and outside the United States: deconstructing stereotypes and vivifying Italian diasporic activism while offering "tough love" to a community that historically has needed encouragement to examine its own biases.

In chapter 4, I transition to examining how Italian American fiction has presented its own gestures of allyship across diasporas. In *Ask the Dust*, John Fante's Italian American protagonist and first-person narrator has a fraught diasporic identity that translates into toxic forms of ethnic, gender, and socioeconomic prejudice and violence, all targeted toward the protagonist's Chicana love interest. Exploring these failures of solidarity and social protest against the backdrop of Depression-era 1930s Los Angeles, Fante's novel presents a cautionary tale that establishes its author as an antiracist ally in the Chicanx diaspora's battle for respect and recognition from a persistently racist United States. Anti-Black racism, like the struggles of the Filipinx and Jewish diasporic communities in the US, is a more occasional but still important target of the narrative's attention. Fante's narrator has perhaps surprising elements in common with the protagonist of Don DeLillo's classically postmodern novel *White Noise*, and the latter part of chapter 4 rereads *White Noise* through the lens of diaspora studies to reveal the white privilege of DeLillo's protagonist as a sort of deracialized, self-indulgent diasporic identity triggered by unexpected events in the narrative. Viewed in this light, *White Noise* makes gestures of allyship across diasporas despite its apparent abstraction from questions of ethnicity and migration, implicitly acknowledging the struggles of diasporic communities that have had to confront this type of self-indulgent whiteness while making an equally vivid critique of toxic masculinity.

The range of postwar and contemporary Italian American fiction is also on display in chapter 5, which examines Tina De Rosa's *Paper Fish* alongside Mario Puzo's earlier novel *The Fortunate Pilgrim*. Here the primary focus of our Italian American writers shifts to diasporic communities that have historically been perceived as "off-white," while also moving on from aggressively insecure, class-conscious male protagonists to complex, fallible girls and women. In sparse but distinctive references, De Rosa's novel captures the superstitious currents of prejudice against the Romani diasporic community in Chicago, which fetishize that community—particularly its older women—as a frightening yet alluring source of excitement for children of the Italian diaspora. Meanwhile, Puzo takes up the subject of Irish-Italian relations, exploring similarly intersectional fears of old Irish crones, where ethno-nationalism, sexism, and ageism collide, to some degree perpetuated by women and girls themselves. The effect is to simultaneously draw attention to and destabilize two-dimensional images of the Romani and Irish diasporas in the United States.

Taken together, these chapters tell a little-known story of reciprocal representations. US writers across diasporas have rewritten the traditional scripts of the Anglo-American "Italian novel," reimagining *italianità* and confronting Italian racism even as they have interrogated other social ills ranging from the United States' stifling postwar heteronormativity to Americans' penchant for climbing the class ladder rather than knocking it down. In their turn, Italian American writers have attacked similar social problems while deconstructing stereotypes of other diasporas—especially stereotypes that Italian America in its more racist permutations has historically profited from, which these Italian American novels frankly acknowledge. The resulting brand of literary allyship has bridged individual diasporas, shrinking the spaces between them and opening up possibilities for reconciliation and healing without occluding what is distinctive about each community's encounters with and responses to American injustice.

Part I

Representational Roots

Chapter 1

Romance, Liberation, and Peril

Representing Italian Identities from Outside the Diaspora(s)

It is a familiar story. A young American or English person ventures abroad to Europe, seeking some type of education or advancement—artistic, historical, or social—as well as some geographic and ideological distance from his ancestral home. If it is European cosmopolitanism that he craves, perhaps he settles in Paris; or, if he envisions himself immersed in a vaguely premodern and beautiful experience of authentic living, perhaps he chooses an Italian city or town. Whether he seeks out Italy directly or only stumbles on Italian culture when he meets with Italians abroad in another country, he finds himself bewitched by this Mediterranean influence. Suddenly he finds it possible to live more freely, with greater honesty and less attention to the confining social mores of his home country—though often enough, the experiment ends in catastrophe. This narrative is enacted again and again in novels by Anglo-American writers for whom the Italian as an Other simultaneously represents a generative potential and a very real sort of danger.

One of the things we can hear in this familiar story is its masculinist bent. And indeed, a great many of the English and American writers who have indulged in this vision of Italy have been men writing from a patriarchal and sometimes aggressively cisgender perspective; here we might think especially of D. H. Lawrence's phallic musings in *Twilight in Italy*."[1] Yet in works by American men that subversively center the lives of women, like James's *Daisy Miller*, and in works by US women writers from Louisa May Alcott and Edith Wharton to Patricia Highsmith, who assertively take on issues of gender, sexuality, and social class, Italy, Italians, and Italian Americans also tend to figure as flat, picturesque, and sometimes deadly set pieces and backdrops to a separate drama. Because *italianità* is not the central concern in these works, we do not always read them from this ethno-nationally inflected vantage-point. Yet when they *are* read in this less typical way, narratives like *Daisy Miller*, *Little Women*, "Roman Fever," and *The Talented Mr. Ripley* become both fresh and useful foils for literary explorations of *italianità* by non-Italian diasporic writers—authors whose fiction achieves a different vision of Italian and Italian American identity.

In her study of American representations of Italy in the era of Woodrow Wilson, Daniela Rossini recalls how the writings of American authors like James and Wharton both reflected and helped to shape narratives of Italian foreignness that other white Americans applied freely to Italians on American soil as well as to those who had stayed behind in Italy itself. These were widely read authors who spent much of their time "savoring [Italy's] flavors and penetrating the country's allure, and then popularizing them back home" through stories and books that were often quite widely read, consolidating the sense of *italianità* as exaggeratedly different from Americanness even when it was painted as "alluring" or admirable (Rossini 6). *Daisy Miller*, for instance, has been credited with making James into a literary success almost overnight, which means that just as swiftly, his imagined Italy gained a large audience.[2] In this social and intellectual climate, although none of these writers characterizes Italy with the flagrant racism of Lawrence's comments about rural Italians as "ecstatic, sensual . . . raucous, cat-like" members of "the Latin races," even relatively subtle literary stereotypes threatened to negatively influence the actual lived experiences of Italian Americans, particularly the southerners who were increasingly the target of suspicion among American academics, politicians, and others (43).[3]

Despite the voracity of these writers' appetite for travel, it seems that perhaps what these books and their authors were missing was an acute consciousness of the experience of diaspora. For all his internationalism, James had not experienced this kind of collective trauma and upheaval in his relocation from the United States to Europe. In his letters, he wrote of his upcoming "emigration" to London in a casual way that marked it as a very different kind of experiment than these movements of peoples made necessary by physical and economic violence: "Evidently," he wrote, "another winter in Paris will not be worth the candle. I shall try and fix myself in London in such a way that it may become my permanent headquarters (while I dwell in Europe) if not my constant residence" (*Letters* 73).[4] By 1868, Alcott's multiple turbulent family moves had taken her from city to city, but they had not transported her across ethnic and national boundaries, and they were a function of private philosophical and economic struggles—especially her father's mistrust of traditional employment—rather than the sort of public, communal challenges that uproot an entire society.[5] Whether they were writing about Italians in the US or in Italy, these writers approached their foreign subject with a corresponding distance rather than in ways that intimated real identification or allyship.

Henry James: *Italianità* and the Fortune-Hunter

Daisy Miller provides a good starting place for this conversation, since despite its classification as a novella, it is perhaps the most likely of our four texts to come to mind when we talk about the Anglo-American "Italian novel." The compact narrative introduces the eponymous Daisy, a young and headstrong American girl who has gone abroad to Switzerland with her mother and little brother. Daisy arrives in Europe with her own notions about social propriety—for instance, with rather liberal ideas about what an unmarried girl may and may not do without a chaperone. These notions are particularly shocking to the American expatriates she encounters during her travels. Her potential love interest, Mr. Winterbourne, is perennially puzzled by this unique element of Daisy's character, and in that puzzlement lies the root of a series of events that will bring about Daisy's tragic death in Rome. Along the way, Daisy encounters other elitist Americans living abroad, particularly women, whose judgments of her nouveau riche parentage combine with limiting expectations for appropriate female behavior to guarantee that Daisy will be rejected by "good" society while she is away from home.

Part of what makes *Daisy Miller* interesting is that its stance on social issues is ambiguous enough to have made some readers miss its elements of protest altogether. In a 2001 article in *The Henry James Review*, Lisa Johnson neatly summarizes this element of the text's reception history, reflecting that whereas "traditional critics repeat Winterbourne's fatal mistake of evaluating Daisy in terms of regulatory categories of womanhood (good or bad, innocent or wild), calling her 'the wonder and horror of all decorous people,' asking 'What *is* one to do with such a contrary girl?,' feminists embrace Daisy's integration of these qualities, recognizing the protest coiled inside her indecorousness" (41). Others have responded to the novella's element of class critique more than its engagement with gender issues and, in doing so, have questioned where James's own loyalties really seem to lie, arguing that the text explores an "anxiety about what the privileged class perceives as Daisy's disturbing behavior" as it relates to "certain qualities of the marketplace," a "downtown" world of commerce that "James himself would view, rather anxiously, in specifically masculine terms" (Pahl 135). Yet Johnson rightly points out that these issues are intersectional more than they are alternatives to each other. Certainly, as her name intimates, Daisy Miller is not a representative of the old-money elite.[6] She and her family have the same rough edges as the historical hoards of "new people" whose successes in American manufacturing had converted the Industrial Revolution into a catalyst of social mobility for some in the latter part of the nineteenth century United States. Daisy is also a woman, and her position at the center of the narrative allows the novella to explore the sticky intersections of class prejudice and gendered social mores for girls and women in her position.

Ferried abroad on her own reinvented version of the Grand Tour, Daisy Miller comes face to face with intense class elitism in the gardens of Vevey and the drawing rooms of Rome's American expatriates. Daisy is rich, and she has the youthful good looks needed to attract a "gentleman" like the familiar Mr. Winterbourne, along with the frank, fresh intelligence needed to distinguish her conversation and her company from the time Winterbourne seems to have spent with more mature, perhaps more conventional women (32). As Johnson has remarked, Daisy "shoots from the hip," earning the title of "cowboy feminist" (41). Unfortunately, her family does not have the social standing or the carefully polished mannerisms to match these other charms of Daisy's. The family's "intimacy" with the courier who works for them, which Winterbourne's expatriate aunt scornfully condemns, becomes an excuse for the old-money elites Daisy encounters to snub her to the point of mortification and rebellious anger, and it seems to guarantee that the budding affair between the two young people will fizzle (20). Every time Daisy is judged as wanting because of the class rules she breaks in public or because her family's money has been earned rather than inherited, James's novella paints a trenchant picture of class stratification and the stickiness of the American social hierarchy. Through Daisy's experiences in Europe, and particularly her adventures in Italy, it becomes possible to see the fissures that blemished the narrative of US social mobility as the nineteenth century came to a close. This part of James's story could have played out in the same way in the parlors of Fifth Avenue in New York City, where families that had enjoyed their wealth for generations were sending their children to boarding schools in rural New England to avoid their exposure to dangerous young people like Daisy.[7] While perhaps, as Dennis Pahl argues, James "*remains* anxious about the dissolution of otherwise stable boundaries, both social as well as aesthetic," the text itself gives readers license to scrutinize and criticize the antidemocratic elitism of America's Winterbournes (156, italics in the original).

As Johnson remembers, the classic question for earlier generations of critics was whether Daisy is a "coquette," like the dangerous married women Winterbourne has known; "a pretty American flirt," as he at one point judges her to be; or something altogether different that is less familiar and thus more difficult to label (James 15). One more contemporary approach to this dilemma is not to try to answer the question at all, especially since Daisy's words and actions are filtered through the consciousness of Winterbourne, the only person whose inner thoughts and feelings James's narrator provides real access to. Accordingly, though the novella is technically titled *Daisy Miller: A Study*, it is possible to understand the text more as a study of Winterbourne—and to see the ambiguity of Daisy as reflecting more on his own character than it does on hers, rendering the question of Daisy's true nature moot. This version of *Daisy Miller* becomes a portrait and a potential critique of masculine self-centeredness: of the ways men project identities onto women according to the former's experiences and desires, with little interest in asking the direct questions that would allow women to speak their minds and claim identities of their own.

Perhaps counterintuitively, our privileged access to Winterbourne's consciousness is what best validates Daisy's own views when they do emerge. Consider her scornful response to Winterbourne at the end of the novella, when his coldness toward her provokes her to exclaim that she doesn't "care . . . whether [she has] Roman Fever or not!" after being exposed to malaria at the Colosseum (77). As a man who has presumed too much and asked too few questions, Winterbourne seems to deserve this rebuke, as does the larger community of presumptuous and elitist men to which he belongs. Our intimate familiarity with Winterbourne's perspective leaves us closely acquainted with these flaws as Daisy sees them. Meanwhile, Daisy's own troubles become symptomatic of gendered expectations for female behavior and their interactions with socioeconomic norms, not just of class consciousness in isolation. After all, "intimacy with one's courier" and other relationships like it are something that was specifically forbidden of upper-class women in a sociohistorical moment in which, for privileged Anglo-Americans, being male could potentially mean being permitted to forge friendships across social boundaries that women would not be allowed to cross.[8]

Eventually, though, the question arises of where Italy fits into this schema. James's novella and his writing more broadly tend to be understood as contrasting American culture with that of Europe at large, bringing the new into relief by immersing it in the old—and this is no great surprise given James's own words on the subject: "Americans in Europe are *outsiders*," he once remarked, suggesting that residents of the United States found themselves distinguished from the English, French, and Germans in ways in which the latter three did not distinguish among themselves ("Americans Abroad" 787). The Italians, however, are notably absent from James's description, and indeed, *Daisy Miller* depicts Italians not as dignified sophisticates certain of their own superiority or that "the standard of manners—the shaping influences—in [their] own country are the highest," but rather as second-rate gentlemen who are less dignified than they are dangerous (786). This vision of Italy is embodied in the Roman landscape, the figure of the courier, and "the glossy little Roman" named Giovanelli, another suitor of Daisy's, who is allowed as little dignity as a servant although he is not one (64).

Conversations recorded between Daisy and the impertinent courier Eugenio reveal that he cannot be trusted to know his place socially because he is too ungoverned or untroubled by social rules, even as he tries to remind Daisy of the rules that purportedly apply to her own behavior as a young woman:

> "Does Mademoiselle propose to go alone?" Eugenio asked of Mrs. Miller.
> "Oh no, with this gentleman!" cried Daisy's mamma for reassurance.
> "I *meant* alone with the gentleman." The courier looked for a moment at Winterbourne—the latter seemed to make out in his face a vague presumptuous intelligence as at the

expense of their companions—and then solemnly and with a bow, "As Mademoiselle pleases!" he said. (32–33)

Even worse, Winterbourne's aunt tells us, Eugenio "sits in the garden" with the family "of an evening" and "smokes in their faces" (21). Like so many other fictional Italians dreamed up by Anglo-American writers, Eugenio is thus "uncivilized" in his disregard for how the world is supposed to work and in his insistence on poorly copying the mannerisms of high-born men in "good society." He is arrogant, certainly, but he is far from refined. Of course, Daisy herself is painted in much the same way: as ungoverned by needless social strictures. In fact, it is suggested that her nouveau riche impropriety, combined with her mother's equally "new" haplessness, is the reason Eugenio can successfully manage to flout his employers' authority without fear of the consequences. Viewed in a certain light, this characterization of Daisy seems charming, even flattering. However, the figure of Giovanelli and the events surrounding him deepen the narrative's stereotyping of Italy and its distinct significance for James's Italians. Giovanelli proves to be handsome but useless, a professional fortune-hunter with exaggerated mannerisms such as the "too emphatic . . . flourish" of his hat, who fails to protect Daisy from malaria despite being a native of Rome and well-acquainted with its dangers (55). Like Eugenio, Giovanelli is immoderate and overstated in a way that is typical of an Italy imagined from outside, where the climate and the personalities of the people who inhabit it are equally intemperate. More importantly, he is dangerously incompetent and careless, remarking that Daisy "did what she liked!" even as he mourns her death (80).

In a different essay, Johnson suggests that we read Daisy Miller as a "race traitor" whose "race loyalty is called into question by her affiliation with the dark Italian, Giovanelli" ("If this is improper" 71). While it is undoubtedly true that Daisy's behavior resists received notions of Italians as a lesser class of person, this current of resistance is not necessarily shared by the narrative itself. Instead, this pair of Jamesian Italian men even belies what Joseph P. Cosco rightly says of James in his travel writing: that he "does often naturalize and romanticize the Italians through the picturesque perspective," although he also "critiques these tendencies of the sentimental traveler" (92). Neither Eugenio nor Giovanelli is really allowed even the level of dignity that romanticism would confer. They are painted as ridiculous more than romantic, as garish more than picturesque, and as generally lacking in human empathy and remorse. James's unnamed Romans are perhaps a bit more typical of James's vision as Cosco describes it above; they walk slowly and gaze "idly" at their surroundings, with a romantic laziness that recalls Lawrence's characterization of "the Latin races" and their supposed lack of "purposive industry" (47).[9] Yet this characterization stings just as much.

Meanwhile, James's Rome itself proves deadly: not only is it a breeding ground for disease, but it also arouses passionate tempers and a lack of caution among visiting Anglo-Americans like Daisy. As her nighttime visit to the Colosseum and her subsequent death from malaria show, being a "race traitor" seems not to be so advisable after all. This particular stereotype of Italy as a site of death that either kills or makes murderers of American tourists is one that repeats throughout US literature set in Italy, from Hawthorne's *The Marble Faun* to Highsmith's *The Talented Mr. Ripley*. That any tourist survives an Italian vacation unscathed might seem surprising given the catalog of Italian literary catastrophes invented by American writers. While it is the American Winterbourne, not James himself, who asserts that "American candy's the best candy" and "American girls are the best girls," the novella at large has its own way of thinking nationalistically, presenting stereotypes as realities and fashioning Italy into a two-dimensional, deadly backdrop for this story of Americans (6–7).

Louisa May Alcott: Those Romantic Italians

Cosco's study of James and Italy emphasizes that Italians transplanted to American shores could not necessarily expect a less essentializing response from James. Instead, if James's Italians were so often representatives of the "romantic picturesque," his Italian immigrants were either "crude urchin[s] . . . forcing the native-born Americans to eat from a greasy ladle" or assimilationists "bleached of . . . color" by the acculturation process (139). What, then, of bicultural characters with both Italian and non-Italian parentage who are brought up mostly on US soil?

Louisa May Alcott's Theodore "Laurie" Laurence is born in Italy, is raised by his non-Italian grandfather in the United States after the death of his mother and father, and is bicultural from birth due to his parents' differing nationalities. In so many ways, the boy-turned-young-man is a kindred spirit: someone the Marches, as well as Alcott herself, seem to recognize as one of their own. As a desirable male character in a novel that is populated mostly by women and that is not unconcerned with matters of romance, love, and marriage, Laurie also receives his fair share of the narrative's romantic adulation. Still, *Little Women* presents readers with a bifurcated version of hyphenated identity in which the details of the Italian American boy's character are either embraced as familiar or fetishized as foreign according to the ethno-nationality they are associated with in the text. The phrase "the Italian part of his nature," as Alcott's narrator terms it, becomes a kind of shorthand for the typical idea that *italianità* is something to explore superficially rather than three-dimensionally (638). This commentary about Laurie's Italianness unfolds through a series of casual asides as he transforms from a casual playmate of the girls into a suitor of Jo's and eventually—during a trip abroad—into Amy's fiancé and then her husband.

Alcott famously deemed writing projects like *Little Women* "moral pap for the young" (qtd. in Blackburn 98). This commentary, along with some ideological contradictions in her books themselves, has inspired readers to debate whether Alcott's work can be read as feminist as passionately as they have debated whether Daisy is or is not an American flirt. In fact, this is a debate that has spilled over from more traditional scholarly publications into magazines like *The Atlantic Monthly*, the blog for the literary journal *Ploughshares*, and even the website *Vulture*, an offshoot of *New York Magazine*. In 2018, recognizing the 150-year anniversary of the novel's publication, all three of those venues published essays about the embattled feminism of *Little Women*, with conclusions ranging from Janey Tracey's description of "the anti-revolutionary, somewhat contradictory nature of *Little Women*'s feminist leanings" to Hillary Kelly's provocative essay title, "We Regret to Inform You That *Little Women* Is Not a Feminist Novel." Despite taking place largely online in venues whose "comment sections" have allowed loyal readers to weigh in and defend the text, this conversation echoes the ones that previous generations of readers of *Little Women* have had for some time. Consider Jill P. May's 1994 article in the *CEA Critic*, which describes Alcott's work as an example of how "women authors . . . create images of their contemporary society that are opaque enough in design and style to encourage change while recording current societal attitudes" (27). In other words, some of the apparently conservative plot points in the narrative should perhaps be understood as testifying to social realities rather than signaling Alcott's endorsement of the values behind them.

The keyword here is *opacity*; the novel seems to invite ambivalent readings by declining to be as didactic with readers as the girls' mother is with them as children. Linda Grasso explores similar ideas in her discussion of the failings of the 1994 film version of the text, arguing that the film "eradicat[es] contradictions about female power and artistry that are fundamental features of Alcott's novel" (187).

In the end, there is a sense of social daring in *Little Women*, even if it coexists with cloying moments in the narrative that might seem to assert tired values, like the paternalistic place of men at the head of the household or the imperative that women marry eventually regardless of their disposition. The March sisters' diversity of personality plays an especially important role in the novel's commentary about gender roles, suggesting that even when more conventional young women are candidates for our attention, ones who are self-sacrificingly wholesome (like Beth) or who have purportedly traditional feminine interests (like Amy), it is perfectly legitimate for an author and for readers themselves to find a tomboy and her career ambitions to be the most interesting. It's not simply the fact that *Little Women* centers on female experiences that makes it socially powerful—it's which woman Alcott chooses as her priority.[10] Jo, who tends to be read as the closest equivalent to Alcott herself out of the four sisters, is also the sort of girl who describes herself as "homely, and awkward, and odd, and old," without giving us the sense that she is striving for modesty more than accuracy (578). Next to her, Amy seems even more Eurocentrically resplendent, with her "white shoulders and golden head" and with hair that is best left in its natural "thick waves and curls" regardless of the fashions of the day (605). But as much as the narrative seems to luxuriate in these descriptions of Amy's splendor when they arise, it moves on from them quickly enough, always returning to its ultimate focus on Jo as the most prominent "little woman" among the four girls as they grow older. If anything, as I have hinted above, the problem is that Alcott's novel anticipates second-wave white feminism a bit too well, never wavering from its Eurocentric bent even when it shifts from extolling Amy's "white" skin to celebrating Jo's eccentricities.

What's more, the novel focuses on women whose economic position is relatively precarious without making them all the object of a dour, tragic moral lesson, as upcoming experiments in American naturalism like Dreiser's *Sister Carrie* would do, and in this way the novel creates its own current of social protest. Granted, Alcott may stop short of a socialist critique of class inequality. By suggesting that it is possible to be happy and "poor"—"gladly" giving up one's Christmas presents, for instance—and by extolling the virtues of self-reliance and charity, her novel arguably risks excusing the class hierarchy or downplaying its consequences (1–2).[11] There is also the fact that even when they call themselves poor, the Marches are quite a bit more well-off than some of the other truly working-class characters in their midst. This chosen focus on Alcott's part does have its own ramifications. Yet there is always a sense, especially in the first part of *Little Women*, that the Marches are faced with unjust trials—and the moments of "injury and resentment" that do result become a way for the novel, through the emotions of its characters, to register its awareness of the larger inequalities at play, which individual people's charity and generosity can only do so much to counteract (Foote 69). The fact that these women are generally not victimized by the narrative does not do anything to lessen our sense that they and the other women around them deserve better than the existing system has given them, even when things turn out tolerably well for some in the final calculus.

One related view of *Little Women* is that Laurie's relative marginalization as a secondary character is itself a feminist gesture, as again, women are centered at the expense of men in a way that flips the traditional cultural script. The actor who played Meg's husband in the 1994 film version suggested something similar about his own character when he referred to himself as the film's "token penis" (qtd. in Grasso 185). However, because of the way that ethnicities are distributed throughout the novel, this also means that Anglo-Americans are at the heart of the novel, while a diasporic American—an Italian American more specifically—is decentered or marginalized. While it is in the nature of fiction to center some characters and marginalize others, exactly how this casting of primary and secondary characters plays out can have sociopolitical ramifications that are important to recognize. In this case, in asserting its feminist values, *Little Women* assigns a comparatively thin, two-dimensional role to Laurie that has implications for the way ethnicity, too, is treated in the narrative.

This marginalization is visible not just in Laurie's literal lack of presence throughout much of the text but also—and especially—in the comments made about him and his ethnic heritage, in which his identity and backstory are constructed largely from cultural clichés. Consider the scene when Amy goes with Laurie to the Parc Valrose, or Valrosa, as the novel refers to it. While the pair is there, Alcott's narrator makes a set of arresting observations:

> She put [the flowers] in his buttonhole as a peace offering, and he stood a minute looking down at them with a curious expression, for in the Italian part of his nature there was a touch of superstition.... He had thought of Jo in reaching after the thorny red rose, for vivid flowers became her, and she had often worn ones like that from the greenhouse at home. The pale roses Amy gave him were the sort that the Italians lay in dead hands, never in bridal wreaths, and for a moment he wondered if the omen was for Jo or for himself, but the next instant his American common sense got the better of sentimentality, and he laughed a heartier laugh than Amy had heard since he came. (638)

Here, Alcott's narrator confidently expresses a vision of national identity that aligns Americanness with logic and reason and Italianness with superstition and sentimentality. Not only is Laurie's ethnic heritage reduced to a tired stereotype that Laurie himself seems to subscribe to, but Laurie's own identity is reduced to his ethnic affiliations. Writing in the midst of Italy's unification, Alcott propagates ideas about *italianità* in general that are quite similar to the ones northerners would peddle about the south as they came to terms with their shared membership in the newly established state, as well as the ones that Anglo-Americans would project onto Italian American immigrants, particularly these same southerners who would begin arriving in greater numbers as the nineteenth century drew to a close, eventually numbering 80 percent of Italian newcomers in the US.[12] The mutually constitutive relationship between literary and social attitudes about Italianness becomes visible in this passage.

Similar complications arise with Laurie's informal and eventually his legal attachment to the March family. With only his grandfather present in the narrative to give him some semblance of a "blood" family, it seems more that Laurie has joined the Marches on marrying Amy than that Amy has joined the Laurences—and indeed, long before he becomes their brother legally, the March girls refers to Laurie as a family member, with Jo using her own pet name for him and proclaiming that her family "includes Mr. L. and a young man by the name of Teddy" (543). Under these circumstances, it is not unreasonable for Jan Susina, in his reading of masculinity in *Little Women*, to refer to Laurie as "the honorary fifth sister" (168). On the one hand, there is something exhilaratingly matrilineal about all this. It upends the traditional Western order of things, in which women were dislocated from their paternal homes to those of their new husbands on their marriage, cast uncomfortably as chattel.[13] In Laurie's case, the opposite seems true: that as a man, he is joining a household and a community made up primarily of women by accompanying his new wife into her preexisting world. This textual detail has clear feminist implications. On the other hand, Laurie is also an Italian American joining an Anglo-American family, his ethnic identity subsumed within their more unambiguous forms of whiteness and citizenship—and this is something the novel celebrates rather than problematizing. Laurie's marriage to Amy is painted as unambiguously joyous, with the two lovebirds "as happy as people are but once in their lives" (702).

Alcott's manner of representing Italy is quite consistent across the genders. Unlike many other Anglo-American novels, this one also features an Italian woman—Laurie's mother—alongside its Italian men. Laurie's Italian mother inspires his American father to marry her despite his family's disapproval, and Laurie emerges as the product of this rebellious union, after which, quite predictably, his parents die. All this happens before the action of the novel, so that Laurie's mother, who is not even given her own name, is woven into the backstory as well as the background of the text. She is more of a type than an individual, with none of the luxuries of representation that the novel's Anglo-American women characters receive. Her story is predictably deemed "romantic" by girls like Meg, who responds to it with a shocked and excited "Dear me!" (86). Meanwhile, that story reinforces the imagined idea of Italian spaces and people as inspiring heedless, rebellious actions in otherwise calm and obedient Americans. While Alcott stops short of suggesting that Laurie's father dies *because* he has married an Italian woman, readers of typical Anglo-American "Italian novels" would not be blamed for wondering if the marriage somehow, even indirectly, has something to do with his demise.

At the same time, just as "real" Italian Americans faced substantially fewer barriers to equal treatment than have people of color in the United States, Laurie and his family are afforded forms of privilege in the narrative that are not assigned to other nonwhite families or even to other white ethnic families. Janice M. Alberghene comments on "the virtually subliminal status of African Americans in *Little Women*," which persists despite the fact that the novel was "set during the Civil War and written at the start of Reconstruction" (347). In fact, Alberghene reveals that for the famous scene of Amy's near-drowning in a pond, Alcott mined from an early childhood experience of her own in which she recalled being "rescued [from drowning] by a black boy" (Alcott, qtd. in Alberghene 352). As Alberghene points out, it is Laurie, not an African American child, who rescues Amy in the novel—that is, "the black boy is erased completely from the scene and the whole scenario must be rewritten" with a bicultural Italian American boy cast as the hero instead (352). Even other white newcomers such as the Irish diasporic community fare rather poorly in the novel, a fact that Grasso notes in her analysis of how the 1994 film sanitizes the original text:

> In the novel, when Amy's authoritarian male teacher commands her to throw away the "oh, so plump and juicy" limes that are then "exulted over by the little Irish children, who were their sworn foes," Alcott not only figures frustrated desire as food denied; she also conveys the ultimate indignity of class infraction: [t]he lower-class Irish, who "shout from the street," get to "feast" on what the white, middle-class girls rightfully deserve. (179)

While this analysis might blur the boundary between Alcott herself and the Marches, additional references to Irish characters in the novel similarly reduce these characters to overburdened women with too many small children "roar[ing]" at once or to domestic helpmates like the woman who takes over Meg's kitchen after the birth of her twins (525). The repeated references to large numbers of Irish children in particular, sometimes by Alcott's narrator and sometimes by an adult Jo whose views readers have generally been taught to respect as sound, suggest that Grasso is right to point out Alcott's mother's anti-Irish sentiment as an influence on the novel, with her concern that the Irish "have come over to take cupboard, tub, and all" (qtd. in Grasso 179). Like the history of Italian America in general, the history of literary representations of *italianità* cannot and should not be separated from these other conversations about ethnicity in American literature and society.

During Alcott's own time abroad in 1870, she once wrote a letter to her mother in which she described what she referred to as "the trouble about getting into Italy," proclaiming that "civil war always breaks out there and things are so mixed up that strangers get into scrapes among the different squabblers" (*Louisa* 242). Alcott's knowledge of the fight for Italian unification is admirable from a certain perspective; she clearly was more familiar than the average American would have been with the political goings-on of the territory that would ultimately become the unified Italian state. Still, there are a few moments in this commentary that deserve extra scrutiny. Alcott's use of the word "always" positions Italy as a perpetually rioting nation in much the same way that the American press now condescends to "developing" nations abroad, rather than casting Italy's unification as a critical, finite, and legitimate process of nation-building. In referring to the Italian soldiers as "squabblers," Alcott also gives their efforts a trivial and petty air, painting them as superficial in a way that mirrors *Little Women*'s flat representation of Laurie, whose lack of dimensionality has deeper sociopolitical ramifications when read in the context of Italian immigrants' contested status in the United States.[14] As a second exemplar of how nineteenth-century American writers both reflected and helped to generate prevailing American attitudes toward the Italians in their midst, Alcott has left behind an illuminating, if sometimes troublesome, legacy.

Edith Wharton: An American Secret in Rome

Ushering in a new century of Anglo-American representations of Italy, Edith Wharton had a more than passing acquaintance with the country that had undergone so many changes in the decades since it had first captured Alcott's and James's attention. Wharton's nonfictional works include the travel narrative *Italian Backgrounds* and another text specifically focused on Italian "villas and their gardens"; as William L. Vance points out in his article "Edith Wharton's Italian Mask," her less commonly read first novel *The Valley of Decision* is also set in Italy and is very much occupied with the "political and intellectual history" of the north in the second half of the eighteenth century (176). Yet Vance suggests that the novel's Italian protagonist functions more usefully as a stand-in for Wharton herself, and Hermione Lee agrees in calling the novel "profoundly autobiographical" (110). The novel's great success seems to be the way it uses Italian history, scenery, and personhood as an implicit vehicle for self-exploration, a tool for reflecting on the "suffocating nature of the society in which Wharton herself lived" (Vance 177). This instrumentalism of Wharton's approach ensures that the foreign space that is captured in such meticulous historical detail is in some sense not actually the focus of the narrative.

This starting point for Wharton's career as a novelist becomes doubly interesting in light of later works like her 1934 story "Roman Fever," which is similarly set in Italy and yet is decidedly not about the background Wharton has chosen for the drama that will play out within its pages.[15] In the story, two well-to-do, respectable New York matrons have gone on holiday with their marriageable daughters, one of whom is determined to capture the affections of an Italian "Marchese" and aviator (11). While their daughters wander unaccompanied through the Roman landscape, their mothers sit on a terrace and reminisce about their own earlier visits to the storied city, where, it is finally revealed, they were rivals for the affections of the same young man—a man who had an affair with one and then married the other. This emotionally charged subtext is at first obscured under a veneer of gentility, and Wharton's matronly ladies speak fondly of times gone by. They recall multiple generations of women under surveillance due to the city's apparent dangers: the genuine threat of "Roman fever"—or malaria—when their mothers were young and the city's supposed social perils during their own girlhood adventures. One of the women remarks,

> I always used to think . . . that our mothers had a much more difficult job than our grandmothers. When Roman fever stalked the streets it must have been comparatively easy to gather in the girls at the danger hour; but when you and I were young, with such beauty calling us, and the spice of disobedience thrown in, and no worse risk than catching cold during the cool hour after sunset, the mothers used to be put to it to keep us in—didn't they? (10–11)

The shift in time and perspective foreshadows Wharton's decidedly twentieth-century approach to issues of gender and sexuality at the close of the story—an approach that, decades earlier, likely would have shocked the genteel readers of Alcott and James.

"Roman Fever" does something extraordinary by refusing to pretend that premarital sex does not exist among moneyed New York women, instead providing a fictional model for talking about sexual liaisons in "polite company."[16] The tensest moments of the narrative center on a conversation in which Grace Ansley, the mother of the Marchese-hunting young person, admits to having had sex with her friend's now-deceased husband in the time before they were all married. At the story's outset, Grace appears "old-fashioned" and even a bit shabby in contrast to her old friend and rival, the showier and more confident Mrs. Slade (5). Though she certainly never uses the word *sex* explicitly, Wharton effects a brilliant reversal by making Grace the woman who not only has sex before marriage but admits it—and admits that the forbidden act produced a child. Grace's final words, "I had Barbara," are spoken in triumph, suggesting not only that it is permissible to reveal a long-hidden and taboo secret but that doing so, openly and verbally reckoning with one's sexuality, can be an incredible source of power for a woman whose silence would have been socially expected of her based on her gender. At the same time, as Janet Mason Ellerby notes, the fact that Grace is ultimately the more likable and "generous of spirit" of the two women assists in "remov[ing] the immoral implications of premarital sex" from the world of ideas swirling around the narrative (81).

A healthy measure of class critique is also palpable here, as Wharton skewers social rules and expectations that were necessary to maintain the New York elite's sense of genteel superiority during the period of Mrs. Ansley's girlhood. Given that "late Victorian Americans of all social classes simultaneously romanticized the image of motherhood and feared extramarital female sexuality," it is not as though the expectations that governed the society of Grace Ansley's teenage years and that she ultimately rejects are exclusive to her social rank (Broder 125). Nevertheless, it is also true that this moneyed, urban American upper class saw the sexual respectability of its women, like its avoidance of discussing taboo topics in public, as a marker of its special social status. In this context, Grace's disclosure not only resists confining expectations for women's sexual behavior but also destabilizes these fictions of class difference and economic elitism.

While moving forward so decisively from *Daisy Miller*'s timid allusions to female sexuality, "Roman Fever" also becomes important because of what stays the same in the transition to a new era. Wharton's narrative gives a new meaning to the phrase "Italian backgrounds," as here it is even more literally true that Italians exist in the background of the story, where there is only room for them to be represented two-dimensionally. Like James's and Alcott's works, this short piece features an Italian love interest, indirectly mining a stereotype of Italians as passionate, sensuous lovers: a construction of *italianità* that continues to appear in American cultural artifacts ranging from novels to chocolate bar and ice cream commercials.[17] The Italian love interest never physically appears or is given a first name in the story, referred to only as the "Campolieri boy" and as "one of the best matches in Rome" (11). As they evaluate the young man as a source of money and social standing for Barbara, the narrative's more unambiguously white matrons point out the social caché that Italians of a certain class have in the eyes of Americans from Wharton's set. This instrumentalist vision, not unlike Wharton's own relationship to the protagonist of her first novel, is simultaneously flattering and flattening.

Rome itself, as the actual backdrop or setting of the story, is fancifully stereotyped in ways that match Wharton's treatment of the Campolieri boy, contradicting some critics' interpretation of the narrative as capturing "a new Rome grounded in the present" (Elsden 127). In the imagination of Wharton's narrator, Rome is a beautiful, ancient place that has remained governed by its past, sheltered from the prosaic modernity of the Anglo-Americans who tromp though it. The Roman landscape is dotted with picturesque "ruins" and architectural marvels like "the outlying immensity of the Colosseum" (11). In the shadow of these long-standing wonders, small details like the "feeble string of electric lights" that "flickered out" in the restaurant where the women are seated assert the distance between Wharton's aesthetically rich Italy and the contemporary scientific world of working electricity (19). Occluding relevant aspects of Rome's own modernity, such as its status as a forerunner in utilizing new types of electric power as early as the late nineteenth century, this detail pointedly echoes earlier English figurations of Italian infrastructure as perennially failing or being overtaken by the premodern, as when Forster writes in *Where Angels Fear to Tread* about "the dry white margin of the road" being "splashed" with violets "like a causeway soon to be submerged under the advancing tide of spring" (19).[18] This primitivist detail gives new significance to Mrs. Slade's assertion that the view from the Roman terrace is "still the most beautiful view in the world," so that Mrs. Slade's fetishization of Rome as an aesthetic object becomes an echo of the story's larger impression of Italy (4).[19] Importantly, this narrative vision of Italy's "feeble" resources cannot really be explained away as a function of Wharton's rightful concerns about the impact of World War I or of Mussolini's burgeoning influence. In fact, the rise of fascism in Italy had actually corresponded with nationalist investments in its domestic infrastructure and in industries including electricity.

Instead of unromantically representing issues in contemporary Italian life between the wars, then, such details paint the story's eponymous city more whimsically, underscoring Rome's purported Otherness and obfuscating its actual, deeply problematic modernity. This pattern of interpretation echoes Wharton's musings about the place and its identity through the centuries in many of her nonfictional writings. In *Italian*

Backgrounds, when Wharton protests how "for centuries it has been the fashion to look only on a city which has almost disappeared, and to close the eyes to one which is still alive and actual," she is referring not to the "alive" modernity of early-twentieth-century Rome but to its seventeenth-century architecture, which she describes as being neglected by "the purist" whose attitude she decries in calling the city "the best defence of the baroque" (*Italian* 84, 86–87). Additional references to Rome elsewhere in the book emphasize the varied landscapes and vegetation surrounding the city along with "the pacific ruins of pagan Rome" (64). Later, in a 1931 letter written on her return to the city, Wharton would describe it as principally unharmed by war and fascism, with some of its old landmarks newly "uncover[ed]" and "disengaged from rubble" (qtd. in Elsden 127). In wishing to see Rome unchanged, and in resisting Mussolini's own challenge to tourists' vision of Italy as "the country of sun, oranges, songs, stones and venerable fragments," Wharton also seemed to consign the city to that same "venerable" past, denying Italy's membership in a more protean contemporary world even as she expressed justified fears for its future (qtd. in Arthurs, 26). While Annamaria Formichella Elsden is right to note the incorporation of other details into "Roman Fever" that at least allude to the existence of a Roman present, such as references to the US embassy there, I would argue that the designation of this site of modern diplomacy as "a romantic meeting place" makes it more difficult to read these moments as successfully liberating the narrative from old ideas about Italy (Elsden 129).

One more familiar cliché remains for the story's climax to draw on when Grace finally speaks out, liberated to disclose the affair that she has kept hidden for decades in New York. Not only has the Rome of her girlhood allowed Grace to exercise a form of youthful adventurousness and sexual daring, qualities of personality that by all accounts she has never shown since then in her life in the United States, but it is Rome again that makes it uniquely possible for her to resist social convention by revealing this history and her child's identity. In the same Anglo-American tradition glorified by Forster in novels like *A Room with a View* as well as by James and other writers across the Atlantic, Italy here becomes the place where social experiment is permitted, where the limitations of home can be thrown off. In one respect, this is a flattering light in which to place the Roman landscape, since it transfigures its visitor and seems to leave an indelible positive mark on her life. Grace does not die in Rome like Daisy, nor does she find that she must protect herself from the dark "superstition" of *italianità* as Laurie does. Instead, she leaves the narrative a fully confident version of herself, powerful in self-disclosure because of her Italian sojourn. Both she and her daughter are indeed "confident women on the cusp of a new era," unlike Daisy, who "dies for attempting independence" (Elsden 129). A balanced reading of "Roman Fever," however, is also obligated to recognize how casting a foreign space as a site of successful liberation can also instrumentalize and fetishize that place, fashioning it into a playground for foreigners' self-realization rather than recognizing it as the home of its own multifaceted people, cultures, and identities. The difference between the putatively foreign and familiar spaces becomes exaggerated in the process, not unlike in much of colonial fiction, where "the overvaluation of selected aspects" of the culture of the colonized space allowed European writers to "express . . . their disillusionment" with their own society (Dobie 159).

To some extent this is simply what Wharton's characters do—a set of social dynamics that the story faithfully records much as *Little Women* records the pressure on women to marry or *Daisy Miller* records the emotionally painful effects of class elitism. Still, by suggesting that Grace's liberation could only take place in Italy, "Roman Fever" continues to emphasize the transfiguring function of the Italian landscape for Anglo-American people rather than the real life that goes on there after the tourists have returned home. As in so many Anglo-American "Italian novels," this form of fetishism plays out interestingly in "Roman Fever" despite the quite different (noncolonial) political relationship between the United States and Italy and the legally codified, if socially ambiguous, whiteness of Italians in the eyes of America.

Patricia Highsmith: Murder in Italy

One of the most interesting perspectives to emerge on Patricia Highsmith's *The Talented Mr. Ripley* comes from Anthony Minghella, who directed the film adaptation of the novel. Minghella's family hails from central Italy originally, and in an interview, he once commented on what the interviewer perceived as an intriguing difference between the film and the original text:[20]

> NJ: I remember a quiet Italy of ease and comfort in the novel—not a jazz fan's Italy.

> AM: Because of my Italian blood I didn't want to go to Italy and just have lots of postcard views. And Italy in that *La dolce vita* period of *il boom*, as it's called, had changed. Ten years after the war they'd started to escape poverty and discover style and Vespas. So the film had to buy into that.... Actually, Highsmith writes almost nothing at all about the places. There's much more about how you make a Martini, or adjudicating people by what drink they order in a bar. Where the bar was, who was there—so much about the striations of class and personality by choices of costume and hair. (78–79)

As Minghella's comments suggest, nowhere in this range of texts is Italian identity more entirely in the background than it is in Highsmith's novel. The choice of Tom Ripley as the novel's centerpiece allows Highsmith to foreground issues of class as well as sexuality and gender that ultimately make for a skewering critique of postwar American culture. At the same time, Highsmith's narrative is limited in the ways it engages with the modern Italy that Minghella describes, instead presenting a backdrop that appears largely frozen in time.[21] Like the film itself, the novel also invokes lurid Anglo-American visions of deadly Italy, swapping Roman fever for murder in its updating of James's text.

The plot of Highsmith's novel might be called deceptively complex rather than deceptively simple. The father of a rich young man pays another young man to go abroad on a Jamesian mission and convince his truant son to return home to the United States.[22] The emissary is a class imposter, pretending to have been a college acquaintance of the truant when he is not nearly rich or posh enough to have attended Princeton. Still, he worms his way into the wealthy young man's Mediterranean social circle as they live together for a time in a fictional Italian town. The imposter seems to develop feelings for the wealthy young man, although there is some sense that perhaps he also envies him and wishes to take his place. Before long, the imposter has been scorned and rejected by his love interest, then has murdered him and assumed his identity. The rest of the novel is consumed with his attempts to avoid detection by the young man's friends and by law enforcement. The twists and turns of the plot, distilled in this way, leave readers with a rather sensationalist piece of crime fiction with far deeper social implications. That Italy is nearly invisible in this description of the novel so far gives a good sense of how the narrative overall treats Italian people and spaces.

Readers who know that Alcott resisted the idea of marriage as the pinnacle of a woman's life are sometimes among the most disappointed to see that *Little Women* accurately chronicles a woman's imperative to marry in nineteenth-century New England rather than imagining something bolder. Highsmith's reputation as a queer writer and as the author of *The Price of Salt*, which centers on a love affair between two women, likewise complicates the conversation about *The Talented Mr. Ripley* and the entire series of Ripley novels by raising questions about how they fit within this framework of personal and creative life.[23] Joan Schenkar recalls the words Highsmith herself recorded while in the process of composing *The Price of Salt*, which reveal how conscious she was of the distance between this work and her earlier writing. Schenkar writes, "*The Price of Salt* allowed Pat to release herself from what was to become her most reliable artistic forgery: the male 'voice' of narration and an apparently heterosexual orientation. She never again published another work like it. 'How grateful I am at last,' she wrote while working on the manuscript in December of 1949, 'not . . . to spoil my best thematic material by transposing it to [a] false male-female relationship'" (272). Following just three years later, *The Talented Mr. Ripley* was similar in centering on an (in this case ambiguously) queer protagonist; even this, in a way, was revolutionary for 1950s America. But Tom Ripley is also a murderer, leading Michael Trask to wonder whether *The Talented Mr. Ripley* merely encourages sexual panic by "equating homoerotic and homicidal tendencies" (585).

Of course, this is a conversation that readers and moviegoers working in queer studies have been pursuing for some time. Harry M. Benshoff notes that some "have decried Hollywood's killer queers as negative and dangerous stereotypes, while others have argued that New Queer Cinema's killer queers represent sophisticated attempts to deconstruct the Hollywood stereotype, and/or show how social and cultural forces can shape murderous identities" (172-73). Benshoff's argument that the film adaptation of Highsmith's novel raises similar questions—"Does it merely link together queer desire and criminality, or does it attempt to explain how violence can and does arise from conflicted social and sexual identities?"—arguably applies equally to the original text (173). While there are relevant and unsurprising differences between the written narrative and its on-screen equivalent, those aspects of the original narrative often work in the service of its scrutiny of "the dynamics of the closet" and the toxic influence of postwar American homophobia (179). Thus, it is possible to read Highsmith's original rendition of *The Talented Mr. Ripley* as justifiably "panicking" about American homophobia (not to mention socioeconomic inequality, which plays a tremendous role in Tom's responses to Dickie throughout the novel), just as many have ultimately done with the film.[24] Read in this way, the novel follows a long line of socially aware American narratives from this period, including both fiction and memoir, that have tackled the erosion of the self by racism, sexism, and classism and the connections of that erosion to eruptions of violence.[25]

While an extensive discussion of Highsmith's treatment of queerness in the *Ripley* series would be outside the scope of this chapter, some of these moments that readers have noticed as unique to the novel provide an interesting window into this aspect of *The Talented Mr. Ripley*. David Greven has commented on the doggedness with which Dickie's friend Marge scrutinizes Tom's sexuality in the narrative; she "consistently insinuates as well as explicitly asks if Tom is 'queer,'" with the implication being that such a revelation would eliminate Tom's already tenuous place in their social circle (132). This aggression on Marge's part gives new meaning to the response that Tom has when he sees Dickie kissing Marge and protests that "he knew Dickie didn't mean it, that Dickie was only using this cheap obvious, easy way to hold on to her friendship" (76). In this reading, Marge is more than just a rival of Tom's for Dickie's affection, and Tom's rather naive interpretation of the scene becomes an attempt to explain away Dickie's hurtful liaison with a woman who has repeatedly taunted him. Meanwhile, the specter of physical violence posed by Dickie's friend Freddie Miles as "an actual, homophobic threat to Tom" in the novel clarifies that the danger of a homophobic world in Highsmith's rendering is physical as well as social. If, as Slavoj Žižek has argued, Tom's sexual identity in the written narrative is more ambiguous or "equivocal" than it is in the film, then perhaps one effect of this ambiguity is to place into relief the starkly unambiguous current of prejudice that shapes the events of the novel (Myers 58).[26] What is most certain here is the homophobic terror that so many of Highsmith's characters feel and that the book exposes and critiques.

Class issues sometimes arise as an afterthought in this conversation about Highsmith, yet they are equally essential. We can see this, for instance, in how Highsmith explores the tricky act of "reading" other people—what psychologists sometimes refer to as cognitive empathy. Elsewhere, I have written about how Tom Ripley's uncanny but inconsistent capacity for "everyday mind-reading," as William Ickes calls it, draws attention to class injustice in scenes where he succeeds in mentally manipulating members of the 1950s American "1 percent." When Tom feigns ambivalence about his availability to travel abroad at the start of the novel, speaking "carefully, with the same pondering expression, as if he were even now going over the thousands of little ties that could prevent him," he is hoping to trigger a flash of recognition in Dickie's father that will mark him, falsely, as a member of the upper class (15). He ultimately does dupe the elder Mr. Greenleaf, his success raising questions about the legitimacy of elitist class distinctions. After all, if membership in the elite is so easy to fake, then perhaps the persisting mythology of essential differences between the classes becomes easier to argue against, with its social Darwinist explanations of "disparate rewards for different efforts" that have historically claimed a superior set of personality traits for the wealthy (Goldstene 18). At the same time, the fact that Tom is even in this position, left without a job despite his "talent for mathematics" and relying on his wits instead, speaks to "the disjuncture between the freedom promised by a world of material abundance" in the United States of the 1950s "and the consequences of . . . the Fordist regime of capital accumulation" (14; Pepper 91). Similar ideas arise from Tom's unsuccessful efforts to anticipate the nuances of Dickie's sexuality and the extent of Dickie's homophobia through a form of sociosexual "mind-reading" necessitated by the characters' inability to talk candidly about any form of sexuality besides the most heteronormative. Where he fails at this type of cognitive empathy, Tom and his experiences become a marker of the repressive hold of regressive ideas about sex on the postwar American consciousness.

    Contrasted with the nuance of these ideas as they emerge in Highsmith's novel, Italy in *The Talented Mr. Ripley* comes off quite differently. In this context, Italy plays its recurring role as the liberator, a foil for these comparatively inhibitive American social values. The charmed fictional village of Mongibello brings the two men together: local strangers who "seemed to understand" guide Tom to the right house, where the sun drives him to expose himself "pale and naked" to Dickie on the beach (46, 48). Rome and Naples, the quintessentially southern city, provide a space for the two men to "walk . . . with their arms around each other's shoulders, singing"—a space where they are able to urinate in public, eschew sexual contact with women, and develop an intimacy that seems to extend beyond the traditional bounds of homosocial acquaintance (67). As closeted as he may be, even in Italy, this trio of Italian locales allows Tom to momentarily resist the stranglehold of his home culture and its toxic antiqueerness, engaging in behaviors that contrast with his comportment in the US, where he terms any man who might approach him in a bar "a pervert" (10).

From the perspective of Tom's victims, Highsmith's Italy is also simply a place that can get you killed with impunity, as these wild and ungoverned fictional Italian spaces allow Tom to murder his love interest and survive undetected. In this imagined Italy, unpunished murder is facilitated by the provincial incompetence of a procession of stock characters that includes the exaggerative, unhelpful journalist, the "naively curious" hotel employee, the masses of men "babbling away like a madhouse," and the "short, middle-aged" detective "who looked like thousands of other middle-aged Italians" (168, 250, 149-50). Highsmith's Italy thus is simultaneously flattened and distanced from the ordered, "civilized" world, as much a threat to unsuspecting travelers as a potential site of liberation. The only difference is that in Highsmith's novel, an Anglo-American tourist in Italy is likely not just to die of malaria or to be seduced into a sexual indiscretion but to die a painful death at the hands of a murderer. Through these recycled stereotypes of Italian spaces and their influence, the outsider's vision of *italianità* as exotic, liberatory, and dangerous repeats and is reified.

As a writer embedded in the Anglo-American literary tradition, Highsmith was far from alone in mixing this sensationalist version of Italy with a resistance to heteronormative values. Some of the best examples of this literary pairing, Forster's "Italian novels," come from English rather than American literature. In *A Room with a View*, the novel's central romantic relationship and its existential line of inquiry are catalyzed by the murder of one Italian by another during a dispute over five lire. The event so shocks the novel's timid and polite English protagonists that it dismantles their complacency about their own existence. Likewise, when the Italian dentist's son Gino assaults his English wife in *Where Angels Fear to Tread*, Forster paints Gino's rage as so monstrous that it becomes physically transformative: "His figure rather than his face altered, the shoulders falling forward till his coat wrinkled across the back and pulled away from his wrists. He seemed all arms" (44). And while Forster's novels set in Italy are not overtly queer in the way that *Maurice* is, for instance, both novels contain sexually subversive material—like the homoerotic bathing scene in *A Room with a View* or the unconventional love triangle between Gino, Philip, and Caroline in *Where Angels Fear to Tread*.[27] Even when the homoerotic subtext is not directly acted out against the backdrop of the Italian landscape, as in the English country bathing scene, Italy functions as the initial catalyst that challenges English inhibition and makes these moments of subversion possible. The mere specter of Italianness—and particularly Italian violence, which brings the English almost perversely to life—becomes a source of what Margaret Goscilo calls "Mediterranean erotic-spiritual salvation" (203).

Recognizing these literary ancestors of Highsmith's also helps to clarify what was at stake when, in the year after *The Talented Mr. Ripley* was published, the literary world was first introduced to James Baldwin's *Giovanni's Room*. This was a novel set in Europe, a novel that was very much about sex and Italians, yet it seemed to envision Italy differently, with an Italian character at the center of the narrative who was himself allowed to speak, not just in cultural clichés but about raw, real things. Chapter 2 will turn to Baldwin along with Bernard Malamud and their departures from Highsmith as well as her earlier American counterparts.

Looking Forward

This chapter does not pretend to be a comprehensive overview of all of the Anglo-American literature that featured Italy and imagined *italianità* in the time between Alcott and Highsmith. What it does offer, however, is a few vivid examples of the kind of thinking about Italianness that proliferated in the Anglo-American literary imagination even among writers whose approach to other social issues was at times quite progressive. If Daisy Miller models an admirable blend of proto-feminism and class-based resistance, it is perilous Italy that converts her acts of rebellion into something deadly. Alcott's Jo may face an ending that speaks to the constrictive social expectations for women in nineteenth-century New England, but the narrative problematizes those events and forces in such a way that its narrator's bald statements about "the Italian part" of Laurie's personality are not called into question. The New Women of "Roman Fever" carry themselves with an air of modernity that stands in contrast to the flickering electricity of Wharton's Rome, which may hold traces of its more recent historical self in the wake of the Great War but which harkens back as much if not more to old Anglo-American ideas of premodern, romantically liberating Italy: a place Wharton herself sometimes suggested that she did not want to see change. And despite the ambiguity that has led critics to argue over *The Talented Mr. Ripley*, the critique of antiqueerness and its effects in Highsmith's narrative is rather more nuanced than its portrayal of the country that forms the charming and dangerous backdrop for most of the novel. What these illustrative examples show is the persistence and the prevalence—though not necessarily the universal acceptance—of these received cultural ideas about a putatively foreign space in both literature and popular culture. At various moments, such ideas would critically shape the social if not legal reception of Italian Americans at home in the United States.

These four narratives also show the room left for diasporic US writers to say something different that countered this prevailing understanding of Italy. The narrative tradition of the "Italian novel," as it can be understood from reading James, Wharton, and their compatriots, critically shifts in the hands of writers like Baldwin, Malamud, De Robertis, and Lee. These writers forge interethnic and interdiasporic alliances simultaneously with other forms of social protest, opening up alternate ways of seeing a community of Americans that has at times directly threatened their own communities' survival in America.

Part II

Diasporic Writers on Italian America

Chapter 2

Sex and Diaspora in the New "Italian Novel"
James Baldwin and Bernard Malamud

With the publication of *Giovanni's Room* in 1956, it quickly became clear that this was not a novel that was going to please everybody. In a *New York Times* review of the text, Granville Hicks praised "Mr. Baldwin's subject, the rareness and difficulty of love," and the "rather startling way" in which he had handled it. Though Hicks was notably circumspect in his references to sexuality in the novel, his reaction was positive on the whole. Yet what was most "startling" to some other readers was how, in this new novel, Baldwin had taken up a story of two white men. That one of them was Italian did not lessen the feeling of skepticism among these readers: a feeling that Langston Hughes had already expressed about Baldwin's earlier work in calling *Go Tell It on the Mountain* "a low-down story in a velvet bag—and a Knopf binding" (qtd. in Rampersad 205). Critics' objection to *Giovanni's Room* in particular tended to be that the book "defied the prevailing tacit assumption . . . that black authors must write about what was euphemistically, and characteristically, referred to as 'the Negro problem'" (Jarrett 317).

More recently, some have reinterpreted *Giovanni's Room* as in fact being about Black identities, reading *italianità*, queerness, or both as an allegory for Blackness in ways that even Baldwin's own comments would seem to disavow.[1] Asked by one 1984 interviewer when he had "conceive[d] of leaving black characters out of *Giovanni's Room*," Baldwin responded in an illuminating way. "I suppose the only honest answer to that," he said, "is that *Giovanni's Room* came out of something I had to face. I don't quite know when it came. . . . I certainly could not possibly have—not at that point in my life—handled the other great weight, the 'Negro problem.' The sexual-moral light was a hard thing to deal with. I could not handle both propositions in the same book" (Elgrably and Plimpton 239). Keeping Baldwin's words in mind, I tend to read *Giovanni's Room* not as a novel about Blackness per se but as a "white life novel" that, in the midst of this "sexual-moral" conversation, interrogates multiple significations of whiteness. Significantly, Baldwin's narrative positions its Black author as an authority on the anatomy of this racial construct and its various falsehoods. What is particularly interesting for the purposes of this book is how, in the process, Baldwin's novel takes up the question of *italianità* and becomes an ally text that reaches out to Italian America across diasporas.

A year following the publication of Baldwin's narrative, Bernard Malamud would publish his second novel, *The Assistant*. While sympathetically representing working-class Jewish American immigrants in Brooklyn, New York, Malamud would put these characters in conversation with an Italian American with a more checkered nature: a young man named Frank Alpine, whose portrayal throughout the text is rather problematic. The trouble with Malamud's rendering of Frank is not that he is unsympathetic; in fact, there are elements of his backstory that encourage readers to look more kindly on him than he might otherwise deserve. The trouble is not even that Malamud makes Frank seemingly suspicious of Jewish people; unfortunately, this narrative detail is far from unfair to Italian America, instead accurately capturing an ethno-religious prejudice harbored by many Italian Americans in the mid-century United States. What is actually troubling about Malamud's Frank is the way his character fits and reinforces the stereotypes of his own ethnicity: stereotypes of a violently impulsive, emotional Italian America. So it is perhaps surprising that by 1969, just over a decade later, Malamud was ready to go in a different direction with his renderings of Italianness. In *Pictures of Fidelman*, we can see Malamud begin to rewrite some of these traditional ethnic scripts as he examines relationships that also explicitly resist the conventional wisdom of postwar US heteronormativity.

This chapter explores the more nuanced vision of race, ethnicity, religion, and *italianità* that Baldwin's and Malamud's narratives project amid their explorations of sex. Diaspora figures prominently in both of these ventures: while *Giovanni's Room* probes what occurs when the queer diasporic trajectories of a white American and an Italian intersect,

Pictures of Fidelman imagines a Jewish American protagonist whose time in Italy functions as a form of double expatriation that rewrites his sexual identity. These intersections and repeated displacements gradually reveal a more three-dimensional version of Italianness, despite moments in each book when Italy is familiarly painted as a liberating antidote to a homophobic home culture. In the process, the two fictions call on genre conventions of the African American passing novel as well as recurring Jewish American literary tropes, creating complex literary currents of Black-Italian and Jewish-Italian allyship. The problematic genre of the "Italian novel" receives a critical revision in these quintessential works of diasporic fiction.

Rethinking Sex through Diaspora

Giovanni's Room opens with a consummate moment of resistance: a sexual encounter between male friends, an experience that is fraught and terrifying because it is forbidden in a mid-century America that is obsessed with all things heteronormative. The actors involved are David (Baldwin's first-person protagonist) and a childhood friend named Joey. The backdrop for the scene is an American city rather than a European one, although the encounter eventually inspires David's flight to Paris, where he will meet and begin an affair with the eponymous Giovanni, who will eventually be sentenced to death for committing murder. As it unfolds, this chain of events will invite readers to appreciate Baldwin's manner of rethinking sexual identities, to recognize the place of discourses of diaspora in this project of reinterpretation, and, finally, to trace the work that the novel simultaneously does to reenvision *italianità*.

In the meantime, this early event receives all the attention of the novel's readers, setting the stage for the rest of the narrative with its breathless quality of fear and disbelief. David recalls both of these feelings:

> Then, for the first time in my life, I was really aware of another person's body, of another person's smell. We had our arms around each other. It was like holding in my hand some rare, exhausted, nearly doomed bird which I had miraculously happened to find. . . . I was afraid. I could have cried, cried for shame and terror, cried for not understanding how this could have happened to me. (8–9)

To hear David tell it, the two boys' kiss is accidental, yet Baldwin casts the experience not as a fleeting, aberrant moment of rebellion but as a lasting marker of David's queer identity. "I feel in myself now," he reflects, "a faint, a dreadful stirring of what so overwhelmingly stirred in me then, great thirsty heat, and trembling, and tenderness so painful that I thought my heart would burst. But out of that astounding, intolerable pain came joy" (8). At the same time, Baldwin's use of the words "dreadful" and "intolerable" gestures toward the source of David's "shame and terror"—the impossibility of comfortable, unambivalent homoeroticism, or of moving beyond what Donald E. Hall calls "a simple, fixed hetero-homo binary" in a homophobic cultural climate (102). The opening of *Giovanni's Room* therefore says a great deal not just about who David is but about the nature of the world that surrounds him.

In a sense, the entire problem of the novel is revealed in these few short lines, as David's narration exposes both his indelible difference and his ceaseless capacity for self-hatred: his susceptibility to the social messages of a home culture that he will be unable to forsake. In fact, *Giovanni's Room* resists the doctrine of heteronormativity by representing the strength and consequences of its grip on David's consciousness. David passes for heterosexual throughout the greater part of the story, if not the actual plot of the narrative, and the cornerstone of the novel becomes the doggedness and destructiveness of his attempts to project the air of heterosexual masculinity that American society seems to expect of him—as this is a pressure that he continues to feel even when he is abroad. But what is most painful is how David appears to need to convince himself, not that he might find pleasure in sex with a woman (as this is not necessarily untrue either for Baldwin's protagonist or for Giovanni), but that heterosexual desire represents the sum total of his sexual identity.[2] In the scenes that show him engaged in these efforts, the word "darkening" appears repeatedly, underscoring the somberness and claustrophobia of these moments of denial and pretense (10, 123). Accidental flashes of public honesty are "happily" forgotten, as David's susceptible mind cannot bear the weight of self-recognition (27). Ultimately, David's fear that others may discover the "specifically queer mutability" of his sexuality is more than just a fear of scorn, of being lumped in with "the desperately well-dressed nymphomaniac or trollop" (Hall 157; Baldwin 92). It reflects the desperation of Baldwin's protagonist to disassociate himself from forms of desire that he himself is incapable of recognizing as valid. What's more, these feelings will be what prompts David to leave Giovanni, indirectly bringing about the act of murder that Giovanni commits as well as his execution. Through David's acts of self-denial, Baldwin's novel recognizes the personally destructive influence of American heteronormative values. As Matt Brim puts it, "Giovanni's execution and David's crushing alienation literalize the stakes of failing to love queerly" (60).[3,4]

There is an interesting link to Highsmith here, even if—as we will see—the two novels' approaches to representing Italy and Italianness are deceptively different. Like *The Talented Mr. Ripley*, *Giovanni's Room* is very much about attempts at and failures of cognitive empathy, chronicling the efforts of David's narrator to anticipate what others might believe about him and to shape observers' perceptions of his sexuality so that they might fail to "read" what is on his mind. We can see this in the way that David responds when his older patron Jacques suggests that he strike up a conversation with the young and handsome Italian bartender who will eventually become his lover. David's response is tailored to obscure the very real possibility of his own attraction to Giovanni: "'But man,' [David] said, grinning, 'think of the confusion. He'll think that *I'm* the one who's lusting for his body. How do we get out of that?'" (30). Later, the game of deception escalates when David and Giovanni connect intellectually and, despite David's attempts to remain at arm's length, Giovanni seems poised to act: "I was going to have to tell him that he had made a mistake but that we could still be friends. But I could not be certain, really, that it might not be I who was making a mistake, blindly misreading everything—and out of necessities, then, too shameful to be uttered" (47). At the same time as David seeks to obfuscate his own thoughts, he feels a desperate need and a critical inability to intuit the sexuality of others as he scans for threats to his heteronormative facade. As in Highsmith's novel, the problem of cognitive empathy in Baldwin's narrative becomes a testament to the entrenchment of the antiqueer attitudes that make it so difficult for Baldwin's American narrator to openly claim a more complex and varied sexual identity than the socially sanctioned heteronormative one.

Giovanni's Room also enacts a more direct form of resistance by imagining a brief interlude in the life of Baldwin's protagonist when he does openly acknowledge and act on this complexity. David and Giovanni develop a bond that David describes as instantaneous, organic, and unbreakable by human interference. As David explains, the two men "connected the instant that we met. And remain connected still, in spite of our later *séparation de corps*" (42–43). The exquisite naturalness of the relationship is visible in seemingly incidental narrative details that form a counterpoint to the dark, rather morbid imagery associated with David's self-alienation. While David and Giovanni are living together, spring arrives in Paris, and David recalls how "the river stretched before [them] with a greater haze of promise" (77). Here, the seasonal rhythms of the natural world synchronize with the two men's relationship, working as an arguably cliché symbol of the joint potential for rebirth and fulfillment that they find in one another. The cliché serves an essential function, however, since it destabilizes the specious distinctions that have so often been drawn between queer relationships and the heterosexual ones that such language has most traditionally been used to describe. With this conventional symbolism, Baldwin refuses to paint David and Giovanni's relationship as aberrant, even if the prevalent values of David's (and Baldwin's) American world would have proclaimed it to be so.[5]

By the time Giovanni finds himself face to face with Guillaume, the bar owner he is guillotined for murdering, this happy portion of the narrative has long been over. The story of David and Giovanni unfolds out of chronological order, and the novel ends with David's imagining of what might have occurred—what Giovanni might have felt—that would have led him to this violent act. He narrates the grim scene for us: "For, with his pleasure taken, and while Giovanni still lies suffocating, Guillaume becomes a businessman once more and, walking up and down, gives excellent reasons why Giovanni cannot work for him anymore. Beneath whatever reasons Guillaume invents, the real one lies hidden . . . Giovanni, like a falling movie star, has lost his drawing power" (155–56). With this present-tense narration, David becomes the author of his own fictional metanarrative. In so doing, he not only deepens the sense of sordid pain that permeates so much of *Giovanni's Room* but traces the origins of that pain to both individual causes and larger, more systemic roots. Giovanni is poor and desperate for a job because David has forsaken him. David has forsaken Giovanni because he is determined to deny the complexities of his sexuality that he has been essentially programmed since childhood to reject. Left physically and emotionally vulnerable in the wake of David's betrayal, Giovanni is as fragile as the "rare, exhausted, nearly doomed bird" that David imagines in his initial encounter with Joey at the start of the novel. It almost does not matter whether David is right about how the scene between Giovanni and Guillaume unfolds. Instead, it matters that David is right about these root causes, the very real social forces that the rest of the narrative has already sketched in detail by its sobering end, when Giovanni becomes their ultimate victim in his execution for murder.

What, then, is the role of diaspora in all of this? Giovanni and David are both displaced from home, but their travels, at first glance, are likely to seem individual rather than collective. When David flees the US and Giovanni flees Italy, the upheaval that pushes them abroad is in some ways a very private one. Both are emotionally lost, pained by the scars of their past and seeking a form of escape that they hope will come from a foreign place. This may sound like a personal, emotional kind of exile rather than a diasporic species of displacement. In William Safran's definitional work on diaspora, in contrast, he rightly stresses the nature of such displacements as community experiences: diaspora is something that happens to "expatriate minority communities" in which each individual is only a small part of a larger whole (83). Yet there is in fact an urgently communal component to the displacements from home that take place within the pages of Baldwin's novel. *Giovanni's Room* examines what some theorists refer to as a "queer diaspora," which includes both "the creation of queer spaces within ethnically defined diasporas" and "the transnational and multicultural network of connections of queer cultures and 'communities'" (Fortier 183).

While David, for instance, is not part of a particular ethnic community forced to relocate from the postwar United States to Paris, France, he nevertheless belongs to a diasporic community—a "transnational and multicultural network" that, however hesitantly and intermittently, he joins on arriving on French soil. David's diasporic identity is located not just in the geography of his movements but in his emotions about them as well: particularly the way he "ache[s], intolerably, with a longing to go home," yet feels a "bitterness of spirit" (62) about the home he has fled. This ambivalence tends to be a hallmark of diaspora. Giovanni takes his membership in the community even more seriously; once immersed in a relationship with David, he is determined to continue living with his lover, so that the two men's affective differences testify to the diverse emotional consequences of displacement from home. Despite their differences, both men's flight into the queer "cultural homeland" of Paris can itself be understood as its own type of diasporic movement and affiliation (Schimel 167). By fleshing out the diasporic membership of David and Giovanni in this transnational community, *Giovanni's Room* makes an additional gesture of defiance, recognizing the international architecture of the queer resistance.

Pictures of Fidelman is a very different book from *Giovanni's Room*, and nowhere is this clearer than at the end of Baldwin's novel. The ending of *Giovanni's Room* feels almost painfully sincere, largely as a result of David's narrative voice. In it, we can hear how David has been shaken by his knowledge of Giovanni's impending death and by his imaginings of the events that would have transpired before he was executed: "Perhaps it is only beginning. Perhaps he still sits in his cell, watching, with me, the arrival of the morning. Perhaps now there are whispers at the end of the corridor, three heavy men in black taking off their shoes, one of them holding the ring of keys, all of the prison silent" (166–67). The tone of Malamud's narrative, which reads as an episodic story cycle more than a novel as traditionally conceived, is immediately different. It opens with a frank appraisal of how the eponymous Fidelman, "a self-confessed failure as a painter" and a quasi-tourist in Rome, begins traipsing around the city in "gum-soled oxblood shoes" and "a tweed suit he had on despite the late-September sun," as well as a suitcase "borrowed from his sister Bessie" (3). How the immediacy of Fidelman's dopiness affects the ideological projects and accomplishments of *Pictures of Fidelman* is open to debate, and readers may see the text's resistance to heteronormative values as being undercut by the ambiguously satirical quality of Malamud's narrative voice. As Irving H. Buchen has noted, "Malamud employs an ironic cutting edge" in this particular work, and "to distinguish irony from ideology . . . may not be possible" for his readers (64). Nevertheless, there is a very real undercurrent of subversion in Malamud's story cycle—a resistance to heteronormativity that, informed by its own vision of diaspora, makes *Pictures of Fidelman* deeply serious in its own way.

Fidelman's wanderings through Italy are as much about sexual exploration as they are about anything else. Like any protagonist who begins their narrative with a "perspiring hand" and a borrowed suitcase, Fidelman is neither a dapper figure nor a romantic one (3). Nevertheless, most of the narrative's episodes find him spending at least some time encountering, sizing up, and pursuing physical relationships with people he meets on his travels. This is a project that seems to help him come into his own, though most of the growth occurs through discomfort. That the people with whom Fidelman becomes embroiled in relationships are often women does not diminish the thematic importance of the episode that ends the text, when Fidelman meets Beppo, an Italian glassblower who will become his lover. Instead, as in *Giovanni's Room*, the mutability of Fidelman's experiences of desire is in large part what makes them revolutionary. Beppo's wife Margherita is the one Fidelman initially cozies up to, and the two engage in an affair that takes place under Beppo's very nose, with the Jewish American visitor often invited to stay for family dinners of "ravioli, cheese, bread, white wine" (189). Soon, however, Fidelman falls into an affair with Beppo himself. Their initial encounter is much more comical than romantic—"Don't hurt me, Beppo, please, I have piles," Fidelman protests (199). Yet the tone changes decisively when Beppo commands, "Think of love. . . . You've run from it all your life (199).

Unlike Baldwin's David, Fidelman appears untroubled by heteronormative strictures as this turn in the narrative unfolds: "He said [I love you] to Beppo. If that's the way it works, that's the way it works. Better love than no love. If you sneeze at life it backs off," he muses (199). The lovers' shared determination to seize the life they have been given makes a different type of challenge to antiqueerness. Rather than delineating the painful, inhibiting consequences of prejudice, the Beppo episode and its playful language proffer a positive model for resistance to those received notions, affirming that they do not have to be a death knell for individual happiness. Fidelman's internally untroubled—and ultimately positive—manifestations of queer desire and love save Malamud's text from the ambiguity that has spurred some misguided readers to argue that *Giovanni's Room* illustrates the damaging consequences of homosexuality rather than those of heteronormativity and homophobia. What's more, despite the episode's often-joking tone, Malamud associates the homoerotic with a profound emotional connection that makes it fundamentally unlike the narrative's superficial, cruel affairs between susceptible women and selfish, aggressive men. Malamud's narrator reveals that "Fidelman had never in his life said 'I love you' without reservation to anyone" before Beppo (199).

Meanwhile, Fidelman's heterosexual liaisons tend to bring personal destruction in their wake, even in areas that do not relate to sex. After one such experience, Fidelman is left "depressed" and unsettled about a painting that he has been endeavoring to finish:

> He went over his painting inch by inch and it seemed to him a disappointment. Where was Momma after all these years? He got up to look, and doing so, changed his mind; not bad at all, though Ludovico was right, the picture was dark and could stand a touch of light. He laid out his paints and brushes and began to work, almost at once achieving the effect he sought. And then he thought he would work a bit on the girl's face,

> no more than a stroke or two around the eyes and mouth, to make her expression truer to life. . . . F put down his brush, washed up and returned for a look at the painting. Sickened to his gut, he saw what he felt: He had ruined it. It slowly drowned in his eyes. (146)

Although Fidelman's female lover is the one who cautions him not to change his painting, telling him that he'll "never make it better," the superficiality of their bond leaves Fidelman feeling a kind of dejected restlessness that manifests in the destruction of his art (145). Contrast this with the moment in the final episode when it is revealed that Fidelman, after his relationship with Beppo, has found his vocation as a glassmaker. Even before becoming his lover, Beppo has been daring enough to confront Fidelman with what he already knows—that he is not and has never been an artist—and Fidelman is finally awake enough to listen. With queer love at the root of Fidelman's reckoning with himself, the narrative forces a confrontation with bigoted ideas about gay sex as "debasing." Indeed, in Jerome Hamilton Buckley's schema of "exalting" and "debasing" love affairs as a component of *bildung*, or coming of age, relationships like Fidelman's and Beppo's would be emphatically designated as exalting, for they allow Fidelman to permanently clarify his own understanding of himself and his place in the world (17).

It eventually becomes clear that Fidelman will not remain in Italy with Beppo, and he chooses, instead, to return to the United States. Like Baldwin's David, Fidelman is the one to end the relationship, although he does so at the behest of Margherita, who reveals that with her husband neglecting her and their family, she is "at the end of [her] strength" (207). Like Giovanni, Beppo is hurt, though the hurt comes across differently when translated into Malamud's more lighthearted language. "Before leaving Venice," his narrator tells us, "Fidelman blew a slightly hump-backed green horse for Beppo, the color of his eyes. 'Up yours,' said the glass blower, grieving at the gray in Fidelman's hair" (208). Yet against all odds, Fidelman's return to the US does not spell unhappiness for him. Instead, *Pictures of Fidelman* ends with an image of Malamud's protagonist finding professional and sexual fulfillment on familiar shores: "In America," we learn, "he worked as a craftsman in glass and loved men and women" (208). In an interview, Malamud himself once referred to this ending as "Fidelman escap[ing] his worst fate," and indeed,

Fidelman emerges as a much less self-denying and tortured version of Baldwin's protagonist (Stern 65). Malamud also implicitly suggests that if Fidelman's character has become less self-concerned during the course of these six chapters, this trajectory of growth results from Fidelman's first experience of queer love.[6] It is only when he has attained this level of human connection that Fidelman is capable of meaningfully acting on any impulse besides his own interest. Thus interpreted, even Fidelman's willingness to end his affair with Beppo works in the service of a subversive message. Amid the text's ironies and grotesqueries, *Pictures of Fidelman* proposes queer self-actualization as the catalyst for a broader form of ethical self-actualization. The end result is much the same as in *Giovanni's Room*: both texts strongly resist received postwar American notions of sexual identity.

Of course, none of this transformational work could have happened to the fictional Fidelman without the mechanisms of diaspora, which in his case are complicated by repeated experiences of displacement that leave him multiply removed from his community's ancestral home. When Malamud follows his Jewish American protagonist to Italy, he creates an implicit triangular relationship between the geographic roots of Fidelman's Jewish ancestors, his own home in the United States, and his temporarily adopted homeland of Italy. To really understand how this works, we have to keep in mind that diasporic communities include not just first-generation immigrants but their descendants as well, recognizing the ways that experiences of alienation and longing for home—all defining qualities of diaspora—are emotionally and intellectually inherited from one generation to the next. For Fidelman, about whose life in the US we know little other than that he seems to have been dissatisfied, it is this second dislocation to Italy that brings with it the promise of fulfillment and self-knowledge.

Malamud also further complicates this arrangement by introducing other religious and ethno-national "outsider" characters into the narrative, such as the Israeli refugee Fidelman encounters in the first episode in the cycle, whose collision with the protagonist creates new intersections between (Jewish) American, Italian, and Israeli diasporic identities. These collisions have intriguing implications for Malamud's vision of Italianness, as I will explore later, but they also serve to push Fidelman farther from the comforts of home and toward wanderings that, once he encounters Beppo, will lead him to a new home within himself. In the initial episode, for instance, the Israeli Susskind steals a briefcase containing the Jewish American expatriate's writings. While Fidelman is understandably distraught, Susskind proclaims the manuscript devoid of "spirit" and the theft a "favor" (37). This collision of diasporic communities—or subcommunities, since both belong to the larger diachronic arc of the Jewish diaspora—forces Fidelman to turn his attention to other things, Beppo eventually becoming one of them. We know what chain reaction results from this initial cause. The intersecting forces of diaspora, rather than encounters with exotic Otherness as in Wharton or Highsmith, become a key catalyst of change for Malamud's initially humdrum protagonist.

Like Baldwin's novel, then, Malamud's narrative is colored by the influence of diaspora. And perhaps this is unsurprising given the complex, life-shaping diasporic patterns in Baldwin's and Malamud's own experiences. For Baldwin, Africa, the United States, and Europe had already formed a critical geographical and cultural triangle by the time he began to write *Giovanni's Room*.[7] In Paris, Baldwin's identity became even more complex than previously: already a queer writer of the African diaspora, he also became an American expatriate, a diasporic individual who had moved through and into multiple adopted homelands. *Notes of a Native Son*, Baldwin's 1955 collection of essays, is arguably the first of Baldwin's writings to concretize this experience of double displacement, confronting anti-Black racism in the United States and Paris as well as the complexities of an American expatriate culture necessitated, among other things, by antiqueer prejudice in the US. *Another Country* would also reflect these relationships between geographies and cultures, if with varying degrees of explicitness. For his own part, as a second-generation Jewish American who married an Italian American woman, Malamud lived out another complex form of diaspora, in which two people's diasporic communities collide in the physical and cultural space of a single host country. This particular intersection of Jewish, Italian, and American identities is most closely reflected in *The Assistant*, but it has intermittent echoes in *Pictures of Fidelman* as well.

In their diasporic challenges to the status quo, Baldwin and Malamud uphold an American tradition of literary progressivism—of rewriting social codes related to gender, sexuality, and class—that can be traced to varying degrees from Alcott and James through to Wharton and even Highsmith. What shifts, though, are the other implications of diaspora, as these narratives of displacement propose a vision of *italianità* that rewrites the old scripts, even as it retains some well-worn stereotypes of Italian spaces and people.

Familiar Strangeness and the New "Italian Novel"

In Baldwin and Malamud, Italianness is sexually liberating in a way that we might expect given the precedent set by American writers from Alcott to Highsmith, not to mention their English counterparts. Baldwin's eponymous Italian expatriate quickly develops the power to undo David's barriers to recognizing his own queer identity, even if that power may not effect lasting change in the ways that will ultimately matter most to the happiness of either man. Meanwhile, Malamud's protagonist has transformational experiences in Italy that are painted as though they could only originate in Italian spaces. In this way, Baldwin and Malamud borrow extensively and meaningfully from the paradigmatic "Italian novel." Yet *Giovanni's Room* and *Pictures of Fidelman* still pair their resistance to heteronormativity with a less binary vision of American culture and its Italian alternative. By depicting complex diasporic trajectories that span Israel, the United States, Italy, and France, these novels expand the range of players in the cultural encounter and complicate the conventions of the Anglo-American "Italian novel." In the process, Italy seems to come to life, with fresher and more three-dimensional textures, and Baldwin and Malamud express a sort of tenuous solidarity with Italy and Italian America.

A chorus of critics has affirmed the importance of the eponymous Giovanni as a foil for David where sexual identities are concerned. Cyraina E. Johnson-Roullier describes Giovanni as "the opposing pole within the text, the pole by which its actual reality is given not only form, but depth, meaning, and acceptance" (950). For Mae Henderson, confronting Giovanni is what requires David to "at last and unavoidably . . . come to terms with homoerotic desire. His relationship with Giovanni exposes the falseness and the guilt underlying David's seeming innocence" (312). In essence, Giovanni provides an authentic counterpoint to David's pretense and his willful self-denial. Yet these readings miss the way that this position of Giovanni's within the narrative relies on a vision of his Italianness that will be familiar to us from canonical Anglo-American texts. Baldwin does access the same tired stereotypes of *italianità*—particularly stereotypical imaginings of the rural southern Italian—in considering how this foreign influence might free an Anglo-American from the sociosexual expectations of his home culture.

In the lead-up to Giovanni and David's love affair, Giovanni is characterized in ways that distinguish him from David and that make those distinctions a matter of national or even regional rather than individual or European character.[8] In David's mind, Giovanni is charismatic and alive—"so vivid, so winning"—and neatly fits the Anglo stereotype of the vivacious, irrepressible Italian with his inevitable origins in the rural agricultural south, the seat of so much Italian immigration to the United States in the decades before *Giovanni's Room* was written and the target of so much internal stereotyping on the part of northerners within Italy itself (43). Even before Giovanni reveals that he is from a village "that is very old and in the south," readers who are familiar with this matrix of stereotypes might guess that he is not a northerner from the particular way in which his character is depicted (138). Yet David is a patently unreliable narrator, and readers might fairly suspect that these descriptions stem from his white American subjectivity, whether he is reflecting on Giovanni's charisma or generalizing about how many "kids like Giovanni . . . turn into gigolos and gangsters and God knows what" (134). So it is notable that Baldwin inserts many of the same generalizations into Giovanni's own mouth, inflecting his dialogue with impassioned declarations of difference. Giovanni remarks that

> "[Parisians] are not like the people I knew when I was younger. In Italy we are friendly, we dance and sing and make love—but these people . . . these people, they are cold, I do not understand them."
> "But the French say," I teased, "that the Italians are too fluid, too volatile, have no sense of measure—"
> "Measure!" cried Giovanni, "ah, these people and their measure! They measure the gram, the centimeter, these people, and they keep piling all the little scraps they save, one on top of the other, year in and year out. . . . I do not like to offend your ears by saying all the things I am sure these people measure before they permit themselves any act whatever. May I offer you a drink now," he asked suddenly, "before the old man comes back?" (36)

Giovanni's reply does not challenge or temper David's stereotypical view of Italians as spontaneous and immoderate where others are cautiously reserved. Instead, these remarks endorse David's essentialist vision, asserting a strictly demarcated typology of European national, regional, and cultural identities. David himself may not fully understand what is at stake for southern Italians in these ideas—yet when he paints all Italians with the same brush, the stereotypes that he invokes pose a particular danger to southern Italians and southern Italian Americans who in previous decades had seen themselves maligned on two continents using similar rationales.

Giovanni's comments create a crucial context for later expressions of his sociosexual philosophy, as when he asks David, "And when you have waited—has it made you sure?" (38). Giovanni's earlier remarks suggest that his openness to human connection and persuasive resistance to the American imperative of sexual conformity are byproducts of some essential nature that, even in his own mind, he apparently seems to possess due to a cultural identity tied to national and perhaps more specifically regional origins.[9] The familiar tropes reproduced here are ones that had begun in the nineteenth century to be increasingly associated not just with rural Italy overall but especially with southern Italy and Sicily. Thomas A. Guglielmo relates how the 1911 "U.S. Immigration Commission, throughout its highly influential forty-two-volume report . . . argued that northern and southern Italians 'differ from each other materially in language, physique and character.' . . . [T]he latter was 'excitable, impulsive, imaginative, impracticable,'" and in these ways undesirable to the US (34). The echoes here of Giovanni's own self-concept and self-descriptions are striking.

This manner of imagining *italianità* dovetails with the descriptions of charmingly simple, "uncivilized," and potentially dangerous Italian spaces and customs that are sprinkled throughout the novel, casting Giovanni and his former community as the type of Italians who would have been denigrated by Americans as well as northerners in his own country. Giovanni recounts how before the death of his infant son, he "wanted to stay [in his village] forever and eat much spaghetti and drink much wine and make many babies and grow fat," embracing a life that is "dripping and bursting and beautiful and terrible" (138). Although Giovanni rails against the idea of an older David "telling all the other Americans you meet that they must come and see our village because it is so picturesque," Giovanni's own comments are equally reductive, diminishing his rural agricultural town until all that remains are simple, timeless elements: food, sex, and death (139). Consistent with this vision is Giovanni's account of how he and his "girl" respond when their son is stillborn: they "spanked it on the buttocks and . . . sprinkled it with holy water and . . . prayed but it never made a sound, it was dead" (139–40). This self-characterization is reminiscent of overtly racist late-nineteenth-century northern Italian accounts that painted southern Italians as illogical, superstitious thinkers with "a kind of "strange intelligence" in their "muddled brains" (qtd. in Guglielmo 33). Giovanni also embraces the same stereotypical violent misogyny that Gino does in *Where Angels Fear to Tread*, suggesting that women "need to be beaten half to death so they can find out who rules the world" (80). Resistance to heteronormativity quickly becomes bound up with a stereotypical narrative of Italian sensuality and violence that was peddled increasingly by both Anglo-Americans and northern Italians in the century leading up to the novel's publication. After all, in the supposedly primitive south, what social scientist Edward Ross called "a propensity for personal violence" was to be expected (qtd. in Guglielmo 34).

This line of thinking also raises questions about the murder that leads Giovanni to be executed at the close of the narrative. Somehow, Baldwin does not seem to entirely disavow the idea that Giovanni's sudden act of violence is an outgrowth of something fundamental to the southern Italian nature, the same distaste for "measure" that distinguishes Giovanni from Baldwin's French and American characters. This unsettling uncertainty recalls the flat representation of Italy in Anglo-American novels where Italy and death seem practically synonymous. Yet this is not the only way to read Baldwin's evocations of Italian stereotypes. In his study of African American and Italian American modernity, Pardini takes up this problem in *Giovanni's Room*:

> Of course, this crescendo of lurid stereotypes is a joke, and hardly a bad one, especially because the joke is on the reader and, to an extent, on Baldwin himself, the black homosexual Harlemite writer who plays with the invisible blackness of Italian American men to unmask whiteness in what myopic critics . . . have called Baldwin's raceless novel. . . . Quite the contrary, *Giovanni's Room* is a novel *about* race: the white race. . . . The stereotyping of the Italians ridicules Italian culture and people in order to subvert America's racial discourse and identity. (123–24)

Reinterpreting Baldwin's novel in light of this concept of "invisible blackness," a term that Pardini uses to refer to the de facto or social ambiguity of Italian Americans' racial identities, Pardini ascribes a playful self-consciousness to Baldwin's stereotyping—which, viewed in this light, works in the service of a bigger debate about the nature and the social construction of whiteness, destabilizing conveniently unifying fictions of white American identity. This idea is different from the argument that some scholars have made about *Giovanni's Room* as a coded or allegorical narrative of the "Black gay experience," which, as Stephanie Li rightly notes, "trivializes racial difference while severely curbing Baldwin's artistic freedom to inhabit other subjectivities" and reinforcing "the tacit requirement that for literature to be black it must be about blackness" (135). Instead, Giovanni's concretely ambiguous racialization becomes, like David's "psychic necessity of . . . inventing racial distinctions," a way for Baldwin to critique whiteness as a social construct that can begin to be dismantled and disarmed if its falsity is revealed (136).

Given the centrality of Baldwin's nonfictional writings to whiteness studies and especially to scholars' understanding of the artificiality of whiteness, it is unsurprising that *Giovanni's Room* might play with questions of white identity in this way. In his 1984 essay "On Being 'White' . . . and Other Lies," Baldwin would write eloquently about the fiction of whiteness as distinct from the reality of more specific ethnic and diasporic identities:

> There is, for example—at least in principle—an Irish community: here, there, anywhere, or, more precisely, Belfast, Dublin and Boston. There is a German community: both sides of Berlin, Bavaria and Yorkville. There is an Italian community: Rome, Naples, the Bank of the Holy Ghost and Mulberry Street. And there is a Jewish community, stretching from Jerusalem to California to New York. There are English communities. There are French communities. . . . No one was white before he/she came to America. It took generations, and a vast amount of coercion, before this became a white country. (178)

Baldwin's point, like Pardini's, is not that communities like the Italian American one did not enjoy the advantages of whiteness on arrival that scholars like Guglielmo have described. What he highlights instead is the way that white ethnic communities and individuals progressively came to define themselves personally as white, buying into a fictionalized shared identity that was fabricated "because of the necessity of denying the Black presence, and justifying the Black subjugation" (178). It is not for nothing that Nell Irvin Painter's *The History of White People* specifically cites Baldwin's ideas on this subject, rehearsing his argument that "[e]mbracing white supremacy and losing their ethnic identities . . . were the price second-generation immigrants paid for the ticket to American whiteness" (376).[10]

In *Giovanni's Room* in particular, the monolithic construction of whiteness on which the fiction of white supremacy depends begins to crumble under the pressure of distinct European identities, which challenge both white values and the very category of whiteness. Like the various "communities" that Baldwin would describe in his later essay, the Italian and French characters who populate the narrative come from different worlds and partake of different cultural traditions that point to the absurdity of attempting to lump them together under the artificial heading of a supposedly shared racial identity. Baldwin points out these fissures in the American racial narrative with comparatively little cost to the real Italians who will quite obviously fail to live up to Baldwin's caricature of their identities, as David's Italian love interest is so blatantly typecast that we cannot possibly read him "straight" or believe in him as a realist representation of Italianness, whatever region he hails from. In a sense, Baldwin enlists southern Italians as his allies as he appropriates Anglo stereotypes of *italianità* to dismantle this larger set of Anglo-American ideas about race that have been so central to white supremacy and especially to anti-Blackness. *Giovanni's Room* asks these Italians—and by extension their Italian American counterparts—to accept being the butt of a good-natured joke with a punch line far greater than themselves or their own experiences of anti-Italian prejudice.

This is also not the only way that Baldwin interacts with Italianness, especially where questions of diaspora are concerned. For one thing, Baldwin's narrative deviates from the stereotypical "Italian novel" by lifting its eponymous Italian out of Italy. This shift creates a dynamic that is distinct from the dichotomous relationship between the American or English expatriate on Italian soil and the Italian villager or city-dweller at home—the sort of relationship that we see between Daisy and Giovanelli in *Daisy Miller*, for instance. Baldwin moves his Italian character to the center of the narrative not just by naming the book after him, at least after a fashion, but by allowing Giovanni his own experience of expatriation and diasporic identity, rather than making his American protagonist the only character who experiences these dynamics of displacement.[11] In fact, Baldwin endows Giovanni as an expatriate with a voice that often echoes the thoughts and experiences of characters in earlier Anglo-American "Italian novels," effecting a significant shift in roles. In Giovanni's comment that "I have only just found out that I want to live," the echo of Forster is unmistakable, yet Baldwin has flipped the script (49). Giovanni, like the English hero transfixed by death in *A Room with a View*, begins to express a joyous openness to experience as his new life in Paris unfolds to include the possibility of love with David.[12] Baldwin casts Giovanni in this moment not as a stereotypical peasant but as a man transformed by experiences of migration, separation from his homeland, and connection with strangers in new spaces. In this way, the intersection of Giovanni's and David's diasporic trajectories in Paris gives Giovanni the same complexity and development that we might expect from an American or English hero in the traditional "Italian novel," instead of imposing a static, predictable identity on an Italian stock character. Thus transfixed, Giovanni offers perfectly reasoned "queer critique[s]" of David's self-destructive attitudes, his character disrupting larger ethnocentric fictions of logical, cool-headed northerners and destructive, unthinking southerners (Brim 60).

At other times, Baldwin uses these diasporic collisions to equalize the relationship between the two men, who are in some ways mirror images of one another. Both have been geographically displaced by past traumas—in David's case, sexual nonbelonging and fear of his father; in Giovanni's, the unexpected stillbirth of a child. Both maintain complex internal relationships with their home countries after arriving in Paris, and both have a critical influence on each other's experiences of dislocation from home. Earlier "Italian novels" segregated Italians from Anglo-Americans by making Italian "natives" the unidirectional agents of change for English or American travelers abroad. Daisy dies through Giovanelli's negligence, but despite the sorrow Giovanelli may feel about Daisy's death, the ending of James's novella provides no evidence that his existence will critically change as a result of her influence. In contrast, Baldwin suggests that David and Giovanni as expatriates act as mutual catalysts and, in so doing, gestures toward their shared diasporic identity rather than toward the boundaries of nationality and ethnicity that separate them. The effect is to recuperate Giovanni's *italianità* by recognizing his fully fleshed out humanity, although in this case, this effect occurs through the collapsing of ethno-national boundaries and distances.

Finally, although Giovanni's stated reasons for leaving home may be largely individual, Baldwin points readers' attention to the wave of the Italian diaspora that occurred after the Second World War, just as he represents the American expatriate communities that existed in Europe during that period and the transnational queer diasporic subculture in

Paris. This encourages readers to see Italy as a modern country with its own regional, national, and international history rather than as a charmingly primal, static, and ahistorical land. As in Alcott's commentary on the *Risorgimento*, Italian history becomes a focus of attention, but without the sorts of oversimplifications that Alcott makes in her descriptions of "scrapes" and "squabblers." If Baldwin's novel asks Italians and Italian Americans to ally themselves with people of color in dismantling fictions of whiteness, *Giovanni's Room* also makes reciprocal gestures of solidarity with Italy and Italian America by rewriting the "Italian novel" in these ways.

These fresh imaginings of Italy make it almost disappointing to return to stereotypes in turning the same critical eye on Malamud as on *Giovanni's Room*. Still, *Pictures of Fidelman* invites this type of scrutiny, as Malamud's narrative presents readers with some undeniably formulaic Italian characters. The Italian Catholic Annamaria "is a stereotypical Italian woman . . . mercurial and volatile," with "a religious obsession" as omnipresent as her superstitions—and notably, she hails from the southern city of Naples (Gordon 44). Fidelman's lover Beppo is irrepressibly violent, playing the part of that resilient stock character fabricated by Anglo-Americans: the Italian brute. Confronted with the mediocrity of Fidelman's art, Beppo does not restrict himself to verbal criticism. In addition to proclaiming that the work "lacks authority and originality," Beppo destroys his future lover's canvases by slashing them with a kitchen knife (197). And this is not all. Beppo is also "handsome, hardworking, and loved to breathe; he smelled (and tasted) of oil and vinegar; he was, after all, a tender man and gentle lover" (199). Readers will recognize Beppo's romantic side from *Little Women*'s Laurie, his zest for life from *Daisy Miller*'s Giovanelli, and his desirability as a lover from the "Campolieri boy" in "Roman Fever." Without too many mental gymnastics, Beppo can be read as a composite of all these Anglo-American renderings of *italianità*. Predictably, these elements of Beppo's character are also what inspires Fidelman to move beyond his previous understanding of love, inspiring social experiment in just the way that we would expect based on these earlier narratives. Fidelman's sexual self-expression is a function of both Beppo's desirability and his forcefulness, which set the stage for Fidelman's happy acquiescence to his advances.

Still, the "oil and vinegar" reference, with its playful Woolfian tone, should be our tip-off that something different is happening in Malamud's narrative than we see in Alcott or Wharton. Like Virginia Woolf's *Orlando* in its satire of the biographical genre, *Pictures of Fidelman* is funny—

bitingly humorous—especially in its talent for exaggeration.[13] Whereas the caricature of Italianness in *Giovanni's Room* still feels quite serious despite its playful quality, as though something deeply important is at stake in terms of ideology, *Pictures of Fidelman* feels uniformly ready to entertain, to be laughed at, to shock, and even to offend, as some of its more sexually explicit moments of narration suggest. So there is already something here that encourages us to read Malamud's composite Italians as a way to poke good-humored fun at the stereotypes themselves, or even at the novels and novelists that begat them. Even more so than in Baldwin, when the stereotypes are made comically ridiculous, they cease to be a believable critique of Italianness, and they may instead become a sort of upbeat critique of themselves. This is made all the more true by the fact that the Beppo episode takes place in Venice rather than in a city or a rural village of the south. The stereotypes evoked here, then, disrupt northern Italian ideas of southern Italian difference through their gentle teasing.

More to the point is how Fidelman's complex, retreaded experiences of geographic displacement help his narrative to move beyond the expected paradigm of the "Italian novel." Early on, Fidelman arrives in Rome only to have his first social encounter be with Susskind, the "Jewish refugee from Israel" (7). In this collision of the American and Israeli branches of the Jewish diasporic community, Malamud locates an important aspect of Fidelman's social liberation, appropriating and recasting another typical plot device from the traditional "Italian novel." At the start of Forster's *A Room with a View*, the novelist Miss Lavish has lost a novel-in-progress to the waves at Amalfi, just as Malamud's protagonist loses his manuscript in the first episode of the narrative. As I have previously suggested, this event becomes a trigger for Fidelman's artistic and social liberation, as well as his sociosexual resistance. Notably, however, the loss of the manuscript is not the fault of the Tyrrhenian Sea or a slow Italian shopkeeper (as in Forster). With the Israeli Jewish refugee responsible for the theft, this pivotal moment in the book involves a more geographically and culturally diverse set of players than the typical "Italian novel" allows for. Suddenly, this simple, humorous plot twist begins to take on further-reaching implications: it complicates the text's vision of *italianità* by playfully challenging the stereotypical Italian monopoly on both destruction and liberation.

Later, Fidelman's double displacement as a Jewish American abroad in Italy has a similar effect. Literary lore suggests that Philip

Roth disliked *Pictures of Fidelman* because Fidelman is "not conflicted about consorting with whores" and is "too free of guilt and shame," which makes him appear "insufficiently Jewish" (Gordon 45). However, the subtext of Fidelman's behavior throughout the narrative is precisely the fraught influence of his Jewishness, which visually manifests in his paintings, giving him a frustrated, complicated diasporic identity as a Jewish American floundering in a string of Italian cities. This aspect of Fidelman's identity complicates the traditional binary relationship between the Anglo-American and Italian that the classic "Italian novel" insists on. Most critically, Malamud depicts Fidelman as a member of a marginalized ethno-religious community that is culturally disenfranchised by the Italian Catholic majority in the novel. As a student of art, Fidelman is incapable of escaping the cultural freight of the Madonna archetype, and he incorporates Stars of David so stealthily into his paintings in Italy that they are eventually rendered invisible.[14] This power dynamic is mirrored in the many experiences Fidelman has in Italian cities and with Italian people, both southern and northern, where he is socially or sexually subordinated—even the (ultimately generative) encounter with Beppo. As a result, through the multiply displaced identity of his protagonist, Malamud shifts the imagined relationship between the Anglo-American abroad and the Italian spaces and people he encounters, eliminating the paternalistic element that earlier writers had insisted on in peddling their visions of a volatile yet charmingly subordinate modern Italy. In thus criticizing and even occasionally villainizing Italian culture, *Pictures of Fidelman* departs from Italian stereotypes through a not unreasonable form of "tough love" that anticipates later novels like Lee's *Aloft*.

Diasporic Literatures and Good Allies

As the history of the Anglo-American "Italian novel" demonstrates, it is not necessarily possible to separate Italy from Italian America in these literary representations. At times, as in James's travel writing, Italians and Italian Americans have been imbued with very different characteristics in the minds of Anglo-Americans and other outsiders. Yet "Italian novels" set in Italy and populated with Italians simultaneously had a real impact on perceptions of Italian Americans back home in the United States. This historical reality raised the stakes for books like *Giovanni's Room* and *Pictures of Fidelman*, which had a similar potential to edit cultural perceptions of Italian Americans despite representing Italy and Italians within their pages. Both narratives ultimately made these gestures of allyship despite the very real threat that *italianità* on American shores had posed to both the African American and the Jewish American diasporic communities in the US: the way that, as Baldwin writes in his novel *Another Country*, the Italian residents of Greenwich Village looked at "black-and-white couples" in the street, "hating them, hating, in fact, all the Villagers, who gave their streets a bad name," when "they might have had an easier time of it [being accepted as truly "American"] if they had not been afflicted with so many Jews and junkies and drunkards and queers and spades" (297). Despite the prevalence of anti-Black racism and anti-Semitism among so many Italian Americans, and despite the ways in which Italians in the US were treated as "white on arrival," these narratives propose sly forms of solidarity across diasporas and suggest literary methods of unlearning old ideas about Italianness. Writing from within deeply rooted literary and cultural traditions of resisting injustice, Baldwin and Malamud better succeed at transmuting the "Italian novel" into something more complex, less culturally essentialist, and, in this way, more interesting.

These inheritances of Baldwin's and Malamud's are further evident in how both texts invoke formal and thematic tropes from the African American and Jewish American literary traditions—tropes that themselves grew out of distinct histories of diaspora—and then employ them in disrupting stereotypes of *italianità*. Much has been made of "the metaphorics of 'passing'" in *Giovanni's Room*, where the concept of racial passing is "appropriate[d]" and becomes a way to characterize experiences of suppressed queer identity after a long history of African American literature in which racial passing was a foundational trope (Rohy 218, 220). Narratives like Nella Larsen's seminal modernist novel *Passing* and Charles W. Chesnutt's earlier *The House Behind the Cedars* would approach the experience of passing in ways that were thematically and formally diverse, yet they shared a palpable awareness of how politically, economically, and socially entrenched dynamics of racial injustice created an incentive or an imperative for Black Americans to pass. They also recognized the practical and emotional burdens of passing as well as its subversive promise, uncovering connections between the project of passing and larger patterns of diasporic alienation. Something similar happens in *Giovanni's Room* when Giovanni says of David's passing, "You lie so much, you have come to believe all your own lies" (140). Tapping into this earlier vein of African American literature without claiming a false equivalence between anti-Blackness and heteronormativity, Baldwin allows Giovanni to wrestle with the philosophical implications of queer passing and ultimately gives his character as much dimensionality and humanness as the perennially questioning English hero George in *A Room with a View*.

Pictures of Fidelman, too, fleshes out its composite Italians with recurring elements from the Jewish American literary tradition that are foundational to the story cycle's treatment of social resistance, sexuality, and Italian identity. The trope of the "passive Jewish man," which is so central to Fidelman's homoerotic experiences, also manifests in novels by other Jewish American writers such as Saul Bellow and Philip Roth (Gordon 44). These novels include Bellow's *Seize the Day* and Roth's *Portnoy's Complaint*—which is also set partly in Italy.[15] The trope is what Kirsten Fermaglich calls "a product of centuries of victimization" in which "Jewish men were constructed as 'others' . . . and legally prevented from participating in traditional masculine activities, such as bearing arms" (33). When mapped onto Malamud's text, this historicized experience of victimization and passivity becomes part of the narrative's alternative envisioning of Italy's position in the global order. As Malamud's Italians contribute to the ongoing abuse of his Jewish protagonist, the satirical vision of *italianità* that emerges implicitly recalls a history of anti-Semitism in Italy that, among other things, had made Italians clearly "responsible for genocide" during World War II, when of "all the Jews sent to their death from Italy, half were seized not by German soldiers but by Italians" (Levis Sullam 3; Kertzer x).[16] It is through his invocation of intensely Jewish American literary tropes that Malamud gives the narrative's Italians this more three-dimensional and historically contextualized identity—which, however painful it may be to recognize, is far preferable to the flat essentialism of so many earlier "Italian novels." In putting a mirror up to the ugly face of a fellow diasporic community or to that of the homeland they have left behind, Malamud suggests that this is sometimes how literary allyship works to heal historical wounds.

Chapter 3 will examine how Carolina De Robertis and Chang-rae Lee bring the "Italian novel" into the twenty-first century, with updates that deepen the literary solidarity between Italian America and other diasporic communities. In the meantime, the intriguing innovations made by Baldwin and Malamud offer a preliminary glimpse into what it has meant to reinvent this familiar, well-loved, and deeply problematic genre. *Giovanni's Room* and *Pictures of Fidelman* harness a familiar vision of Italy as a liberating catalyst of social resistance, particularly where sexuality is concerned. Yet they also deploy unique representations of diaspora that complicate the putative binary relationship between Anglo-American identity and *italianità*, drawing on unique cultural and literary legacies.

Chapter 3

Privileged Italians, Poor Italians
Carolina De Robertis, Chang-rae Lee, and Italy in the Americas

After so many narratives populated with just a few Italian characters or even with a single Italian, Carolina De Robertis's novel *The Gods of Tango* may seem filled with an almost dizzying array of bodies that hail from Italy, speak Italian, and—in the case of those who have left their homeland—dream of Italy at night from foreign beds. This, as it turns out, is an essential ingredient of De Robertis's rewriting of Italian stereotypes into a novel where three-dimensional Italians are allowed to exist as realistically as any other character with any other ethnic or national identity. In this story of a young woman who leaves Italy for Argentina and becomes a celebrated violinist in a tango orchestra, there are cruel Italians and cowardly Italians just as there are brave Italians and gentle Italians. Some of them are visionaries; some of them hold stubbornly onto past ways of being. Some of them are naive; some of them are inclined to imagine the worst, and sometimes they are right. This is part of the experiential richness of De Robertis's novel, which enfolds readers in a fictional world that is as fully fleshed out by people as it is by places. But it is also part of what made the act of writing *The Gods of Tango* an act of literary solidarity.

De Robertis herself was in a fascinating position to write this novel, as she has Italian relatives but "identif[ies] primarily" as Uruguayan and as a Latina (Schiel). In an interview with *Las Comadres*, De Robertis commented, "The world is complicated and there's enough difficulty in the world, particularly for Latina women, most particularly for Latina women who want to stand strong on their own two feet in the world.... I'm proud to be a Latina because it's a beautiful part of who I am. We are an incredible collection of people because we—Latinas—have so much beauty" (Musel-Gilley). Speaking to the *Los Angeles Review of Books*, De Robertis explained her history in greater detail:

> I primarily identify as a Uruguayan or as a US American-Uruguayan person and writer. I also have roots in Argentina, as do quite a few Uruguayans. Uruguay is a very small country sandwiched between two giants—Argentina and Brazil. So Uruguay's national story and cultural story is entwined with its neighbors—especially Argentina because of how much the countries share as far as language and demographic composition. They both had a tremendous wave of Italian immigrants that arrived at the early 20th century—of which my ancestors were a part. (Schiel)

Tellingly, De Robertis mentions Italy last in this description, and she mentions it as part of a family origin story that would ultimately give her the Uruguayan and American identities that she claims more personally for herself. Yet the acknowledgments at the close of *The Gods of Tango* list the names of De Robertis's Italian relatives in Salerno and Prepezzano, both in the southwest Italian region of Campania, signaling their family's involvement in the diasporic waves that brought residents of southern Italian agricultural villages to locations not just in the United States but elsewhere in the Americas around the turn of the twentieth century. So it is clear from the start that De Robertis has a rich and complicated international identity of her own—an identity that is visible in her novel's nuanced approach to experiences of diaspora in general and to *italianità* in particular.

    Chang-rae Lee does not share this quasi-Italian identity with De Robertis, at least not from birth, as he is the child of Korean parents who brought him to the US when he was three years old. But Lee's father-in-law is Italian American, and although Lee has clarified that he appropriated only the "least interesting aspects" of his father-in-law's identity in writing his novel *Aloft*—these being "his age, his ethnicity and where he lived"—there are signs throughout the narrative that Lee knows what he is talking about when it comes to Italian America (Quan). Of course, what Lee also shares with De Robertis, without question, is an intimate understanding of the displacement and alienation, the adjustments and confusions that can stem from diaspora. Indeed, while Lee has spoken candidly about how his writing represents "an accentuation . . . , a kind of crystallization that requires certain dramatic and lingual actions that weren't going on in [his] regular life," his fiction nonetheless "does have [his] experiences in it," including a sense of being "not completely aligned with the context or culture that he inhabits" (Daniel Youngwon Lee). Lee has also spoken about the rootedness of these sensibilities in experiences that he encountered as early as his childhood years, when he became "ashamed that his immigrant family had not assimilated" and felt a "fear of inadequacy" in English (Belluck). Such resistance to assimilation gestures toward the membership of Korean migrants to the United States in the larger body of diasporic communities to which so many living on American soil belong today.[1] The fruits of Lee's authorial perspective are uniquely on display in his 2004 novel, with its Italian American narrator-protagonist and its extraordinarily multicultural cast of supporting characters. Like De Robertis's Italian Argentines, Lee's Italian Americans refuse to obey the literary expectations set for them in traditional "Italian novels" like the ones that I explored at the beginning of this book. More importantly, they refuse to obey any one set of expectations, whether it aligns with or contradicts Anglo-American stereotypes of Italy, instead relentlessly confronting readers with their diversity.

Yet there is also more to each of these books, and especially to their relationships with Italy and Italians, than I have intimated above. Much of this additional complexity is mixed up with issues of class and their intersections with race. While Lee provides readers with a vivid and often unsavory glimpse of the striations of the American middle and upper classes, De Robertis brings to life the collisions of tenement communities and spoiled aristocrats occasioned by the evolution of the tango in Buenos Aires. This difference between the two books is mapped onto their visions of Italy and leaves a different mark on each novel's version of solidarity with the Italian diasporic community. As an ally text, *The Gods of Tango* turns its attention to the struggles of a poor Italian girl displaced from a rural village to 1913 Buenos Aires. De Robertis's protagonist begins to pass as a man to survive alone in this urban landscape and finds her own private sense of her gender identity to be indelibly changed. Even as she and her fellow Italians struggle economically, they encounter a mixture of longstanding ethnic prejudice and distinct racial privilege within the city's ethno-racial hierarchy. *Aloft*'s Italian American narrator, in contrast, begins his conversation with the reader with a description of what it is like to fly a private plane—a used one, he is quick to reassure us—and in that moment leaves little doubt about what type of Italian Americans he represents: the rich ones, the ones who have capitalized on American structural inequalities built on foundations of both racism and socioeconomic injustice. In fact, one of the first things that NPR's 2004 podcast and accompanying write-up about *Aloft* says about the novel is that it "tells the story of a white middle-class businessman searching for identity" and thus offers a different point of focus than Lee's previous narratives about "outsiders." As Mark C. Jerng has pointed out, other reviewers of *Aloft* have relied on the notion of universal immigrant experiences in explaining Lee's novel and particularly his choice of an Italian American protagonist. These reviewers have sought to "flatten out differences between Asian Americans and white ethnic identity as common problems of cultural identity and belonging," avoiding reckoning with the special forms of white privilege that have become progressively more available to Italian Americans in the United States while remaining distinctly inaccessible to Asian Americans (Jerng 189). My contention here is different: not that the novel represents a universal immigrant experience but that certain commonalities—particularly of diasporic identity—seem to have made it more possible for Lee to capture the unique contours of Italian America. Importantly, this vision includes distinctively problematic elements of a disappearing, conformist species of *italianità* with complicated ties to larger issues of class and race.

Where De Robertis acts as a witness to the inequities and inequalities facing working-class Italians in Argentina in the 1910s, Lee doles out a greater measure of "tough love" for contemporary Italian Americans who have "made it," with everything that entails for their approach to the world around them in terms of economic and racial privilege. Both of these become literary methods of standing with Italian America—and here I mean the Italians of the Americas, not just those who have made their home in the United States—by offering what is truly needed. While De Robertis keeps the history of a diasporic class struggle alive even as she records the community's complicated relationship to white supremacy, Lee again holds a mirror up to the hazards of what, in some cases, this diasporic community has become.

Scrutinizing Diaspora and Remaking *Italianità*

De Robertis's protagonist first arrives on Argentine shores during what was historically a period of intense Italian migration to Buenos Aires. In 1912, a year before the starting point of the narrative, Italian immigration to Argentina had been greater than Italian immigration to the United States. This influx of individuals contributed substantially to the diasporic movement that would ultimately result in the arrival of more than two million Italian immigrants in Argentina between the years 1876 and 1915; as Samuel L. Baily reminds us, Italians had "represented 32 percent of the Buenos Aires population" as early as 1887 (75).[2]

The diasporic experiences of Italians in Argentina were not straightforwardly alienating. In her book *Migrant Marketplaces*, Elizabeth Zanoni reflects on the differences between prevailing views of Italian immigrants in the US and Argentina, suggesting that in the latter context, "migrants used . . . markets to construct bonds between Italians and Argentines as members of the 'Latin race,' rooted in assumptions about the superiority of Italian and European civilization," and in this way avoided a large portion of the ethno-national prejudice that Italians on US shores were exposed to (44). In the early twentieth century, such a vision of *italianità* would have been deeply distinct from prevailing US views of Italians themselves—if not of Renaissance Italian art or architecture—and points to the early existence of a particular form of white European privilege afforded to Italians upon their immigration to this more southern point of entry into the Americas. This was the case despite the fact that the Argentine elite in particular tended to see Italian and Spanish immigrants alike as "an enormous mass . . . with no economic or symbolic capital," unlike the Northern European immigrants they would have preferred (Ennis 121). It also helped that Italians in Argentina were not "subjected to religious prejudice" as they were in New York and elsewhere in the United States due to anti-Catholic sentiment and the dominant position of Protestantism within the spectrum of US religions (Baily 75).

Nevertheless, Italian immigrants in Argentine spaces often felt a diasporic pull toward their homeland much like the desire for return that Safran describes, looking "forward to moving back to their motherland and enjoying there their earnings [from] the New World" (Luconi). They also engaged in linguistic forms of "selective accommodation," as evidenced by the development of the Spanish-Italian hybrid dialect Cocoliche, which linguistic experts term a "contact variety" because of its roots in "the local varieties of Spanish and the Italian dialects spoken by the immigrants" (Ennis 112). Tellingly, this hybrid mode of communication shares its name with the literary stock character of the Cocoliche, "a partially socialized 'Italian gaucho' who spoke broken Spanish and did not know how to dress or act his new role properly," so that the term ultimately became synonymous with "any personification of a comic Italian character and . . . bad taste in general" (Baily 82). Certainly there is an element of prejudice and alienation here, even if the character of the Cocoliche also became "a means by which non-elite Argentines and immigrants could 'negotiate their differences through ritual and symbolic confrontations onstage'" (82).

The text's engagement with this real and concrete history of diaspora is mirrored in the vivid realism with which, from its opening pages, *The Gods of Tango* grapples with the emotional lives of diasporic communities and individuals. There are descriptions of diaspora in *The Gods of Tango* that feel as though they could not possibly have been written by someone who did not intimately understand the nature of the experience. Describing young Leda's shift in identity once she has settled in Buenos Aires, De Robertis's narrator waxes poetic in a way that rings intensely true:

> Naples had followed her across the ocean. It surrounded her. It had invaded Buenos Aires. And isn't that strange, she thought, the way one city can swirl inside another; the way you can be in one country yet carry another country in your skin; the way a place is changed by whoever comes to it, the way silt invades the body of a river. She was that, a speck of silt. The thought thrilled her but it also made her want to weep without reason, or for reasons utterly unknown to her. (99–100)

This tension between being "thrilled" and wanting "to weep" captures the intense emotional ambivalence that comes with being displaced from home, while the "silt" imagery gives a kind of concreteness to the processes of hybridity through which the culture of a place gives way to its new arrivals rather than the other way around. In distinguishing diaspora from immigration, James Clifford reflects that the "assimilationist national ideologies" that we typically associate with immigration, especially in the United States, fail to account for the ways that diasporic communities "maintain important allegiances and practical connections to a homeland or a dispersed community located elsewhere" (307). We can see this in the new Naples that has cropped up in Buenos Aires, not as a "separatist" enclave, but as a community that is determined to retain more than a few traces of home—like the persistent rhythms of Italian in the linguistic makeup of Cocoliche—and that, as such, necessarily leaves a mark on the city that surrounds it (308).

Later in the novel, diasporic longing comes to life even more painfully, as De Robertis's protagonist—now called Dante though she still identifies as a woman—remarks to her future wife that she misses Italy but "can't bear the thought of going back" (312).[3] Dante's personal reasons for this are tied both to individual experiences of trauma and to social rules she has broken abroad and cannot break at home. But her feelings nonetheless evoke an experience that is at the very core of diasporic longing: the sense that return is impossible, as desirable as it might be. Stuart Hall comments on this facet of diaspora when he clarifies that his notion of the term "does not refer us to those scattered tribes whose identity can only be secured in relation to some sacred homeland to which they must at all costs return, even if it means pushing other people into the sea" (235). Instead, diaspora has come to include this concept of an impossible return, made so by the march of history or perhaps by the same conditions that made the departure necessary in the first place. De Robertis compactly and precisely captures these complexities of diasporic living, ones that are critical to the Italian experience in the Americas, despite the fact that she herself identifies not as Italian but as "a Uruguayan who grew up in the [Uruguayan] diaspora, accustomed to blank stares upon telling people" her Latina roots ("Uruguay, Little Trailblazer").

By breathing this type of life into one Italian woman's experience of displacement from home, *The Gods of Tango* does something critical to its status as an ally text. Going deep into the emotional complexities of Leda/Dante's migration, De Robertis's novel makes her protagonist into a fuller and more human character than any other Italian we have seen so far within the pages of this book. Even Baldwin's Giovanni, who has similar feelings about the impossibility of return to Italy, is not fleshed out in this degree of emotional detail. If *The Gods of Tango* were a straightforward, slim volume with a near-exclusive focus on Leda/Dante's experiences, the novel would still do a great deal to rewrite Anglo-American notions of *italianità*. But the book does not, in fact, stop there. Instead, as the cast of Italian characters expands to include an almost dizzying diversity of figures, the traditional Anglo-American scripts projected onto Italy and Italians are more sweepingly rewritten.

One of the early scenes in the novel that spotlights this diversity involves the original Dante, a cousin of Leda's whom she is married to by proxy before her voyage to Argentina and who is murdered by a policeman before her ship docks in Buenos Aires. Dante and his friend Arturo, a shipmate from his own voyage from Italy, engage in a heated political discussion about the viability of a worker's strike that some of their colleagues are planning as a way to mobilize for more humane working hours and better pay. Arturo is ablaze not just with righteous indignation at the way he and the other men are being treated but with idealistic fervor and hope that things might genuinely change: "The bosses are nothing without workers," he affirms, determined. "They need us, we'll show them our strength" (66). Dante, for his own part, is less than optimistic, reminding Arturo of another strike that ended in "guns, shots, four workers dead"—and he will be proven right when the event he feared might turn ugly leads to his death at the hands of the police (66). Taken together, the two men form a fascinating and sobering counterpoint to the stereotype of the fiery Italian. At first, Arturo might seem to fit the stereotype, at least in part, with his irrepressible enthusiasm for protest; he finds his home among the anarchists with "their passionate words and ample gestures [that] encompassed a whole golden future with the sweep of a single hand" (62). Yet by pairing Arturo with Dante, De Robertis creates a fictional world in which Italians are neither uniformly fiery nor uniformly dour: in which they are simply allowed to be human beings with diverse and intricate feelings about the prospect of activism in a perilous world. In this way, De Robertis writes back against Othering notions imposed from outside while also relieving her characters of the burden of having to prove themselves to be different from this outsider's view of Italianness. In the context of the long history of "Italian novels," this feels like a revolutionary step in itself.

Both Arturo's and Dante's positions are understandable in a historical moment in which class-based reforms were urgently necessary as well as incredibly dangerous to fight for. In addition to posing the very real threat of physical violence, mobilizing for the rights of workers in Argentina could bar an Italian immigrant from naturalization as an Argentine citizen, as applicants for citizenship "were often disqualified as public officials feared that they would vote for the Socialist Party" (Luconi). Within the novel's older generation, though, more disturbing forms of diversity emerge as a villain is uncovered in Leda's old village: her uncle Mateo, whose abuses of power at the level of the village community are mirrored in vicious acts of abuse against his own daughter, Cora. Remembering her cousin's death by suicide, Leda also painfully recalls one scene at the communal family dinner table, when Mateo bullies his daughter and Leda's own father stays "hunched at the table with a blank look on his face . . . transported by his own cowardice" (122–23). That Ugo is unable to act to save his niece from harm becomes the defining feature of his character. Still, he finds smaller ways to rebel, as when Leda departs for Buenos Aires and he gifts her the violin that has been in the hands of the family's men for generations with the understanding that women are not allowed to play it. Leda reflects that her "father was a kind man, but not a brave one. If he wanted her to break the rules, he would not tell her outright, but perhaps he would sabotage himself, leave the jail key in reach as if by accident and walk away" (96). As a foil for Mateo, Ugo invites readers to consider the ethical ramifications of silence and the moral obligations of bystanders to intervene. He also becomes one more figure in an increasingly vast family of characters whose natures are finely drawn, full of contradictions not only to each other but also to themselves. If, as Alex Woloch argues, the flatness of secondary characters in canonical novels like *Pride and Prejudice* mirrors their marginal place in the economic hierarchy of the world they inhabit, then it seems that the complexity and three-dimensionality of the secondary characters in *The Gods of Tango* conversely operates as a way of asserting their importance and that of the community they represent.

 These examples of character diversity are shot through with issues of class conflict and inequality, and indeed, acknowledging this range of experiences of class becomes another way of honoring the three-dimensional complexity of Italian lives in De Robertis's novel. Recalling how the "Campolieri boy" in "Roman Fever" is fetishized for his tantalizing power as a *marchese* and how the Italian men in *Daisy Miller* are made fun of for their airs of pretense to a higher class status, we can see how earlier Anglo-American "Italian novels" tended to each show a single class of Italian, seemingly untroubled by the oversimplification that these types of representation entailed. In Leda's Italian village, however, the class stratification is palpable, permeating the inner reaches of the Mazzoni family as well as shaping the larger contours of village life. The Mazzonis are the landowning family that enjoys the bulk of the power in Leda's town, with control of "half the land around the village" and employees who live in "one-room hut[s] with a dirt floor" (14, 52). Within the family itself, the tendency of Leda's father toward cowardice is a function of his status as the younger and lesser son, who has no land of his own to give him courage, while Mateo's perverse cruelties are painted as a byproduct of the almost obscene power that he has over the entire village—the ability he has to make "a gift to the church" and buy the complicity of the village priests in covering up what he has done to his daughter (76). These details open the door to the narrative's critique of class inequality and injustice, which I will discuss later at greater length, while also making it impossible for readers to maintain a monolithic vision of Italian spaces or the people who populate them.

What these examples also reveal is that *The Gods of Tango* does something revolutionary by allowing its Italians to have so much in common with their Anglo-American counterparts in other narratives. Like James's Daisy and Winterbourne, De Robertis's Italians occupy diverse places in the social order. Like Alcott's "little women," they have vastly different temperaments. In addition to humanizing Italianness, this approach deconstructs the false barriers of distance and difference that fetishism erects between the self and the Other. Soon, more commonalities emerge between Italy and other places that deepen this effect. For instance, if Anglo-American tourists tended to go abroad with the hazy notion that Italian history ended after the Renaissance, De Robertis is here to frustrate that notion through richly specific historical references that bring a more extended time line of Italian history to life. From its early descriptions of the time when "two nations, Spain and France, [were] vying" for the King of Naples's throne to its remarks about "Garibaldi's army" during unification and eventually to its World War I references, *The Gods of Tango* situates Italy in a larger European and global context across the centuries and affirms that Italy, like any other nation, has a history of its own (8, 111).

Social convention, too, like history itself, becomes a weighty influence in the lives of young Italians who must go abroad to experiment, to rebel, and ultimately to become themselves—just as so many privileged Anglo-Americans did during their Grand Tours and expatriate adventures in Italy. Leda reflects that "if there were any place in the world where it could be possible" to remake one's life, "that place had to be América. Land of self-creation. Of rootlessness. Of New Babel" (126). And Italians prove to be afraid of the putative dangers of Latin American cities like Buenos Aires just as Anglo-Americans were once afraid of "Roman fever" and its associated ills. When Leda loses her way while wandering through the maze of streets outside the *conventillo*, De Robertis deliciously echoes Forster's descriptions of Lucy Honeychurch lost in Florence "with no Baedeker" (18). "She was lost," De Robertis's narrator proclaims. "One turn, two, and she was on a block she'd never seen before. . . . Her arm ached from the basket's weight, she sifted it to the other side and kept walking and walking until she reached the end of a street that let out to the port. . . . You are alone, Leda. Alone. It took her another hour to find her way home" (101). Suddenly, Italians are allowed the dubious but rather hard-won privilege of being just like everyone else, even in their tendency to imaginatively Other foreign spaces, perhaps inspired by their own sense of "the superiority of Italian and European civilization"—which would have seemed to include only a certain kind of Argentine and certain portions of the city of Buenos Aires. While it may not paint Italians in the most flattering light, this narrative turn is rooted in complex truths more than simplistic fictions, and it goes a long way toward destabilizing the more bigoted and flattening Anglo-American fictions about Italy.

Perhaps all of this is unsurprising in a novel that is, after all, focused on an Italian protagonist. Even the eponymous Giovanni is not the real center of Baldwin's narrative, although he shares the spotlight evenly with David in a way that at least lifts him out of the margins of the text. In contrast, Leda/Dante is allowed to remain the focus of the reader's attention from beginning to end, despite short, occasional passages that take on the perspective of another character, like the bunkmate Leda crosses the ocean with from Naples or the old, blind violinist who first teaches her to really play her father's violin. This itself becomes a way for the narrative to remake the "Italian novel," righting the wrong that was done when it was somehow decided that such novels should be focused on Anglo-American protagonists in the first place. Of course, as an Italian protagonist with a regionally specific identity, Leda also becomes a humanizing representative of the southerners who were so derided by both northern Italians and the Americans who referred to them in aggregate as "the little swarthy Calabrian, Sicilian, or Neapolitan" (LaGumina 223). And because Leda/Dante is a gender-nonconforming woman who dresses as a man, passes as a man, sleeps with women, marries a woman, and only at the novel's very end starts to identify as "a he," the multiplicity of Leda/Dante's queer identity becomes its own form of diversity that is impossible to square with artificially imposed visions of romantic Italian men à la Wharton and tragic Italian women à la Alcott (357).

Leda/Dante unflinchingly faces the dangers that exist for her in Buenos Aires regardless of the name she uses, including the danger of an "unmasking" that she fears might lead her to be sexually assaulted or murdered for her gender transgressions (191). In the process, she forges alliances across diasporas that make her the most positive model for interdiasporic collaboration in the string of narratives covered by this book. The greatest expression of this is in the tango music Dante makes with the *orquesta* that will eventually expand to include six and then seven musicians with diverse backgrounds characteristic of Buenos Aires's migrant population. Among the band members is El Loro, who earns his nickname when he is just three years old because he serves "as translator for his parents—Jews arrived from Russia" and thus "is forced to chatter and repeat himself incessantly in both languages" (187). Meanwhile, the person who has brought Dante and El Loro together with the other musicians is a biracial man named Santiago who has "wide curls and olive skin" that lead Dante to believe he might be "Mediterranean" (186). Santiago plays an instrument called the bandonion or *bandoneón*, which, despite its German origins, has "been absorbed into the music" of tango in a perfect expression of diasporic hybridity (201).

While the Italian American novels in the upcoming section of this book largely express their solidarity with people of color by reflecting on how Italian Americans have in so many instances failed to do so, De Robertis proposes a fictional vision of allyship in a shared community that crosses ethnic and national borders just as each individual person within that community has done in leaving home. Among other things, this makes the novel a positive testament to what Italians in the Americas have done and can do again: a reminder of the kinds of activist strength that the community is capable of. Even Dante's death is consistent with this vision of possibility, as when he dies his wife Rosa finds him "facedown on the morning paper, which featured photographs of a huge funeral procession in the United States for Martin Luther King, Jr." (362). In this moment, Dante's death becomes an act of recognition of the activist work being done a continent away, work based in the other end of the Americas and yet very much in keeping with the racial and class-based activism of Dante's tango music. In death as well as in life, then, Dante is allowed to retain this sense of synergy with other diasporic quests for recognition, for fulfillment, and for justice. By painting its Italian American protagonist as this sort of activist, the narrative lends an air of satisfying completeness to a refreshing vision of Italianness, one that focuses as much on Italians vis-à-vis other diasporic communities as it does on the nature of *italianità* in itself.

Doing Tango, Thinking through Class

I have already begun to suggest some of the ways that the novel's brand of class consciousness is intertwined with these reimaginings.[4] What is perhaps most striking about *The Gods of Tango* is its insistence on examining the intersections of diasporic and class identity for the Italian community in Buenos Aires without occluding the very real privileges afforded to Italian migrants—especially Italian men—in comparison with other residents of the city. Given the novel's setting in a historical context in which Italians in Argentina did have substantial unearned advantages rooted in fictions of European cultural supremacy, and in which Italians' whiteness provided them with protection from forms of discrimination that confronted many other Argentines, De Robertis's grappling with these complexities is essential to the narrative's interventions in the genre of the "Italian novel."

Granted, the welcome afforded to Italians entering Buenos Aires for the first time is inflected with more than glimmers of class inequality. Italians are welcomed as potential laborers who will accept the less desirable jobs—jobs like filling interminable cigarettes with tobacco, which Dante does by day while playing her violin at night until she is able to find a better-paying gig as a musician and quit her day job. As Leda notes during the nerve-wracking wait for her examination by men wearing stethoscopes on the deck of the ship that transports her from Italy, "Argentina was promoting immigration. They wanted workers. They did not take the old, sick, or unsound of mind" (37).[5] These are historically accurate statements. Already relegated to a lower class, Italian migrants arriving earlier than Leda have had it even worse, facing accusations from wealthy Argentines who blamed them for an outbreak of yellow fever that led the upper class to flee their expensive city houses permanently. Nestore, the elderly blind violinist, remembers as much:

> When he arrived, there were still two rich families on the block, stragglers caught up in planning their escape. They seemed disoriented and offended by their new neighbors, and never greeted them on the street, never even looked at them, as if they did not exist. *You don't know how bad it got during the sickness,* his Italian neighbors told him. *They blamed us for the outbreak, fired us from our jobs, our people wandered the streets without work, sometimes without a home, men died in the street*

of cold or of the sickness and it took hours for anyone to come for the bodies. Nestore's room gleamed with gold-leaf wallpaper that had not yet begun to fade. (114)

In this collision of the abandoned aristocratic house and its "gold-leaf wallpaper" with the suffering of the impossibly crowded Italian families who would come to occupy such houses, De Robertis serves as a witness to the combined effects of nationality, migrant identity, and class status on the experiences of these desperate men and women. Class and diaspora intersect painfully during the multigenerational history of Italian-Argentine migration, and the novel testifies to these inequities.

At the same time, *The Gods of Tango* is deeply invested in avoiding false equivalences, acknowledging the space between the Italian experience in Buenos Aires and those of the other diasporic lives swallowed up by the city. This emerges in moments when the narrative explicitly confronts the history of slavery in Argentina and the social position of the children and grandchildren of the nation's enslaved people, who continue to meet with overt racism, including deadly racist violence, in the world of the narrative. Tango is described as "a music born among the children of slaves," which "like an orphan . . . will never hear the full visceral story of its birth" (282). We learn that some of Santiago's family members were conscripted "by force" into the Argentine army to fight in the Paraguayan War because, his uncle Palo tells him, "they needed a way to not only win their war but also rid this country of us in the process, two birds with one stone" (282). Later, confronted with an arrogant cabaret owner who presumes to make her own decisions about who can and cannot sing with his band, Santiago finds himself thinking that she has acted "as if she owned him, Santiago, or, more accurately, as if her grandfather had owned his grandfather as in truth he might have and this meant that anything he, Santiago, did or felt or *was* belonged to her even now" (281). This is not just a racial problem but a class problem as well, since the power and wealth of Buenos Aires's aristocracy have been literally built with slave labor, while the vulnerable working-class status of those Black Argentines left in Buenos Aires appears to be predetermined and inevitable. Even Santiago, who manages to partly subvert the social order by playing beautiful tango music until the city's aristocrats are forced to recognize his brilliance, is ultimately killed by a racist and sexist bandmate bent on stabbing Dante.[6] In this context, the successes of Santiago's *orquesta* become a way for the novel to witness the persistence of these inequities as well as a tentative testament to the activist potential of music as a means of resistance for Black Argentines. Meanwhile, *The Gods of Tango* will not let us forget the tricky role that Italians have played in this story as the "white men" who "would pour into the city to replace" its Black residents (283).

Still, the narrative's consciousness of Black Argentine experiences does not just place Italian América at odds with African América. In some ways, De Robertis shows us, the experiences of the two populations are necessarily similar, defined as they are by troubles and complexities that are common to diasporic identities. One scene featuring Santiago's uncle and his friend makes these commonalities plain. In a heated debate over the nature of tango, Palo's friend asks him to put into words his diasporic relationship to Africa: "Look at us: we have the blood of Africa in our veins, but we were born here. Are we African?" "Of course," Palo replies. "And our children?" his friend retorts. "Are they African?" (285–86) Reading this passage for the first time, one cannot help but think of Hall's comments on the difficulty of assuming an African diasporic identity from across vast barriers of time and space.[7] In addition to capturing the tenuousness of African diasporic identity, however, this conversation speaks to the familiar ambivalence of a diasporic consciousness that, it turns out, is shared across Italian and African lives in this city brimming with working-class migrants living in fragile circumstances.

Tango also allows the novel that bears its name to make more sweeping commentaries about class even beyond the specific diasporic frameworks of the novel's Italian migrants and Black Argentine citizens. Covering the period when the newfound popularity of the art form brought it from *conventillos* filled with working-class migrants to the most upscale cabarets owned and frequented by the aristocracy, the narrative thus gives readers special access to an opulent world where a good party means "rare wines, towers of French pastries, several piglets choking on the polished apples in their mouths, and trapeze artists to slice the air between acts" (270). There is an explicit and implied violence in these descriptions of Argentine opulence that emphasizes the unnecessary extremity of the upper class's financial resources as well as the destructive effects of this kind of wealth on the anatomy of an entire society. Not far away, there are parks like Palermo, a more genteel but equally unsettling version of the cabarets in that the rich continue to use them to parade their wealth and their superiority to the few "interlopers" who are present there, the "families on benches, sharing a single loaf of bread" and the "lone girl in a maid's uniform gazing sadly at the water" (224). Read in this light, and combined with earlier moments like the scene of the original Dante's death, the cabaret scenes become very clearly representative of a larger social schema rather than a glitteringly amoral exception to the rules of the city.[8] The extent of class stratification is clear, and we can see that it infects the entire city as badly as the yellow fever once blamed on the Italians. The band's successes, on the other hand, suggest that it may be possible to at least partly "undo" the damaging effects of inequality by transgressing these class boundaries through artistic production.

If I have said relatively little so far about the place of gender and sexuality in this world, it is because this is the part of De Robertis's novel that has already received the most attention and acclaim, though the novel was so recently published that the academic world has scarcely registered its appearance on the literary scene.[9] One thing that *The Gods of Tango* does incredibly well, however, is acknowledge the intersectional effects of gender and sexuality—like those of race—on the architecture and the everyday workings of class stratification. When Dante begins an affair with the wealthy woman who co-owns the cabaret where the *orquesta* has finally become a city-wide sensation, the relationship between the two women (for Dante at the time still self-identifies as such) invites readers to scrutinize these intersections. As the relationship sours, Dante gives voice to the fundamental problem: "She could threaten to expose Carmen as having an illicit affair with a dirty conventillero. Surely that could cause some embarrassment in her world. But the embarrassment of an aristocratic woman, especially one with her own money and cabaret, not to mention a track record of flouting convention, was nothing compared to the ruin Dante faced. It would not be an equal fight" (302).

On the other end of the spectrum from Carmen are the many sex workers whom Dante interacts with, including one nicknamed Mamita who teaches her with infinite patience to make love to other women, all the while believing her to be a young man who reminds her of her son. Since its more intersectional turn in the wake of the second wave, contemporary feminism has become increasingly conscious of how class status can inflect gender issues like the relationships between women and their children. After decades of insistence from working-class women and women of color, "mainstream" white feminists with deep socioeconomic resources finally began to ask what happens when a woman who is obliged to spend long daily hours caring for someone else's children therefore is unable to care for or even see her own.[10] Mamita experiences the extreme version of this problem as a sex worker who becomes pregnant as a result of her job and is forcibly and permanently separated from her child by the men who exploitatively profit from her uses of her body:

> You were fourteen when you conceived him, fifteen when he was born, and the men you worked for let the other whores stand around you in a circle as you labored, then gave you a few days to hold your little boy and give him milk—you gave him your milk and in the hardest times you say that to yourself over and over, *there's that at least, he had my milk*—before the men who owned you took him away. After that you used the herbs the other girls did, every time you needed to, so you'd never have to say goodbye like that again. (231)

Mamita's very name speaks to the ways that her perceived feminine role as a caretaker has been commodified and sexualized even as her actual rights as a mother have been stripped away. *The Gods of Tango* grapples with these intersections of socioeconomic status and gender and ultimately protests them by bringing to life the emotional ramifications of injustice.

Near the end of the novel, De Robertis's narrator takes a moment to remember the various casualties of these intersections of diaspora, class, and gender—a critical moment given the way her narrative will end. After being wrongly accused of Santiago's murder, Dante will be forced to flee the country. Her lover Rosa, the first woman who has chosen to sleep with her already knowing that she is a woman, will insist on accompanying her. This sets the stage for a fulfilling final few pages in which the novel will allow Dante and Rosa, together in Rosa's native Uruguay, to be entirely happy together. Among other things, this ending rejects the frustrating expectation that the marginalized queer characters in a novel will meet some sort of unhappy or even tragic fate.[11] It is important, though, that the mostly happy ending of *The Gods of Tango*—which instead ends with Dante's uneventful death at the age of seventy-two—does not naively overshadow the more sobering realities of the narrative.

The narration that accompanies Dante and Rosa's flight to Uruguay is critical from this perspective, describing what happens in tandem with their escape:

> In a public morgue, the body of a bandoneón player was prepared for burial. . . . [This is Santiago.] At that moment,

in San Telmo, a woman known only as Mamita sat on her bed, a gray-haired man suckling at her large breasts like a baby.... Nine blocks from Mamita, a young man from the Cilento Coast woke with an ache in his arm, which had broken in his youth and never set right. [This is Arturo.] ... Two houses down from them, a blind old man who sensed his time to die was close, but not yet here, dreamed an intoxicating dream. He was walking barefoot on a road that led to Naples, or that he hoped would lead to Naples.... (347–48)

Although most of these characters are at least part-Italian—even Santiago, whose father originally hails from Florence—they also have distinct racial identities in a social environment that distinguishes fundamentally between them on that basis. Mamita's story is inflected with gender-based injustices, too, so that her forced separation from her son, which De Robertis's narrator implicitly evokes in this scene, becomes a somber reminder of the intersection of gender and socioeconomic vulnerability in the lives of sex workers like her. Still, this constellation of lives and experiences is brought together just as potently by class struggles: the improperly treated broken arm, the life ending in a cramped *conventillo*. Even in its relatively rosy ending, the narrative will not let us forget the names or stories of any of these individuals. For *The Gods of Tango*, this is what class consciousness means. In such moments, like *Giovanni's Room*, the novel moves far beyond questions of *italianità* even as it continues to process them.

Indistinguishable Italians?

It would not be precisely correct to say that Italian Americans at the turn of the twenty-first century have encountered no experiences of ethnic discrimination or prejudice. Salvatore J. LaGumina recounts varied and relatively recent instances in which public portrayals of individuals of Italian descent from the realm of sports journalism to that of politics mined and perpetuated derogatory stereotypes of *italianità*. In 2008, Washington State gubernatorial candidate Dino Rossi "was confronted with innuendo-loaded campaign material" in the lead-up to his loss of the election (233). The opposing party had aired a television ad "set against a background of a photograph of Rossi accompanied by the soundtrack of the *Sopranos* television series," invoking the stereotype of Italian Americans as violent *mafiosi* (233). Meanwhile, in 2006, a reporter for *Sports Illustrated* referred to National Football Commissioner Paul Tagliabue as a former "*consigliere*" rather than a former lawyer, drawing the ire of Italian Americans for whom the mafia reference was quite obvious, as well as inspiring comparisons to a similar moment in late 2005 when a prominent radio personality had referred to Italian American Supreme Court justice Samuel Alito—whose family originally hailed from southern Italy—as a "meatball-sucking wop" (qtd. in Kane).

Nevertheless, much like specious white claims of "reverse racism" (a phenomenon that cannot exist in the United States given the institutional, not just individual, character of racism), the arguments made by many writers in response to these incidents ironically typified the reality of Italian American racial privilege. Gregory Kane, for instance, attempted to compare the "wop" incident to another radio personality's "joking reference to the lynching of James Byrd, who was killed by three white supremacists in Texas"; he also suggested that the "*consigliere*" incident was akin to a 1938 *Washington Post* reporter's calling African American boxer Joe Louis a "lethargic, chicken-eating young colored boy." What seemed to be lost on Kane was not only the larger context of structural anti-Black racism and white supremacist racial violence that made the latter two remarks far more significant, but also the incredible positions of institutional privilege from which Tagliabue and Alito had been insulted: positions that today continue to afford them political, social, and economic power that is far more wide-reaching and potent than a single ethnic slur could possibly be. In a sense, because of the individuals involved as well as the false equivalences that were so facilely made in the wake of each incident, these occurrences draw attention to the privileges of white Italianness as much as if not more than they illustrate the persistence of anti-Italian prejudice.

Such willful confusion about the position of Italian America within the broader spectrum of American identities has also not been exclusive to more popular discursive arenas. In his recent book *Guido Culture and Italian American Youth: From Bensonhurst to Jersey Shore*, Donald Tricarico interprets community and media responses to the murder of Yusef Hawkins as evidence of unjustified anti-Italian prejudice rather than as a rational calling to account of Italian America with regard to the persistence of racism in the community. Presenting examples of both Italian and non-Italian individuals' comments on Italian American anti-Black racism and anti-Semitism, Tricarico objects to the fact that "[d]iscrepancies with the dominant interpretation that cast . . . Italian Americans as racists were muted or swept aside" (218). A sort of variation on the tired refrain of "#NotAllMen" or "#NotAllWhitePeople," Tricarico's argument both fails to recognize the greater importance of the extreme violence against Yusef Hawkins relative to the subsequent criticisms of Italian Americans, instead defensively centering "good white people" at the expense of the young Black man who had become the victim of a violent crime, and inappropriately values the task of defending the reputations of Italian Americans over the very real need to grapple with the problem of Italian American racism. While Tricarico's larger point about ethnically prejudiced responses to the "guido" subculture is well-taken, his argument is far from enhanced by his indiscriminately lumping in Yusef Hawkins's murder with snobbish Manhattanites' complaints about Italian American Long Islanders who "turn formerly hot clubs like Marquee and Lotus into B&T [bridge and tunnel] wastelands" and "dilute Manhattan nightlife or pretty much anything else they manage to get their hair-gel stained, grubby hands on" (qtd. in 240).

Considering all of this, it might seem at first as though the Italian Americans who populate Lee's *Aloft* do not belong in this book. Viewed from a distance, they seem not diasporic but almost utterly assimilated in their privilege—a fact that readers of Lee's narrative have tended to lean on in emphasizing the miscellaneous whiteness of Lee's protagonist. Look more closely, however, and you will uncover a more finely tuned vision of Italian identity in Lee's novel of middle-aged disaffection and loss: a vision that recognizes the persistently diasporic character of *italianità* in the United States while refusing to mince words about Italian American complicity with institutional racism and socioeconomic injustice. Read in this light, *Aloft* operates as an antidote to false claims of equivalence between Italian American experiences in the US and those of diasporic communities of color while showing that this species of "tough love" is not at all antithetical to literary allyship across diasporas.

The overt focus of the narrative is its first-person narrator, the nearly-sixty-year-old Jerry Battle, although the cast of supporting characters that swirls around him runs as deep as in *The Gods of Tango*. Jerry is the newly retired owner of a landscaping business, a family enterprise that has been passed down from one generation of Battles—formerly Battaglias—to the next. The novel follows him through an array of personal crises, from his attempts to win back the attentions of a former girlfriend to his efforts to cope with his only daughter's cancer diagnosis during her pregnancy. These are almost aggressively universal problems, problems that in themselves might have little to do with the Battaglia family's history of migration and their integration into American life. But this bare outline of the novel's plot occludes many of the intricacies that make it a distinctive piece of fiction, including the traces of diasporic experiences that color the narrative.

Early on, narrator Jerry explains that the switch from Battaglia to Battle has been inspired by "the usual reasons immigrants and others like them will do, for the sake of familiarity and ease of use and to herald a new and optimistic beginning" (24). This lukewarm report of migrant motivations describes the family's efforts at assimilation without suggesting that the adjustments to the family's name have resulted from any real racism or discrimination. However, rather than setting the stage for a narrative that will ignore the history of anti-Italianism in the United States, this early comment turns out to be inconsistent with other signs scattered across the text that the family's cultural affiliations are more embattled, so to speak, than Jerry wishes to admit. In one moment, Jerry is surprised that an acquaintance's "dago ass" has been admitted into a country club where, in former years or without immense wealth, this would likely have been impossible (62). In another moment, Jerry reflects on his father's anger being caused by "the usual reasons of privation and poverty and general mistreatment by family members and people in the street and at school and by the authorities, which these days you'd call racism and discrimination but then was known as the breaks, how it was, your miserable fucking life" (306). These admissions on Jerry's part underscore his fallibility as a narrator whose family has a history of cultural struggles but who cannot always be trusted to admit it, partly because of a kind of stoic skepticism about the terms and concepts used to describe such experiences, which also seems to make him resentful of anyone who protests contemporary "racism and discrimination" rather than passively accepting it. Despite Jerry's intermittent denials, it is clear that he and his family have felt the sense of alienation that diasporic communities tend to feel in perceiving that they "are not—and perhaps cannot be—fully accepted by their host society" (Safran 83). Thus, while it is written from a relatively outside perspective, Lee's novel nevertheless acknowledges the history of anti-Italian discrimination in the United States. Taken together with *The Gods of Tango*, *Aloft* offers a cross-historical and transnational picture of how racism in the Americas did impact Italian migrants, even if these more overt forms of discrimination have fallen away as Italian Americans like Jerry have neared the end of their middle age.

As in De Robertis's novel, the Italians in this diasporic world are rich in their diversity—diversity of personality, of interests and relationships, all of which are imagined in captivating detail. The Battaglia family itself is full of personalities that exist at odds with each other, even before the collision of diasporas that leads Jerry to marry a Korean American woman and have two biracial children. There is Jerry's brother Bobby, whose irrepressible nonchalance lives on in the family's memory decades after his disappearance during the Vietnam War. He is the sort of young man who "didn't ultimately care," with "a long-ingrained insoluble indifference, which sprang from how easily he could do things, like pick up any instrument, or a new sport, or have a beautiful girl fall in love with him, with what was always this effortless sparkling performance of Himself" (157). There is Jerry's father, "whose firm and sometimes gruff stance . . . is not so much about teaching deference or respect but reminding one and all of his own status as family patriarch/biggest boy" (75). Meanwhile, Jerry himself simultaneously manages to assume bits and pieces of these family identities while also feeling profoundly alienated from them. After his brother's funeral, he has a romantic encounter with a woman who briefly dated his brother and who seems to be attracted to him because of whatever part of Bobby she "sensed . . . as residually expressed" in him (160). Taking on the family business, he exercises a "sagely ever-passive hand" that allows things "to get done" (295). And yet, as Jerry is quick to clarify, he doesn't "give a hoot about Battle Brothers" or in any way feel that he is able to fill his brother's shoes within the context of a family that still idolizes him (295). This multigenerational complexity is worlds away from the flat representations of *italianità* that Anglo-American readers came to expect and believe in during the eras of Alcott and Wharton.

Across the Italian American world of the novel, the wider array of people who hail from the "old neighborhood," this same breadth of experience and perspective repeats to create a kaleidoscope of diasporic identities (263). On the one hand, Jerry's old school classmate Richie pads his existence with comforting tokens of his success as a legal practitioner, like "dusty, moldering leather-bound volumes of late-nineteenth-century English maritime law" and other "custom material . . . the kind of prime antique furnishing and ornamentation that you would never be able to put together if you weren't bred in the life, or didn't handsomely pay someone who purported that he or she did" (185–86). On the other hand, Lee's narrator has a daughter named Theresa, as Italian as she is Korean, who uses what Jerry sees as "snide deconstructive terminology" to critique her father's world travels "for the rapacious, hegemonic colonialist 'projects' that they were" (28–29). Bobby plays baseball before he is killed in Vietnam, at least temporarily embracing the sport for which Italian Americans became so well-known thanks to stars like Joe DiMaggio and Yogi Berra. Jerry, meanwhile, prefers tennis and makes somewhat sardonic comments about the baseball diamond as his "people's pattern supreme" (2).[12] As the generations shift and evolve, so, too, does the range of cultural affiliations permitted to exist alongside *italianità*. Echoing De Robertis's early Italian Americans and their implications for the "Italian novel," the cast of characters in *Aloft* becomes a way for Lee to reach across diasporas, imagining these vibrant variations on the idea of Italianness.

This diversity, of course, is unremarkable in the sense that it is utterly normal, the sort of variation we would expect in any run-of-the-mill family home or in any small town—even, arguably, in the suburbs, where conformity is at a premium. But again, as in *The Gods of Tango*, what feels fresh and exciting about Lee's narrative is partly that its Italians are allowed to be like everyone else, no longer fetishized or exoticized in their difference, though they may be fairly criticized for their conformity. Rather than being the object of the touristic gaze, Lee's Italian Americans become themselves the tourists; Jerry remembers himself "leafing through [his] tattered *Baedeker's Italy* for the umpteenth time" in the good days before his girlfriend Rita left him (4). Like other "typical" Americans, they wallow in indecision and tentativeness, shaking off the stereotype of the impulsively impractical Italian, as Jerry does when he refuses to fly his plane unless "the sky is completely clear, with no threat of weather for at least another day" (152).[13] As a pilot, Jerry blends in with his pampered suburban surroundings to such an extent that it would not be unfair to call him normal, which may seem damning but which is also something of a step forward for a community that has been so used to being Othered, in literature and otherwise.

Lee's Italian Americans also wax melancholy about their aches and pains, their pasts and futures and those of their loved ones, as Jerry does when looking back on the death of his wife and his son's adolescence:

> I suppose the Grandeur of Life does this to all of us, forging us into figures more like ourselves than we'd otherwise be, for

better and/or worse, and so you wonder what ramifications in substance and detail there'd be, say, what kind of house Jack would be living in, had his mother never died, whether he would have married an altogether together woman like Eunice, whether he would have taken up the business of Battle Brothers at all. (71)

This is a far cry from the bland remarks about innocence that Giovanelli makes at Daisy's gravesite and even from Giovanni's stereotypically mournful remembrances of his infant son. In his intricate and painful philosophizing, Jerry sounds more like Forster's Mr. Emerson advising Lucy Honeychurch on the virtues of Love, although Jerry is also the bearer of the sort of (self-)deprecating attitude toward intellectualism that has commonly been passed down through generations of working-class Italians—that is, he distrusts academia and doesn't necessarily think he's very smart.[14] As Stephen Hong Sohn has commented and as Lee himself has confirmed in interviews, that Jerry is allowed to produce this sort of philosophical discourse becomes a way to "challenge stereotypical conceptions of Italian Americans" and how they talk and think, though reviewers of the novel have instead attempted to frame these moments as times when Lee has mistakenly allowed his own voice to creep in a bit too much, in this way showing their own prejudice as they resist the textual reality of Jerry-as-intellectual (38).[15]

As Jerry's inner consciousness comes alive, it becomes clear not only that Jerry is at the center of the narrative but also that he is in control of its telling. In this way, Lee goes one step beyond De Robertis as well as earlier writers like Baldwin and Malamud, offering narrative self-determination along with attention to his Italian American protagonist. Jerry tells his own story on his own terms, complete with criticisms, justifications, contradictions, and evolutions that bring the humanity of his character fully to life. The novel begins with him waxing poetic about the glories of the small plane that he flies to escape his family but ends with him sitting in a hole in the ground where the soil has been removed to make way for a swimming pool, reveling in "the smell, which is loamy and fat and sweetly vernal, not at all of extinction" and taking satisfaction in the way the hole makes "a perfect frame of firmament for flights endless, unseen" (364). While we may not fully trust Jerry's apparent transformation from high-flying avoidist to grounded family man—after all, isn't he still obsessed with the sky?—there is real privilege in the way he is allowed to operate as the architect of his own story. There is no external third-person authority in *Aloft* who is allowed to side with Anglo-America in the contest between "North" and "South," as England and Italy are tellingly referred to in Forster's *Where Angels Fear to Tread*.[16] In this context, Jerry's very fallibility as the narrator becomes a way of honoring his dimensionality as a human being, the complexities that keep him from being a flat stock character like the Italians of *The Talented Mr. Ripley* or "Roman Fever."

Critically, however, Lee is unwilling to let readers ignore the Faustian bargain that Italian Americans have so often made to achieve this degree of normalcy, not by fully relinquishing their Italian identities but by assimilating where it most counts: in their attitudes toward race. While *Aloft* makes gestures of solidarity with Italian America by recording injustices and frustrating stereotypes, it also functions similarly to Malamud's narrative in the moments when the border blurs between *italianità* and anti-Jewish sentiment. Allyship here means truth-telling—forcing your compatriots across diasporas to confront the uglier parts of themselves. We can see this ugliness in Jerry's skepticism about discourses of racial injustice, whether or not they might have applied to his own family's experiences of discrimination. We can see it in his reluctant self-editing, how he agrees to stop referring to Asian Americans as "Oriental" but still insists on clarifying that he doesn't "quite yet appreciate what all the fuss is about" (30).[17] We can see it when he repeatedly describes women of color using food imagery, engaging in a form of dehumanization that Italian American fiction from Fante to DeLillo will also testify to.[18] Like the Italian American writers in this book, Lee turns a critical eye toward these sorts of practices by Italian American men, which are far from exclusive to them but which are especially uncomfortable to witness when the perpetrators are people who ought to know better because of the ways that they themselves have historically been treated. While Sohn is absolutely right to characterize Jerry as painfully unaware of and clearly complicit in "the long history of American white supremacy," it is also important to recognize how this critique fits into a larger rewriting of the "Italian novel" and a pattern of expressing solidarity by reckoning across diasporas with these more than unpleasant realities (50).

Intersectional forces make Jerry's relationships with diasporic women of color the places where his racism, shaded by some very typical forms of American sexism, comes most obviously to light. Jerry's Korean American wife is named Daisy, and her death by drowning, which seems likely to have been a suicide, recalls Cora's death in *The Gods of Tango*. However, in its ambiguous self-destructiveness, this tragic event also resembles the way that James's Daisy, her namesake in the classic novella, almost wills herself to contract malaria by going to the Colosseum at night. Jerry unemotionally relates the story of her death, how "she, unclothed as preferred, drifted floatless into the pool, perhaps paddling a calm yard or two, before flying, like a seabird, straight down to the bottom" (130). Like James's Daisy, Lee's Daisy has had to cope with the influence in her life of a man who is certain of what she needs, how it is best for her to behave, and what she should do to "cure" herself of her unconventional personality. Lee's Daisy has been found naked in the park at night and is subsequently forced to take Valium in a joint effort by Jerry and his doctor to control her bipolar disorder—presumably to make her fit the stereotype of Asian female docility that she has increasingly been resisting by refusing to treat the doctor with "respect" (128). The two men's role in the affair is not unlike the one that Winterbourne and socialite Mrs. Walker assume when they attempt to keep James's Daisy from walking in public unchaperoned with Giovanelli the fortune-hunter, given that the nineteenth-century Daisy's actions are treated as equally scandalous and sexually inflected at the time. The critical difference is that Lee's Daisy is a woman of color married to an Italian American rather than a white girl attempting a flirtation with a quintessentially Anglo expatriate in Italy. This is a new way of flipping the script that assigns new responsibility for the struggles of diasporic women to men whose freshly assumed whiteness becomes as dangerous an influence as their gender in a patriarchal society shaped by urgent, persistent issues of race.

Elsewhere, despite being more adjacent to than personally immersed in Italian culture, Lee precisely captures the power of patriarchal values as a specific architectural feature of the Italian American family in isolation. It would have been easy for the novel to fall into several traps here—for instance, making its Italian American women into caricatured victims or making its father-son relationships cartoonishly unemotional. Instead, Lee handles this tricky subject with grace, without oversimplifying the complex ethical and emotional ramifications of these family arrangements. The sexual indiscretions of Jerry's father are denied a certain overdrawn pathos that has been typical of some American fiction when Jerry admits that he is not particularly devastated to learn of his father's affairs.[19] He tells us, "I was too young to think too much about it, and to be honest it never bothered me as it might have" (310). Alternatively outspoken and quietly dignified, Jerry's mother is allowed in one moment to threaten "to gut them both," her husband and her husband's lover, and then in another moment to cloak herself in the trappings of her domesticity, continuing "to make a meal from what was at hand" rather than being emotionally undone by her husband's flirtations with her daughter-in-law (46, 123). Neither portrayal squares with the idea of Mrs. Battle as a victim. Lee shows an uncanny ability to hold a mirror up to complicated issues within Italian diasporic families while avoiding the clichés of victimization and villainy that made patriarchal Italianness seem like a rationale for Anglo-American superiority in the minds of English novelists and American social workers alike.[20]

If *The Gods of Tango* reaches out a hand to Italians in the Americas by scrutinizing what the people of the Italian diaspora have achieved and can achieve again in collaborating with other diasporic communities, *Aloft* approaches the question of solidarity with a more cynical eye. In fact, there are times when Jerry laughs at the very idea of "solidarity"—as when he remembers one painful scene between himself and Daisy—and Lee's narrative raises similar questions about whether the Jerry Battles of the world have what it takes to be good allies once they have given up their real surnames and everything that went with them (116). Still, like De Robertis, Lee also acts as a witness to anti-Italianism in the Americas, and both of these approaches—the witnessing and the "tough love"—become forms of literary allyship in Lee's textual relationship with Italian America.

Whose House Is This, Anyway?

Whether or not they have wrestled with the complexities of Jerry Battle's racial and ethnic identity, critics have tended to emphasize the definitional power of Jerry's suburban milieu in shaping his identity.[21] From the very first page of *Aloft*, it seems likely that the Faustian bargain made by Lee's Italian Americans has to do with more than race. Narrator Jerry's relationship to his private plane does a great deal to demonstrate the evolving class position of the Battaglias-turned-Battles, showcasing the extent of the disposable income swirling around even the older generations, who balk when their sons purchase 6,000-square-foot houses with separate wings but who don't mind a few indulgences of their own. In fact, much of the advancing whiteness of the Battles is dependent on their class position, which gives them the money to plan expensive vacations straight out of the pages of *Baedeker's Italy* and to enjoy hot drinks freshly made by a "push-button automatic Italian coffee machine" (142). The richer men like Jerry Battle become, Lee suggests, the whiter they seem—and the more likely they are to begin consuming Italy in the typical tourist fashion like any other good American, going abroad and bringing home (or importing) souvenirs.

The intermittent glimpses we receive of the Battaglias in their earlier years tend to drive the point home just as emphatically. The Battaglias were once working-class migrants who used to "repoint the top of . . . fireplace chimney[s]," and through the evolution of their landscaping business, the distinction between white-collar and blue-collar work emerges and reemerges throughout the book, invoking not just the differences in the work itself but also the larger class hierarchy upheld by that distinction (308). In a sense, the discursive shift that occurs when Jerry's son Jack starts to refer to their business as "the firm" instead of "just a shop" says it all (141). The youngest-generation Battle Brother has bought into the lie that self-worth, like success, requires an air of "professional" respectability, one that can be purchased only by pretending that no one at his company works with their hands. Still, the earlier roots of the transition seem to lie somewhat further back—perhaps in the aftermath of World War II, when "the challenge was . . . considered not a matter of *re*-integrating white ethnic enlisted men like Hank [the Battaglia patriarch] into their former lives but of molding them into a new social order that would align with the economic interests of the established order," more specifically "by way of the GI Bill" (Knapp 29). In exploring these intricacies, Lee yet again proves himself to be precisely familiar with important details of not just the long arc of American history but also the more specific historical narrative of Italian America, where the specter of blue-collar work has followed many a family from one generation to the next, whether they embraced it or scrambled to distance themselves from it through higher education or other avenues. As the houses of Italian American families get larger and more opulent, *Aloft* seems to ask us, *Whose houses are these, anyway?* Or, to put it another way, whose ambitions are these? Who are these sprawling properties really for?

One answer to this question is that the houses are purchased by men for women based on their sense of what these women want, which is often quite far from the truth. This is easy to see in one episode near the middle of the novel, a sort of figurative "pissing contest" between Jerry and his childhood classmate Richie, now both rivals for the affections of Rita Reyes, Jerry's former and future girlfriend (200). It is Richie's idea to make a bet with Jerry that is tied to the outcome of a tennis match between the two men. If Richie wins, Jerry's plane is his; if Jerry wins, he takes home Richie's Ferrari for good. Meanwhile, Rita is beside herself with anger at the juvenility of the two men's behavior, which objectifies her by extension, suggesting that she, too, like the Ferrari and the plane, can be won by whoever is a good enough tennis player or a rich enough consumer—whoever, in short, is the most masculine according to the most suffocatingly traditional definition of the term. Richie is sure that in order to "keep" a woman like Rita, he will need to be "a partner at a top law firm with a big house in Muttontown and five Ferraris," especially with his bookishness and physical markers of his ethnicity like his height and shoe size working against him (264). Yet Rita refuses to stick to this traditional playbook, rejecting an engagement ring with a "stone as big as a hazelnut" and moving out of Richie's mansion although it is even more sprawling than Jack's house and is made of more expensive materials (263). When she leaves, it seems clear that Richie's emotional immaturity, more than his stature, is what has pushed her to reject him. While again critiquing the objectification of women of color by Italian American men, Lee frustrates stock expectations for female desire and asks readers to reinterrogate their notions of how it might intersect with experiences of diaspora and difference.

While making a compelling critique of Italian America, this part of Jerry's story opens up the world of the novel to a wider critique of its class structures and issues. As much as it is animated by questions of diaspora and social integration, *Aloft* is also about the desperate emptiness and loneliness of a consumerism that has permeated the bulk of the United States and the world beyond its shores as well. In one particularly depressing episode, an English billionaire named Sir Harold Clarkson-Ickes takes to the sky in a hot air balloon in an attempt to "balloon around the world, solo," only to be presumed dead after an encounter with vicious weather (131). Closer to home, Jerry's son Jack is caught up in a whirlwind of consumption-as-expansion at the Battle Brothers headquarters:

> Jack has changed quite a few things since I early-retired, including the old hand-painted script signage of "Battle Brothers," which he switched out for hefty three-foot-high stainless steel

letters that were drilled into the building.... A few months ago construction was finally finished on a new suite of offices that were built on the street side of the double-height eight-bay garage, a funny-looking free-form mass of an addition (based loosely after the style of some world-famous architect), which itself has three different kinds of façade claddings and colors and oddly placed windows cut into it like a badly done Halloween pumpkin. (141)

Jack spends far beyond the company's means, keeping this up until the multigenerational family business is bankrupted and forced to close, confronting readers with the most obvious practical lesson of the novel. And although Jerry is vocal in his criticisms of Jack's materialism, wondering if "all these bulwarks of his prosperity . . . are maybe too much for anyone to handle, and especially Jack," Jerry's plane becomes a way for him to distance himself from people, so that he soon embodies the mantra of the plane's former owner: "There's no point in flying if you can't fly alone" (70, 21). Jerry's neighbors, the Guggenheimers, have a similar experience when winning the lottery leads Mr. Guggenheimer to develop an agoraphobia and germophobia so strong that they cause him to physically isolate himself from his own wife as "a ready importer of contagion" until she leaves him (287). All across the novel, people are separated by possessions from other people and from the larger things that they have built for each other.

For their own part, Jack and his once-materialistic wife Eunice are remarkably happier when the bankruptcy forces them to move out of their McMansion and into Jerry's ranch house, where they will live together with Jerry; Jerry's aging father, who has been liberated from his adult living facility after running away; and Jerry's son-in-law Paul, who inhabits the basement alone after Theresa's death, waiting for his preemie son to grow old and strong enough to leave the NICU. This stunning experiment in communal living harks back to a time when multiple generations of Italian American family members would indeed share the same house, but it also says something critical about the importance of people in the novel—people sharing space, time, emotions, and ideas with each other, and in this way displacing the possessions they have all become used to idolizing. Perhaps, in this decadent and vacuous culture of "the rare and cher, artisanal meats and breads and cheeses," it is not too late for material objects to be dispossessed of their hold on the American psyche (84). The end of the novel finds Jerry behaving accordingly, sitting in the future site of the swimming pool to be built for the entertainment of his grandchildren instead of escaping the noise of the family. As I have suggested before, however, this final scene also raises questions about the addictive power of flight—not in the literal sense, but the flight of the individual into the soothing haze of materialism evoked by the "nifty little Seahawk" from day one (1). This ambiguity in the ending of the narrative means that it retains a cautionary quality, suggesting alternatives to fetishistic consumerism and the inequities it maintains while continuing to sound the alarm about the enduring resilience of the system. Meanwhile, *Aloft* teaches us—again from its precise external vantage-point—that Italian America cannot be understood apart from these questions of class.

Looking Forward

While working from a very different perspective, Lee's novel makes a vital contribution to the conversation that De Robertis would continue with the publication of *The Gods of Tango* just over a decade later. Poor Italians mix with privileged Italians—in terms of race as well as socioeconomic status—in these contemporary portrayals of diasporic identities, which continue the acts of rewriting *italianità* begun by Baldwin and Malamud in their fiction half a century before. In the process, like their literary forebears, Lee and De Robertis also take part in an authorial tradition that is reciprocally linked to decades of Italian American texts from Fante to DeLillo, where Italian diasporic authors have turned their own critical gaze on the community and have taken up the task of representing diasporic experiences outside their own, writing in solidarity across diasporas.

Part III

Returning the Favor: Italian Americans Write Back

Chapter 4

"Mayan Queens," Secondhand Suits, and Toxic White Masculinity
Fante and DeLillo

With novels like Lee's *Aloft* raising essential questions about the place of Italian America in a nation of diasporas and stressing the tenuous quality of Italian American allyship, it becomes critical to reread Italian diasporic fictions from a similar perspective: with attention to the ways that they admit the failures of their own communities and work to disrupt white supremacist narratives that at times have asserted a distressing influence on Italians in the United States. As the earliest and latest novels by Italian American writers in this book, John Fante's *Ask the Dust* and Don DeLillo's *White Noise* hold an important place in this discussion because of their unflinching confrontations with American masculinity, whether Italian or otherwise, as a key ingredient in the struggles of diasporic communities of color coming face to face with a self-indulgent culture of whiteness. At the same time, class-based struggles and issues of economic privilege are interwoven into these already brilliantly crowded narratives in ways that uncover urgent intersections of socioeconomic status with gender and ethnicity in the complex relationships between people across diasporas. The result is a literary gesture of reciprocity that echoes across Italian American writing from Fante to DeLillo and beyond—though of course, Fante's work technically predates and in this way anticipates even Baldwin's and Malamud's acts of allyship.

Colliding an aspiring Italian American writer named Arturo Bandini with a Chicana waitress named Camilla Lopez in the stressful milieu of Depression-era Los Angeles, *Ask the Dust* creates its own set of diasporic intersections, connecting the movement of generations of displaced families from Italy and Mexico as they meet in their shared adopted homeland of the United States.[1] Rather than modeling the type of solidarity that might stem from such collisions, *Ask the Dust* instead presents a cautionary tale of explosively intersecting diasporas: Fante illustrates what occurs when one diasporic community competes for class standing and acceptance into white "majority culture" rather than resisting claims of white superiority and socioeconomic elitism. At the center of Fante's narrative is a young man who inhabits a complex web of racist judgments, classist ambitions, and aggressive, sexist displays of masculine bravado. At times when the aspiring writer becomes aware of his own missteps, he morphs into an intermittent voice of protest against his own bigoted views. In other moments, the young man regains his appetite for white supremacy; he also proves himself to be simultaneously naive and egotistical, so clearly self-deluded that he loses all narrative authority, his racist elitism and misogyny discredited along with him.[2] In contrast, waitress Camilla emerges as the novel's best voice of reason when it comes to the class hierarchy, developing this stance from a world of kitschy pop-cultural artifacts that also vividly contradicts Arturo's matrix of ethno-racial fetishism and gender stereotypes. As the narrative's plot moves from one fraught romantic encounter to the next, punctuated with traumatic scenes of sexual violence and relationship abuse, the novel thus allies itself with the other diasporic communities within its pages. In offering his "often profound critique of the racism within 1930s Los Angeles society," not just as it was directed toward Italian Americans but as it was perpetuated by them as well, Fante provides an example of what it means to write across diasporas from a position of multivalent, self-critical solidarity (Laurila 119).

Meanwhile, DeLillo's *White Noise* confronts readers with the fissures in the aspirational narrative that young men like Arturo Bandini subscribe to by closely scrutinizing generically white toxic American masculinity—which, like Raewyn Connell and others, I define not as "a fixed character type, or an assemblage of toxic traits" but as "common masculine ideals" that "become problematic when they set unattainable standards," so that "[f]alling short can make boys and men feel anxious and insecure," triggering aggressive compensatory behaviors (Connell and Messerschmidt 854; Salter).[3] By far the most widely read Italian American novel covered in this book, Don DeLillo's *White Noise* is also the least Italian American by some metrics. Neither Italy nor Italians are a focus of DeLillo's narrative, which is also not explicitly centered on issues of diaspora or intercultural alliances, and there is no reason to suspect Jack Gladney of having any Italian heritage. Yet readers have gradually come to resist this understanding—or misunderstanding—of the *italianità* of DeLillo's work, finding other ways to define and locate that elusive quality in narratives like this one.[4] I am similarly interested in the subtle ways that *White Noise* parallels diasporic narratives like *Ask the Dust*, even as its characters traverse paths that at first glance may seem wildly different from the ones cleared by Fante's protagonists. Rereading *White Noise* through this diasporic lens makes it possible to understand the white, comparatively wealthy, male privilege of DeLillo's professor-protagonist Jack Gladney as a sort of self-indulgent diasporic identity.

At home in routines, in possessions, and in feelings of certainty about the identities of others, particularly his wife, Jack has carved out a secure home for himself in the midst of a disorienting postmodern America. When an "airborne toxic event" forces him and his family to leave that home for nine days, it foreshadows a larger figurative displacement, a more permanent dislocation from these trappings of home that occurs when he is forced to rewrite his understanding of his wife's psychological and sexual identity in the aftermath of the evacuation (105). With the revelation of his wife's fear of death and her resulting affair, Jack embarks on a strangely diasporic existence, one marked by mental wanderings, feelings of alienation, half-hearted attempts at assimilation, and the desire for a return "home" to a supposedly simpler and less fraught existence. Through all this, even with Jack as the narrator of his own tortured existence, the professor-protagonist betrays a spoiled, self-centered egotism in reacting to his own life and the lives of others—especially those who come from places with languages he cannot identify or histories he cannot clearly remember. Despite its apparent abstraction from questions of Italian American migration and prejudice, *White Noise* therefore becomes its own gesture of allyship, implicitly and sometimes explicitly acknowledging the struggles of diasporic communities of color that have had to confront Jack's type of self-indulgent whiteness and its effects on their own lives. As one way of imagining the fraught conclusion to Arturo Bandini's desired path, the novel fits decisively within the conversation established in *Ask the Dust*.

Uncovering Diasporas

From Mexican repatriation to the Zoot Suit Riots, events surrounding the publication of John Fante's *Ask the Dust* add critical context to the expressions of anti-Chicanx sentiment by the characters in his novel. Yet the story begins much earlier than that. Almost a century before, the Mexican American War had led to the transfer of ownership of nearly half of Mexico's land to the United States—an ethical detail that is often conveniently ignored in today's migration debates.[5] In the wake of the war, economic policies encouraged by American political leaders and grossly in favor of American businesses in Mexico had helped to create financial conditions that had spurred on large-scale emigration out of Mexico and into the US. Raul E. Fernandez and Gilbert G. Gonzalez describe this history thus:

> [T]he story of U.S. domination of Mexico dates to the last three decades of the nineteenth century. . . . Domination of a new type by the United States increasingly undermined the social and political cohesion of Mexico, causing dislocation to its domestic agriculture and industry as well as migration to the United States-Mexico border and to the United States itself. . . . Washington preferred economic domination by U.S. corporations to the direct annexation of Mexico. (29–30)

This economic violence inflicted by the United States thus provided a steady stream of easily exploitable labor that, among other things, played an essential role in growing and sustaining California's commercial agricultural industry through the "war emergency" of the 1940s and beyond (Mitchell 10).[6] Meanwhile, Chicanx residents received little thanks from white Americans for their contributions. Instead, Chicanx workers in rural and urban contexts, both adults and children, faced denials of their basic human rights, from adequate wages to access to education and medical care, a problem rooted in what activists justifiably termed "the fundamentally racist nature of the health care system" (Hoffman 155). Anti-Chicanx sentiment was visible at all levels, generating profound social alienation for individuals in the diaspora. Daily interethnic interactions on Los Angeles streets echoed the same large-scale patterns of bigotry that fueled the forced deportation of Chicanx individuals and families (even US citizens) during the federal government's repatriation campaign of the 1930s, when a "million or more Mexicans . . . were repatriated or deported," including individuals who left on their own due to "local harassment" as well as those whose deportation was officially ordered (Balderrama and Rodríguez 237, 149). Equally concerning were the currents of violence against pachucos and other Chicanx residents of Los Angeles during the same World War II–era riots that made African Americans there the target of vicious attacks. These events were an extension of explicitly racist ideology that cast the city of Los Angeles as playing a vital role "in the long saga of the Aryan race," and they shed a different light on the waves of displacement of Mexican citizens into cities and towns across an often-hostile adopted country, calling for these movements to be understood not just as instances of migration but as part of an ongoing diaspora (Carr qtd. in Laurila 116).[7]

This context was the backdrop for a letter Fante sent to his cousin Jo Campiglia in 1938, detailing his intention to write a novel about "a beautiful Mexican girl who somehow didn't fit into modern life" (6). As envisioned in this early letter, Fante's conception of his project was intensely problematic, playing on primitivist visions of Chicanx identity. In an earlier letter from 1936, Fante had criticized his friends for similar views of Mexican culture, though he also engaged in stereotyping of his own. Writing about a friend's planned trip to Mexico, he commented, "Of course Ross twitted me about Mexican senoritas [sic] and hot nights beneath the Mexican moon and such romantic bosh, and I replied succinctly: look out for the clap!" (*John Fante Selected Letters* 126). There is a frustrating duality in Fante's dismissal of these clichés as "romantic bosh" coupled with this racist joke of his own.[8] Still, Fante had expressed to his publisher that he was interested in writing a novel that would examine currents of anti-Chicanx prejudice in Los Angeles and that his Italian American protagonist would be sensitive to those experiences due to his own confrontations with ethnic discrimination, telling his Chicana love interest that she should be "proud [she] was a Mexican" (*Prologue to* Ask the Dust). And as a literary artifact with a life apart from its author's, *Ask the Dust* turns out to be an ally text that preemptively returns the favor the US-Italian diasporic community would receive from writers like James Baldwin and Carolina De Robertis, doing antiracist work by deconstructing stereotypes and interrogating the complexities of allyship across diasporas—especially the Italian one and the one spurred on by the United States' imperialist maneuverings in Mexico. Written nearly seven decades before, it also neatly anticipates Lee's critique of the toxic Italian American male, not to mention DeLillo's critique of the generically white one.

From the start of *Ask the Dust*, it is obvious that Arturo Bandini himself is not to be trusted to do this sort of self-reflective work. This is a young person without the mettle or the stability of character of De Robertis's Leda. On moving to Los Angeles from Colorado, he cherishes dreams of glamorous success in a new city, dreams that are incompatible with the city's prevailing attitudes toward Italian Americans. Fueled by hope and egotism, he finds himself almost obsessively angry at men and women from other diasporas, misdirecting rage that should more properly be targeted toward the American architecture of white supremacy. Neither the African diasporic community nor the Filipinx one is safe from his wrath, although the Chicanx community in Los Angeles bears the brunt of his abuse.[9] Still, underneath this veneer of bravado lies a layer of insecurity internalized from anti-Italian prejudice during a time when, as Gardaphé points out, the rise of Italian fascism threatened to intensify those sentiments.[10] As these psychological wrinkles emerge in Fante's narrator, they become a way for the narrative to pinpoint the complex and painful instabilities of Italian America's alliances with other diasporic communities, and to make a literary gesture of solidarity that in its own way reciprocates the future work of *Giovanni's Room*, *Aloft*, and other texts.

In this case, the histories of diaspora that color the narrative are largely unseen. The diasporic shifts that have occurred are part of the narrative's backstory rather than its plot, in which no one moves overseas or recalls a foreign homeland personally lost in the throes of political or personal upheaval. Yet *Ask the Dust* does indirectly reference the historical realities of the Italian and Chicanx diasporas through Arturo and Camilla—particularly the diverse "collective histories of displacement and violent loss" that precipitated Italian and Mexican emigration in the late nineteenth and early twentieth centuries (Clifford 307). On Arturo's side, we see the narrator recall his family's poverty during their time together in Colorado, proclaiming that he was "born poor, son of miseried peasants" (20). While the moment is over almost before it has begun, the word *peasants* calls up a vivid image, not of an American family but of the Italian agricultural laborers who were driven from their homeland by national economic policies in the wake of Italy's unification. One short clause marks Arturo's presence in Los Angeles as the diasporic legacy of this socioeconomic persecution. Later, when Arturo proclaims the glory of the US "empire" and passes judgment on the Mexican people as a "bashed and busted race," Fante indirectly acknowledges how the American neo-imperialist foreign policy in Mexico has wreaked havoc with Mexico's socioeconomic framework, tracing the unique contours of this particular diasporic history (44, 24). The political commentary is subtle and indirect, but Arturo's cruel emotion makes it easier to see how the US's machinations in Mexico functioned as an economic form of "structural violence" and precipitated the diasporic displacement of Mexican individuals and families (Bourdieu 40).[11] When diaspora is recognized not simply as a scattering of people to diverse locations but more complexly as movement triggered by diverse forms of violence, Mexican migration as diaspora becomes easier to understand.

Whether their focus is Arturo's soul searching as an Italian American or the noxious effects of his racism on others, many readers have commented that Fante's characters flirt with the possibility of assimilation rather than committing altogether.[12] What is less commonly acknowledged is how this flirtation complicates the way that diaspora in particular manifests in *Ask the Dust*. Fante's narrator repeatedly suggests that his connections to the diasporic community of Italians living abroad are weaker than his affiliation with US culture or with the landscape and community of Los Angeles. He refers to the United States as "my country" and at one point exclaims, "I was an American and goddamn proud of it" (47, 44). Speaking of the "dust and sand . . . from the Mojave and Santa Ana deserts," Arturo displays a knowledge of local geography that bespeaks this intimacy (16). Obliged to debate with the owner of a Los Angeles hotel who insists that Boulder is in Nebraska rather than Colorado, Arturo reveals a more experiential knowledge of the makeup of the American West than many others have:

> "Mr. Bandini," she said, looking at me coldly, "Boulder is *not* in Colorado."
>
> "It is too!" I said. "I just came from there. It was there two days ago."
>
> She was firm, determined. "Boulder is in Nebraska. My husband and I went through Boulder, Nebraska, thirty years ago, on our way out here. You will kindly change that, if you please."
>
> "But it *is* in Colorado! My mother lives there, my father. I went to school there!"

> She reached under the desk and drew out the magazine. She handed it to me. "This hotel is no place for you, young man. We have fine people here, honest people."
>
> I didn't accept the magazine. I was so tired, hammered to bits by the long bus ride. "All right," I said. "It's in Nebraska." And I wrote it down, scratched out the Colorado and wrote Nebraska over it. She was satisfied, very pleased with me.... (49)

In this scene, Arturo's protests give voice to his desperate desire to have his Americanness recognized. It is fundamentally important to his own self-concept that he identify and be identified as assimilationist. While it may be the case that the hotel owner qualifies as one of the novel's "wonderful comic characters," this is a serious interchange from the perspective of Arturo's identity as an American citizen born in the American West (Fine 188).

Ask the Dust as a diasporic novel also hangs on such moments. If Safran had had his way, discussing the Italian diaspora would be impossible today because the migration of people from Italy in the wake of unification would not qualify as diasporic, despite the economic and other forms of violence that precipitated these flows of people. Still, reconfigured in a more flexible form, Safran's ideas are useful here, particularly his understanding of social alienation as a key element of the diasporic experience: a deep sense of estrangement from the space "expatriate minority communities" had relocated to and from the people they would encounter within it. This concept of social alienation becomes a helpful touchstone as *Ask the Dust* sweeps its narrator from one scene of estrangement to another, forcing him to grapple with precisely this experience of distressed misunderstanding and insulation from "majority" US and Los Angeles society, even as he scrambles to claim his own Americanness. Viewed in this light, Arturo's encounter with the hotel owner is vividly illustrative. There, he encounters a kind of illogical nativism that paradoxically requires him to invalidate his own American identity to gain acceptance by more unambiguously white Americans with more obvious insider status. Although he is a US-born American citizen, he must cede to the claims of another American who interrogates him about his ethnic background or perhaps even his national origins, asking him if he is "a Mexican" and then presuming to know more about his own country than he does, simply because he appears to be more foreign (48). The only way that Arturo is able to gain acceptance into the hotel community and avoid being expelled onto the street is to humbly deny what he knows is true about his own hometown, acquiescing to pressures that he has felt since childhood. Indeed, in another passage, he recalls having been verbally abused and socially marginalized as a child, exposed to the hatred of other children and even their parents: "When I was a kid back home in Colorado it was Smith and Parker and Jones who hurt me with their hideous names, called me Wop and Dago and Greaser, and their children hurt me" (46). While *Ask the Dust* does not directly depict the extreme forms of physical violence that did confront some Italians in the United States during historical moments in which their whiteness was treated as suspect, it does capture the xenophobic condescension and cruelty of these other Americans, reactions that foster quite understandable feelings of diasporic alienation.

The religious references that Gardaphé recognizes as a possible factor in Fante's marginalization within American literary studies further intensify this push and pull between assimilation and belonging in the diaspora. There it becomes increasingly clear how, to borrow Clifford's language, Arturo's tactics for coping with Los Angeles life "encode practices of accommodation with, as well as resistance to," the culture of the country and the city in which he has found himself (307). Sometimes Fante's narrator appears quite eager to accommodate social norms that encouraged Italian Americans to assimilate by deemphasizing their Catholic roots.[13] He imagines himself writing a letter that begins, "Dear Mother: I went to Mass last Sunday," then clarifies that, as "an atheist," he has only gone to church to catch a glimpse of the Mexican women who attend the service (15, 22). Yet in the end, the pull of spirituality as a diasporic tie is equally strong, and Arturo is more linked to the Catholic faith of his ancestors than he might wish to admit. He even moves toward reclaiming this spiritual inheritance as the novel progresses. Promising to "return to the church" if God transforms him into "a great writer," Arturo takes part in a tradition among "less affluent Catholics in Italy" of "bargaining with God, Mary, or a local saint, promising to perform certain acts of devotion in exchange for some requested blessing" (Jacobsen 348). In this case, the "act of devotion" is also a signal of his nonbelief, since he rebels to the point of refusing to associate himself with the church at all unless the "requested blessing" materializes. When considered alongside the "masochistic form of Catholicism, partly southern Italian and partly American Irish, in which suffering and self-abnegation" are highly desirable of worshipers, the brazen egotism of Arturo's approach to religion may appear starkly nonconformist—even heretical (Casillo 393). Still, his mentality also indicates the ways that his identity continues to be influenced by the religion of his family and his diasporic community, and an element of "resistance" to typical Anglo-American culture remains, immersing *Ask the Dust* in a larger history of displacement and unbelonging.

In the story of Camilla, Arturo's love interest, Fante creates another seeming parable of assimilation that connects to a larger diasporic history. Camilla rejects the subversive hybrid possibilities that would eventually come to be associated with the term *Chicanx* when she claims, "I'm *not* a Mexican! . . . I'm an American" (61). As Elizabeth Martínez notes, "During the 1960s and 1970s, in an era of strong pressure for progressive change, the term became an outcry of pride in one's peoplehood and rejection of assimilation as one's goal" (1-2). To call oneself "Chicana" also immediately suggests a dualist identity, where Mexican and American heritage and cultural affiliations merge and blend, each equally legitimate, and where Mexican identity itself is understood as encompassing European and indigenous elements. For Camilla, however, there is no liminal social space where she can feel comfortable locating these hybrid identities within herself—and so, over and over throughout the novel, Camilla chooses to emphasize her Americanness. She purchases a car under the name of Camilla Lombard rather than Camilla Lopez, justifying her selection to Arturo by asking him whether he sometimes wishes his name were "Johnson, or Williams, or something," though her choice of name is even more complex and interesting because it has the potential to function as an Anglicization of an Italian one (64).[14] Her plaintive comment makes her desire for assimilation plain; however, like Arturo's protestations about American geography, it also converts Camilla's story into one of diasporic rejection and alienation. Meanwhile, more typically American residents of the city persistently label Camilla as Mexican—often in ways that are explicitly denigrating. Her bartender colleague refers to her as "the Little Spick" and proclaims, in a clear and compact display of intersectional racism and sexism, that "Mexican women . . . don't like to be treated like human beings" (121). In this context, the huaraches that Camilla intermittently wears are more than simple shoes; they are a symbol of cultural identification, and she ultimately chooses them despite briefly experimenting with "new white pumps, with high heels," whose assimilationist implications are equally clear (60).[15] In Arturo and Camilla's collision, then, *Ask the Dust* models twinned experiences of diasporic struggle, not just assimilationist obedience.

Racial Anxiety, Class Consciousness, and Toxic Masculinity

It seems obvious in Fante's narrative that these echoed struggles could lead to intercultural allyship, but it is almost more thematically important that they do not. As a son of the Italian diaspora, Arturo is a shamefully bad ally. The novel tracks his movements as he vacillates between sweetly essentializing compliments and irate insults, incapable of understanding that both are hypocritical betrayals of what he should have learned through experience. That is to say, the expressions of prejudice that Arturo and Camilla both face on behalf of their communities are far from identical but remain symptomatic of the same overarching system of white supremacy. They therefore call urgently for collaboration, a shared resistance to that system that might leverage the tenuous but real white privilege Arturo enjoys despite his Italian parentage. In one sense, Fante's novel is a disillusioning exploration of what happens when someone in this precarious position chooses to ignore that call, competing for scraps rather than committing to allyship in any real way. It witnesses and critiques the actions of Italian Americans in the 1930s and beyond who leaned into the power of their increasingly perceived whiteness as they sought to climb the racial hierarchy in the United States rather than attempting to disassemble it. At the same time, Camilla's own brand of progressivism disrupts this problematic model, not only with regard to whiteness but also where issues of gender, conspicuous consumption, and class aspirations are concerned. As diasporic trajectories collide, that collision becomes a vehicle for moving us into this new conceptual space, and Fante's tenuous allyship with the Chicanx diaspora emerges in the contours of Camilla's character.

Understanding race and ethnicity in *Ask the Dust* requires readers to reject the fallacy of the so-called positive stereotype, since Fante's narrator expresses desire more than disdain when he first speaks of the Chicanx community in Los Angeles. "Oh for a Mexican girl!" he exclaims. "I used to think of her all the time, my Mexican girl. I didn't have one, but the streets were full of them" (15). Arturo defines his imaginary future lover in terms of her nationality or ethnicity, and he clearly expects a woman of Mexican descent to have particular attractions because of her heritage. What attractions these are become apparent when he describes "the Plaza and Chinatown" as "afire" with Mexican women, when he refers to them as "Aztec princesses and Mayan princesses," and when he describes them as "so happy when you acted like a gentleman and all that" (15). Arturo simultaneously indulges in the stereotype of the passionate or "fiery" Latina while imagining Chicana women as exhibiting a kind of docile gratitude for the patronage of white "gentlemen." In making flat, vague references to Aztec and Mayan women, he also associates Chicanx culture with cartoonish imaginings of its pre-Columbian past and casts himself implicitly as the white colonizer.[16] The second half of the narrative finds Arturo similarly obsessing over the supposed primitivism of Camilla's identity. He imagines her specifically as a "Mayan princess," proclaiming, "All of this land and this sea belongs to you. All of California. There is no California, no Los Angeles. . . . This is your beautiful land with the desert and the mountains and the sea. You're a princess, and you reign over it all" (94). This series of images primitivizes Camilla and her diasporic community by continuing to situate them in an exaggerated version of the pre-Columbian Americas.[17]

When Camilla enters the novel, Fante also brings to life the intersectional fetishization and disparagement of nonwhite women's bodies, for centuries a mainstay of American racism. Consider Arturo's first description of his waitress and love interest, which implicitly contrasts Camilla's "muscle" and her "strong silk legs" with the stereotype of delicate white female beauty, notes that Camilla's lips have "the thickness of a negress's lips," and proclaims that she is only beautiful relative to other nonwhite women: "She was a racial type, and as such she was beautiful, but she was too strange for me" (34–35). In another instance, Arturo describes Camilla's hair using language that recalls the white tradition of objectifying and primitivizing nonwhite bodies by associating them with nature, particularly with food: "Her hair was so black, so deep and clustered, like grapes hiding her neck" (41).[18] The moment is similar to one in which Arturo goes with Camilla to buy marijuana and describes the eyes of the African American men and women he sees as "wide and grey and oyster-like," fixated on their race as he repeats the words "Negro" and "Negroes" over and over (141). Later on, Fante's narrator will intensify this rhetoric by literally equating Camilla with the landscape of California ("she was all of those calm nights and tall eucalyptus trees, the desert stars, that land and sky, that fog outside"), showcasing a way of thinking that makes it much more difficult to read the ending of the novel as "an undoing of a bitterly reactive subject toward a reconfiguration of a man . . . who can finally be 'a credit to' Bandini himself" (123; Verdicchio 66). At the beach, he will describe her diving "ahead of the next breaker with all the grace and perfection of a seal," troublingly invoking the same white supremacist discourse that historically has used such figurative language to dehumanize people of color in general and women of color in particular (67). In Fante's hands, Arturo becomes a mouthpiece for racist rhetorical strategies, allowing the novel to record the role of Italian America in perpetuating them.

While this racialized vision of gender is toxic enough and represents a clear betrayal of solidarity, collisions of masculinities trigger further expressions of bad allyship in *Ask the Dust*, as the young writer loses himself in vitriolic comments about a Chicano rival for the attentions of a white sex worker:

> The girl was gone. I walked on: perhaps I could catch up with her. At the corner I saw her again. She stood talking to a tall Mexican. They walked, crossed the street and entered the Plaza. I followed. My God, a Mexican! Women like that should draw the color line. I hated him, the Spick, the Greaser. They walked under the banana tree in the Plaza, their feet echoing in the fog. I heard the Mexican laugh. Then the girl laughed. . . . A half hour passed. There were sounds on the steps. The door opened. The Mexican appeared. He stood in the fog, lit a cigarette, and yawned. Then he smiled absently, shrugged, and walked away, the fog swooping upon him. Go ahead and smile. You stinking Greaser—what have you got to smile about? You come from a bashed and a busted race, and just because you went to the room with one of our white girls, you smile. Do you think you would have had a chance, had I accepted on the church steps? (23–24)

In the novel's first encounter between Italian American and Chicano masculinity, not only does Arturo spout segregationist nonsense, but he also situates himself on the "right" side of the so-called color line, asserting his whiteness by calling the sex worker "one of our white girls." Arturo aggressively dismisses the questions that white society has raised about his own ethno-racial identity. Instead, he participates in the white American tradition of seeking to "defend" white femininity against the supposed threat of nonwhite masculinity, a tradition with its own poisonous history of justifying segregation, fueling false accusations of sexual assault against men of color, and generally perpetuating racial injustice in the United States. Arturo's broader judgments of Mexican and Chicanx culture, as when he proclaims that the "Greaser" comes "from a bashed and a busted race," implicitly suggest that Mexico's domination by the US "empire" is further evidence of its inferiority. This declaration gives added weight to the racial slurs Fante reproduces (which, significantly, include one term that Arturo himself has been called) and the derogatory language that Arturo chooses in referring to the man as "stinking." It is unsurprising when he later uses the same language in anger against Camilla, referring to her as a "filthy little Greaser" (44). While Arturo's similar references to Filipino men in Los Angeles are somewhat more restrained, they telegraph a suspicion of what he perceives as the somehow inferior masculinity of these other men as well as a distaste for interracial relationships between Filipino men and white women. At one point, he describes a "gaunt redheaded girl, with brown freckles below the neckline of her dress" walking with "a short Filipino holding her arm," noting that "even with the high leather heels he was a foot shorter than she" (51–52).

That Arturo views the Chicanx diasporic community through the same stereotyping lens turned on him and his ancestors by Anglo-American society is not just a matter of ironic hypocrisy.[19] Arturo's perspective on the Chicanx community and other diasporic communities in Los Angeles is causally shaped by his own traumatic encounters with discrimination and their persisting psychological weight. Although Fante importantly does not cast these forms of prejudice as equivalent or excuse Arturo's racism by diagnosing its origins, Arturo's progression from victim to aggressor helpfully draws readers' attention to the self-perpetuating quality of ethno-racial prejudice, a very real barrier to allyship. Speaking to Camilla in a rare instance of emotional vulnerability, he explains, "[W]hen I say Greaser to you it is not my heart that speaks, but the quivering of an old wound, and I am ashamed of the terrible thing I have done" (47). Here, *Ask the Dust* admits the connection between anti-Italian prejudice and racism in Italian America: the way white supremacy became a cudgel for Italian Americans seeking to distinguish themselves from their neighbors of color, beset with anxiety over their seemingly ambiguous semiwhiteness. Jennifer Guglielmo reminds us that because "many Italians remained poor and working-class longer than most other European immigrants, they have often lived in the nation's blue-collar neighborhoods, amid people of color," and that "this proximity—in terms of class, color, and geography—has given Italians a particular anxiety to assert a white identity in order to effectively distance themselves from their Brown and Black neighbors" (4). True to form, Arturo uses his interactions with Camilla as an opportunity to distinguish himself as more white and more American than the diasporic community she represents. Hurling slurs at his love interest makes him more convinced of his own Americanness, more "goddamn proud," euphoric at the thought of the social membership he has purchased by verbally abusing her. Arturo's inability to break the cycle of racism serves a cautionary function for readers, and the novel enacts a key method of witnessing—itself a form of allyship—by recording the genesis of these hypocritical reactions to the Chicanx diaspora. The same is true of Arturo's negative responses to the Filipinx diaspora in Los Angeles, to African American communities there, and to Jewish working-class characters like Vera Rivken. Fante reaches out to every one of these diasporic communities by making the target of his attention a young person whose own history of abuse leads him to betray them all—and by locating the roots of that betrayal.

Despite the fissures in Fante's own understanding of racism and its workings, as evidenced in his 1938 letter and in some of his other correspondence, *Ask the Dust* makes a challenge to the very forms of fetishism that those nonfictional writings express. Out of a modernist tradition of narrative unreliability comes Arturo's untrustworthy persona as the novel's storyteller, which makes it easy to see his fetishism of Camilla for what it is and suggests that *Ask the Dust* is far more antiracist than its narrator. In the second half of the novel, an increasingly violent Arturo writes a vitriolic letter to a rival for Camilla's affections. The man is terminally ill, and Arturo tells him to put his "idiotic soul in order," calling his writing "literary manure" (119). When a rare burst of humanity inspires Arturo not to send the letter and instead to write an actual critique of his rival's manuscript, he lauds his own generosity: "How wonderful I really was!" he proclaims. "A great, soft-spoken, gentle man, a lover of all things, men and beast alike" (120). But the young writer has proven to be anything but "gentle"—he has mentally, verbally, and physically abused anyone who has threatened him, with fits of arrogance punctuating these scenes of abuse. In classic modernist fashion, Arturo's self-delusion suggests that the novel's narrator cannot be trusted to see himself or others clearly. By the end of the text, this unstable impression of Arturo will color his description of Camilla, too, making it seem like the misguided vision of an egotist. *Ask the Dust* capitalizes on what Jessica Berman calls an "ironic stance" to move beyond the ideological limitations of its narrator, calling very much into question the idea that "the narrator, the implied author, and perhaps even the historical author are not sufficiently differentiated" where "Bandini's relentless racism" is concerned (123; Harrison 228).[20]

Deepening this instability, the novel also plays with ways that even in a first-person narrative, other characters—their words, their actions, and the environments they choose to inhabit—can undermine a narrator's authority to define the identities of those around him. Camilla is neither a fiery sexpot nor a docile girl-child, and her life and personality are much more familiarly contemporary than Arturo's primitivist caricatures allow for. Early in their relationship, Arturo spurns Camilla's kind gestures in especially showy displays of toxic masculinity: made insecure in her presence, he becomes aggressively nasty. In response, Camilla expresses herself with insults that are decidedly of-the-moment: "I hope you die of heart failure," she says with near-medical precision (37). Happier times find Camilla driving Arturo around town with her foot dangling out the window and her leg exposed, shouting that the men who catcall her "ought to mind their own business" (64). While Camilla is passionate, she uses that passion to defend a strikingly contemporary view of gender relations. She rejects the conventional wisdom that nonwhite women's bodies are objects for men to visually consume and scorns that classic hallmark of rape culture, the idea that women must hide their bodies if they want to avoid unwanted attention from men. When Arturo suggests as much, she merely scoffs. And while Arturo imagines Camilla as a "princess" in a "castle," Camilla lives in an unrelentingly contemporary apartment littered with objects that have a pop-cultural resonance: "a Murphy bed, a radio . . . a movie magazine. . . . [K]ewpie dolls standing about, souvenirs of gaudy nights at beach resorts" (43, 141–42). Even the objects that show signs of "disuse" still function as symbols of modernity: a bicycle and a shotgun (142). Arturo takes in this scene and reflects that Camilla "would ruin any apartment" because she "belonged to the rolling hills," but by this late moment, his interpretation reads as the projection of an exoticizing fantasy onto Camilla's messy, quotidian, working-class life—a life that marks her as entirely distinct from Arturo's exaggerative rhetoric (142).

It is in the area of class consciousness and commentary that *Ask the Dust* allows Camilla the most power to counter Arturo's vision. Camilla is not always more progressive than her would-be suitor; she makes racist remarks on occasion about both Fante's narrator and other characters, such as the Japanese children whom she refers to as "Japs" (132).[21] She is also not the main focus of the novel, and as she disappears for whole chapters at a time, her insights punctuate the narrative rather than guiding it throughout. Still, as the narrative's intermittent voice of reason where matters of class are concerned, Camilla has a role to play that also disrupts and resists Arturo's interwoven expressions of racism and sexism. This role of hers is particularly essential given *Ask the Dust*'s status as a chronicle of Depression-era class struggles and anxieties that, for instance, was written just a few years after the Los Angeles Chamber of Commerce would give "its chilling recommendation that a hard-labor concentration camp for vagrants be established to cope with unemployed transients already in the county and discourage others from coming" (Starr 227). For Camilla to be right about one of the most pivotal historical issues of the novel—the damaging social influence of class inequality and the savagery of the "haves" and "almost-haves" in their dealings with the "have-nots"—gives her character a different aura that turns out to be quite important to a range of conclusions reached by the close of the narrative.

Just as Arturo subscribes to the same racist ideology that helps make him vulnerable to ethnic discrimination, he lusts after the same economic resources and social position that, while enjoyed by others, help to keep him poor in the intensely stratified environment of Depression-era Los Angeles. Struck by the sight of a man outside the exclusive Biltmore Hotel, Arturo recalls that the man "looked rich; and then a woman got out, and she was beautiful, her fur was silver fox . . . and I thought oh boy for a little of that" (12-13). Arturo's socioeconomic aspirations are as plain as his objectifying attitude toward the woman he refers to as "that." He wants to "look rich" himself and acquire women like so many objects. This is clear when, a moment later, he envisions himself in the wealthy man's shoes. It is the man's possessions and his social cachet that he imagines first, with sex appeal as a potent afterthought: "I . . . saw myself a great author with that natty Italian briar, and a cane, stepping out of a big black car, and she was there too, proud as hell of me, the lady in the silver fox fur" (13). I read this scene as a vivid example of pecuniary emulation and conspicuous consumption, concepts introduced in the decades before the novel's publication in Thorstein Veblen's *The*

Theory of the Leisure Class. Veblen's capitalist consumers were people who would seek to secure their social standing and even their personal sense of self-worth by emulating the consumption patterns of their neighbors, or of individuals in higher classes than themselves. Operating in the same way, Fante's narrator embraces a conformist mode that accepts the tacit assumptions of classism rather than challenging them. He might seek to improve his socioeconomic status or project an image of greater wealth than he actually has, but he will never seek to dismantle the class hierarchy itself. Through Arturo, Fante directs our attention to the power of the dominant system to control its victims, drawing a painful parallel between the allure of whiteness in this diasporic community and its materialist aspirations.

Meanwhile, familiar-seeming limitations arise from Arturo's unwillingness to develop solidarity with other members of the working class. The narrator's positive feelings about the display of wealth that unfolds in front of the Biltmore are matched by his negative feelings toward others at the hotel who are nearer to his own position in the socioeconomic hierarchy. He remarks, "I was passing the doorman of the Biltmore, and I hated him at once, with his yellow braids and six feet of height and all that dignity" (12). Whereas Arturo covets the immense wealth of Los Angeles's upper class, he despises the "dignity" of other working-class people, especially those who seem to have achieved a more secure position within the lower echelons of the hierarchy. This contrast speaks volumes about the barriers to socioeconomic resistance and allyship. Not only does Arturo aspire to join the ranks of the wealthy, but he actively rejects possibilities for human connection and solidarity within his current class, seeing only competition where he might forge an alliance. Working-class people enjoying their leisure time are equally vulnerable to Arturo's scorn; surrounded with others of his class at a burlesque show, he labels them "dirty lowbrow swine," again using the word "hate" (21). This passionate emotional response suggests how deeply Arturo has internalized elitist messages about the repulsiveness of the poor, despite being poor himself. The repetition of familiar diction from the "Greaser" scene in the Plaza also suggests a potent link between denials of class identity and breakdowns of allyship across diasporas. The same mentality is at work in both failures, feeding dominant social structures and protecting them from the threat of would-be rebels—who, rather than knocking the entire social ladder down, instead choose to knock others off of nearby rungs so that they can rise beyond them. *Ask the Dust* begins to suggest that racism is not the only problem standing in the way of collaboration across diasporas that are also marked by their working-class origins, as both the Italian diaspora and the Chicanx diaspora historically have been.

Like antiracism, class critique is something *Ask the Dust* intermittently models as Arturo muses on the socioeconomic injustice facing his own diasporic community. When reflecting on his identity as the "son of miseried peasants," he underscores the intersectionality of class inequality and ethnic prejudice that left displaced southern Italians doubly disadvantaged.[22] Arturo's social alienation in Colorado results from his socioeconomic status as well as his ethnicity, which prompt the neighborhood boys to taunt him because he is "poor" and his "name ends with a soft vowel," until he not unreasonably plots to become a famous and wealthy author, hoping to quiet the ethnic slurs they shout at him (47). While material resources may never have fully neutralized ethno-racial prejudice in America, they have historically promised to eliminate at least one dimension of the disadvantage that has haunted poor Americans with diasporic histories, especially when the new arrivals in question have been white. Arturo's pragmatic self-awareness draws attention to these multidimensional burdens and unearned advantages as he seeks to navigate them.

Arturo admits that his consumerist aspirations are problematic, and his economic motivations for writing drive him to self-loathing: "[I]t would be better if you died," he laments (20). The same intermittent and painful self-consciousness is at work when Arturo receives a check for $175 for a short story and immediately spends the money on new clothing that is intended to make him appear wealthier than he is. Trying on his new purchases, he recalls, "The image in the glass seemed only vaguely familiar. . . . All at once everything began to irritate me. The stiff collar was strangling me. The shoes pinched my feet. The pants smelled like a clothing store basement and were too tight in the crotch" (59). Arturo is only able to find comfort when he retrieves his old clothes from the wastebasket and puts them back on, literally and symbolically rejecting the conformity with classist norms with which he has briefly experimented. If there were any questions about Fante's position on the virtues of "selling one's soul," Arturo's intermittent self-criticism should begin to clarify things, as the novel carves out its initial stance on class issues in these fleeting moments.

Throughout the rest of the novel, Fante aggressively underscores the dangerous attractions of materialism as Arturo reverts to self-destructive and anticollaborative behaviors designed for him to get ahead, often by exploiting other working-class people from other diasporic communities. Fante's narrator finally attains financial success by appropriating and rewriting the story of a Jewish American woman named Vera Rivken, who is "a housekeeper for a rich Jewish family in Long Beach" (85). In a distinctly poor showing of allyship, Arturo capitalizes on Vera's trauma by using it to secure a book contract and an unnamed but clearly substantial sum of money. With the proceeds, he also attempts to secure Camilla's affections by renting an expensive beachfront house for the two of them to live in, uncritically reproducing the strategies he fantasized about at the start of the novel. *Ask the Dust* is far from endorsing these tactics. Instead, the same egotistical unreliability that undermines Arturo's judgments about Chicanx culture also casts doubt on his approach to socioeconomic issues. In one scene, Arturo proclaims that his novel "is more important than Hitler" and laments that his neighbors "preferred the war in Europe" (146). Fante continues to emphasize Arturo's inability to see himself and others clearly, making it difficult to give credence to the young writer's larger vision of class—an unfortunate product of foolish egotism, selfishness, and discrimination, the narrative implies. Near the close of the action, when Camilla disappears and Arturo reflects that he has started "to hate" the expensive house he has rented with her, this almost seems to serve Arturo right (160). Arturo's unreliability gives readers permission to criticize and ultimately to reject his obsession with upward mobility, recognizing it as a misguided source of misery as well as a primary reason for the failure of alliances across diasporas—in this case the Jewish one as well as the Chicanx one.

Supplementing Arturo's erratic example, Camilla tries to break through the facade of his pretension, encouraging him to proudly claim his membership in the "proletariat" and attempting gestures of socioeconomic solidarity with him (38). Even after Arturo gives up his new clothes, he maintains an air of superiority. Returning to the diner where Camilla waitresses, he orders an expensive cigar and proclaims that he "used to be" but now is no longer poor (60). Arturo seems to expect Camilla to be impressed, but she resists the classist assumption that he will be more desirable to her if he is wealthier: "I liked you better the other way," she tells him (61). In an earlier scene, when Arturo reveals that he would "drink beer too" if he had the money, Camilla responds by buying his beer herself "from a handful of coins she dug out of her smock"—clearly her tips (42).[23] Camilla has a greater appetite for class solidarity than her admirer, who remarks that her actions "hurt" him and, in a "devilish" response, "poured the beer into the spittoon" (42). For Arturo, Camilla's offering is waste to be discarded in a display of toxically masculine bravado. Yet Camilla's actions simply and effectively illustrate the potential for diasporic communities to give each other concrete assistance in resisting the class hierarchy. They also make Camilla a foil for Arturo and for the portion of Italian America that he represents: those who have chased material wealth in white America at the expense of their ties within the working class and across diasporas.

In an interview where he discussed his enthusiasm for *Ask the Dust*, poet Luis J. Rodríguez once said of Arturo, "He's poor. He's hungry. Some people turn to racist ideas when they're desperate" (Dick 187). In other words, perhaps Arturo's class status and class ambition are themselves a driver of his racism, not just an accompaniment to it. Likewise, Camilla's proven ability to challenge the classism of her dysfunctional admirer becomes a way for the novel to invalidate its narrator's racist thinking. By positioning Camilla as the novel's clearer-headed, more progressive thinker about class issues, much in the way that Baldwin makes Giovanni more fully self-actualized in his embrace of queer love, *Ask the Dust* makes a new gesture of solidarity, destabilizing racist ideas about the superior wisdom of white maleness. The novel also proposes an implicit rationale for Camilla's class resistance that is linked to her own recent diasporic history and that of Chicanx immigrants more generally, recalling the cruel intersections of diaspora, class, and empire in the Americas during the mid-nineteenth through early twentieth centuries and beyond. In *A Century of Chicano History*, Gonzalez and Fernandez remind us that "historically, Mexican workers begin to come to the US Southwest and into the bottom layers of the US labor force at a time of generally rising standards for the rest of the working class," filling the role of the "working, propertyless class" necessitated by the capitalist system in the wake of the Mexican American War (124–25). Beyond the general struggles of diasporic peoples in the United States, this more particular reality is visible in *Ask the Dust* through Camilla's class position, which Arturo scornfully invokes in calling her huaraches "desperately ragged" and in ridiculing her "rattling Ford" (35, 63). By refusing to buy into the American capitalist value system, Camilla stages an effective protest for herself and for other abused diasporic communities. Simultaneously, Fante effects his own act of allyship by testifying to these abuses through Camilla while shaping her into a character who is thoroughly of her own historical moment, and whose empowerment belies the primitivist stereotypes projected onto both the men and especially the women in her community.

This context also sheds a different light on the events at the close of the novel, in which Camilla is physically abused and rejected by her white love interest, begins using marijuana, is evicted by her white landlady for supposedly erratic behavior, and, thanks to the Los Angeles police, lands in a mental institution for the poor. Camilla's fate becomes a testament to a particularly insidious collision of racism and classism, one in which the United States precipitated a diaspora and then economically and personally subordinated the individuals displaced by this neo-imperial aggression. That Camilla is a woman and thus is uniquely vulnerable to being perceived as "crazy" only deepens the injustice she encounters. In telling Camilla's story alongside Arturo's, Fante makes a gesture of interdiasporic allyship that is more nuanced and more successful than readers might expect given his initial intentions with regard to Camilla as expressed in his personal correspondence. As much as Arturo himself does not, the novel does the work of challenging stereotypes while encouraging readers to acknowledge problems of racial fetishism and racial hatred; class prejudice; and insecure, aggressive masculinity left unchecked in Italian America and the United States at large.

Perhaps there will always be some readers who will conflate Fante with his narrator, assuming that Arturo Bandini's prejudices are identical to those of the man who created him. As recently as December of 2016, the Los Angeles Review of Books published an essay by Rob Sternberg in which he lamented "Fante's hysterical treatment of marijuana—specifically, his depiction of Camilla as a 'hophead'"—suggesting that "her downfall is attributed . . . explicitly to the effects of the drug." Yet this is more properly an attribution that Arturo makes than one that the nuances of the narrative themselves support, and *Ask the Dust* can just as easily be read as satirizing such views. Since the book was published, the roots of this type of misreading have most often seemed to be in the correspondences that do exist between Fante's life and Arturo's, as when reviewer E. B. Garside lauded Fante for capturing "a whirligig American existence" and suggested that "Fante must have lived this out at some time" (qtd. in Collins 91). If anything, however, Fante's biography sheds light on his uniquely diasporic perspective as it appears in the novel and throughout his writings. Fante faced explicit ethnic prejudice from more traditionally white Americans, including his own mother-in-law. His letters recount his lies to his mother about attending Catholic mass; they also condemn the Italian government's treatment of its peasantry, and at times they proudly proclaim his own Italian identity. These snippets of day-to-day life testify to Fante's own ambivalence about his cultural inheritance and his selective accommodation of purportedly mainstream American cultural norms. Fante's painful awareness that he would be unable to return to Italy even if he wanted to because of the threat of fascism recalls another quintessential element of diaspora: the desired but impossible return.[24,25] It also dovetails with his recognition of the economic violence in Italy that had forced so many families to emigrate to escape the exploitation of southern agricultural communities by the north. With Fante's own personal and familial experiences of alienation, accommodation, violent displacement, and impossible return driving his writing, it is perhaps unsurprising that the book capitalizes on these same sensitivities. In colliding two distinct trajectories of diaspora, however, Fante creates the narrative conditions necessary for a literary gesture of reconciliation and solidarity rather than a myopic study of his own experience, and *Ask the Dust* takes its place in a series of diasporic narratives that will eventually include novels like Lee's *Aloft*, with its "tough love" approach to Italian American identity.

At Home and Displaced in Postmodern America

If Arturo Bandini is critically shaped by the liminal status of his ethnicity in a city and country beset by their racism, DeLillo's Jack Gladney seems at first to have virtually nothing in common with Fante's protagonist or his predicament. Tim Engles reminds us that for the first decade and a half after the novel was published, "almost all critiques of DeLillo's portrayals of postmodern identity formation" failed to analyze "the persistent whiteness of his protagonists" (756). Meanwhile, to read *White Noise* as diasporic fiction remains understandably rare, since Jack has a literal home in a way that is traditionally inconsistent with the concept of diaspora. This is not Arturo's cramped Los Angeles apartment, nor is it the crowded Argentine tenement flat sketched so vividly by De Robertis. Instead, DeLillo transports us to a small college town whose inhabitants—especially its college professors—live in houses instead of apartments. So when we first find Jack describing the contours of his home, we are treated to a description of a house "at the end of a quiet street in what was once a wooded area with deep ravines," in a place where some of the other houses have "turrets and two-story porches where people sit in the shade of ancient maples" (4). What is most immediately striking, though, is the more figurative set of features of home that Jack has accumulated to provide the comfortable foundation for his day-to-day life. Routines, objects, beliefs: these are what moors Jack to the place where he lives and especially to himself—and they will similarly displace him from home when they unexpectedly disintegrate.

Take the cyclical rhythms of the academic year, which transform the town every September into the home Jack will know from fall through spring. The opening of the novel recalls what is now an iconic scene in postmodern American fiction:

> The station wagons arrived at noon, a long shining line that coursed around the west campus. In single file they eased around the orange I-beam sculpture and moved toward the dormitories. The roofs of the station wagons were loaded down with carefully secured suitcases full of light and heavy clothing; with boxes of blankets, boots, and shoes, stationary and books, sheets, pillows, quilts; with rolled-up rugs and sleeping bags; with bicycles, skis, rucksacks, English and Western saddles, inflated rafts. As cars slowed to a crawl and stopped, students sprang out and raced to the rear doors to begin removing the objects inside. . . . (3)

Recalling the scene to his wife Babette, Jack is triumphal in his satisfaction at its familiarity: "It's the day of the station wagons. . . . They stretched all the way down past the music library and onto the interstate. Blue, green, burgundy, brown" (5). That the occasion has its own nickname in Jack's household marks it as a family tradition of sorts, something that gives a comforting shape to Jack's existence. Day-to-day family interactions form a microcosm of this larger annual cycle, especially in the kitchen, where food is unloaded into the refrigerator and cupboards to be satisfyingly consumed or, in the case of Babette's neglected "wheat germ," to be reluctantly thrown away (7). As objects and bodies flow in and out of the kitchen, appearing and disappearing with a diurnal rhythm that mimics the annual flow of people and their possessions onto and off of the college campus, they obey a routine that forms the heart of the family's life together. It is no wonder that Jack reflects that other than the bedroom he shares with his wife, this one room of the house is the place that is most like home to him. "The kitchen and the bedroom are the major chambers around here," he muses, "the power haunts," whereas the rest of the house functions "as storage space" (6). In truth, it is the routine that the room promises, as much as the physicality of the place itself, that allows DeLillo's spoiled professor-protagonist to feel at home.

Acts of possession and consumption do remain an essential component of these routines, despite the "foreboding" quality that Jack assigns to some of the objects in the house (6). Like Arturo Bandini wishes to be and sometimes is, Jack is a conspicuous consumer in the Veblenian sense, not only using objects to shape others' perceptions of his identity but using the act of consumption itself for the same purpose.[26] To solidify his position of influence at the college where he chairs the department of Hitler Studies, he invests in "glasses with thick black heavy frames and dark lenses" to match his "medieval" academic robe (17, 9). While he admits that these accessories represent him somewhat falsely to onlookers, he also revels in the feeling of "romance" that the robe confers, so that the object becomes part of what makes him feel at home in his own skin (9). When a colleague sees him off-campus without these accoutrements and deems him "harmless," Jack shores up his social image through a shopping spree at the mall, in which his children giddily select items for purchase while he gestures "in what [he] felt was an expansive manner" (83–84). In these moments, what Jack is mostly securing is his own sense of self, refracted through his perception of others' perceptions of him. To be at home in his body, he requires objects that can shape what he knows about how he appears to the world outside himself. For him, then, home is defined by objects not just through the comforts that they provide—as in the domestic space of the kitchen—but also through the feeling of self-definition, the fleeting but potent confidence that they confer.[27]

Understanding these aspects of home, figuratively speaking, will help to illustrate how DeLillo's protagonist and narrator can be permanently dislocated from home even without physically leaving his house for much longer than the duration of the average American family vacation, creating a figurative and satirically shaded experience of diaspora that will become essential to the novel's social critique. Equally vital to Jack's sense of home is his understanding of his wife Babette—and the architecture of Jack's displacement from home will ultimately hinge on her. From the start of the narrative, Jack as narrator prioritizes asserting his authority on the subject of his wife: her habits, her cares, and what she stands for symbolically in the context of his own life. Babette is the sort of woman who volunteers her time reading from the tabloids to an elderly blind man, who runs up the stadium steps at the high school to improve her figure, who cries when her stepdaughter breaks one of the bones in her hand while away at camp. She is conscientious; she cares deeply, but about concrete, tangible aspects of the world that surrounds them. "The point," as Jack puts it, is that "Babette, whatever she is doing, makes [him] feel sweetly rewarded, bound up with a full-souled woman, a lover of daylight and dense life, the miscellaneous swarming air of families" (6). She is someone who does not feel "estranged from the objective world" as his former wives did (6). For Jack, Babette exists as an antidote to the complex, abstract subterfuges of Jack's previous marriages, including one to a spy. Her body, to him, *is* home—at least as long as she continues to be the Babette that he knows, allowing him the sense of gratification that comes from being certain of what he believes about her. Jack's unearned sense of certainty about Babette's identity is what he returns home to with the greatest enjoyment and relief in the evenings after his work at the college. Still, like Arturo, Jack knows much less about the woman he loves than he believes he does. This version of Babette-as-home is precisely what disintegrates as the narrative accelerates through the famed airborne toxic event and toward even more unexpected and sociopolitically charged revelations.

The temporary exodus of Jack's neighbors out of their quiet, uneventful neighborhood is described in terms that give the journey a diasporic air, as though it is a dystopian reenvisioning of the "caravan" of students that Jack, in Orientalist fashion, describes arriving on campus every fall (5):

> Slowly we approached an overpass, seeing people on foot up there. They carried boxes and suitcases, objects in blankets, a long line of people leaning into the blowing snow. People cradling pets and small children, an old man wearing a blanket over his pajamas, two women shouldering a rolled-up rug. There were people on bicycles, children being pulled on sleds and in wagons. People with supermarket carts, people clad in every kind of bulky outfit, peering out from deep hoods. (118)

Some of these details are satirically nonsensical, showing why Frank Lentricchia has called DeLillo the "last of the modernists, who takes for his critical object of aesthetic concern the postmodern situation" (14).[28] At the level of perception of characters like Jack, they also evoke the feeling of traumatic departure that is at the core of diaspora and that both Arturo's and Camilla's ancestors once faced in their actual displacement from home, though the exaggerative quality of some responses to the event paints DeLillo's characters in a markedly less sympathetic light. Once inside the "abandoned Boy Scout camp" where some of the displaced residents have been relocated, they also begin to develop a makeshift community shaped by their circumstances, not unlike a diasporic enclave in a foreign country (117). Jack's son Heinrich plays a particularly formative role in this process, shaking off the trappings of his insecure adolescence as he educates listeners about the properties of the escaped chemical Nyodene D: "This large gray area, dank and bare and lost to history just a couple of hours ago, was an oddly agreeable place right now, filled with an eagerness of community and voice. Seekers of news moved from one cluster of people to another, tending to linger at the larger groups. . . . People listened attentively to this adolescent boy in a field jacket and cap, with binoculars strapped around his neck and an Instamatic fastened to his belt" (126). This passage evokes Clifford's description of how diaspora "involves dwelling, maintaining communities, having collective homes away from home" (308). At the same time, for most of the family, these adaptive half-measures prove inadequate to compensate for the feelings of discomfort they experience as they are shuffled from one location to another with the movements of the toxic cloud, feeling "subdued, worried, confused" (120). While one of the children refuses to take off the mask she's been wearing, which leaves her sensitive "to episodes of stress and alarm," Jack himself wanders the shelter looking "haunted, ashen, lost," terrified by the news that his health may have been negatively impacted by exposure to the toxic chemical (154, 156). Once the toxic cloud dissipates, we are primed to think about these sorts of experiences of dislocation at the same time as the figurative foundation of Jack's home begins to shift—displacing him mentally and emotionally in ways that, from his pampered social position, he experiences as diasporic.

Here, a few reminders about the plot of the novel may be useful. The airborne toxic event, despite having uniquely captured the attention of DeLillo's readers, is not the real root of the narrative's eventual climax.[29] Rather, the hidden source of the novel's defining conflict is Babette's fear of dying, itself obscured until late in the novel due to the obliviousness of DeLillo's fallible narrator, who has no idea she is thus afflicted. Jack's own fear of death has been exacerbated by the toxic cloud, which he has been exposed to while pumping gasoline for the family station wagon on the way to the shelter. When Jack plots to hunt down the man Babette has repeatedly slept with in exchange for a bottle of Dylar, an experimental drug designed to cure her fear of death, he claims that his motivation is his own fear; he wants to steal the man's supply of the drug and use it himself. But what recurs throughout this ominously shaded final section of the novel is Jack's obsessive imaginings of his wife and this nameless male figure (eventually revealed to be a man named Willie Mink) having sex in a nameless, cheap motel.

Babette, as it turns out, is not so different from Fante's Camilla, who endlessly frustrates Arturo because she refuses to conform to his imaginings of feminine docility, so that "[i]nstead of cooking and cleaning and staying home, she smokes marijuana and, from time to time, runs away" (Guida 139). For Jack, who has taken so much for granted, having to rewrite his understanding of his wife's identity is akin to making a painful departure from a home that he will never be allowed to return to again. His first response to Babette's disclosure of her infidelity is disbelief that Babette would betray him—not exactly by sleeping with this unidentified man, but more by destroying his image of the woman he has married. Repeating the syntax of his earlier descriptions of his wife, he protests, "The whole point of Babette is that she speaks to me, she reveals and confides" (183). Moments later, he complains, "That's what I can't forgive you for. Telling me you're not the woman I believed you were" (188). Similar refrains echo throughout the remainder of the novel as Jack chides his wife repeatedly. "Babette is not a neurotic person," he tells her. "She is strong, healthy, outgoing, affirmative. She says yes to things. This is the point of Babette" (210).

This primary experience of displacement begets secondary effects as the other elements of what Jack experiences as home begin to fall away. Always brooding in his own thoughts of death, Jack begins to find his mind more and more uncontrollable as he ruminates on the "hazy gray seducer moving in ripples across a motel room . . . their purling foreplay, the love babble and buzzing flesh" (230). Instead of taking comfort in familiar objects, he consigns them to the garbage: "I threw away shelf paper, faded stationary, manuscripts of articles I'd written, galley proofs of the same articles, the journals in which the articles were printed" (249). This becomes its own sad ritual as Jack repeats it without feeling any solace, later discarding a "battered khaki canteen" and "ridiculous hip boots" as well as "candle stubs, laminated placemats, [and] frayed pot holders" (280). The abandoned possessions notably include things that have propped up his identity in the eyes of others, items related to his academic life—not only the copies of his articles but also the army paraphernalia that we might imagine as a byproduct of his specialization on Hitler. (Such details recall Arturo's fit of frustration in which he consigns his newly acquired suit to the dustbin.) Even Jack's old routines cease to be pleasurable, instead becoming something sinister. Parroting the cynicism of his colleague Murray, a New York émigré, he begins to refer to routines as "deadly" (237). With all of these moorings of his life torn from him, Jack floats aimlessly in self-pity until he develops a plan to shoot and kill the man who has destroyed his image of his wife. He has, in a metaphysical sense, been violently displaced from home, swept up in his own private diaspora—though this form of angst often reads as wallowing.

Feelings of alienation follow as Jack begins to perceive himself as increasingly distant from the people and places that surround him. This hallmark of diaspora finds new life in Jack's reflections about whether he is actually alive or dead. "I don't know what I mean," he whines. "I only know I'm just going through the motions of living. I'm technically dead. My body is growing a nebulous mass" (270). In short, Jack is consumed by what David Cowart calls "a latter-day plague, a mental and spiritual wasting" (77). Already unhealthily attached to the doctor who he hopes can reveal whether he actually has health problems following his exposure to the toxic cloud, he increases the frequency of his doctor's visits after Babette's revelation. The obsessive tenor of these meetings becomes a signal of his escalating distraction from the people in his personal life, causing his physician to praise him for taking "[h]is status as a patient" seriously (247). As in any good narrative of diaspora, this sense of alienation is matched by Jack's half-hearted attempts to assimilate into a world that he now sees with new eyes. Never particularly eager to "talk about gaskets and washers, about grouting, caulking, spackling," he finds himself acquiescing to the demands of Babette's father by accepting a quintessentially masculine gift from him—a gun (234). Murray receives similar consideration when he floats a typically abstract and absurdist argument about mortality, suggesting that to kill a person is "to gain life-credit" in a world separated into "[k]illers and diers" (277). Jack's plan to kill Willie Mink is born of these developments, which paint Jack as a lost wanderer scrambling to adapt to a new land.

DeLillo's professor-protagonist never loses his desire to return "home" to Babette, which is so strong that it would make Safran proud.

In Safran's vision of diaspora, displaced people "regard their ancestral homeland as their true, ideal home and as the place to which they or their descendants would (or should) eventually return" (83). Viewed in this light, Jack's continual efforts to find comfort with his "head . . . between [Babette's] breasts" take on new meaning, even beyond the self-indulgence and self-concern that they signal (282). When Jack returns and re-returns to the physical space of his wife's body, we see a homesick displaced person attempting an impossible act of return, seeking the old comfort and security he has left behind on meeting the new Babette. Of course, these feelings of discontent and displacement are not unique to him but are instead shared by many in the world of the novel—like Babette herself, who constantly seeks a return to the life she lived before she began to fear death, or like Jack's ex-wife Tweedy, who asks if he still loves her as she proclaims her newfound unhappiness in another marriage. If, as Gardaphé argues, DeLillo's fiction "dramatizes the effects of living life the American way," this sense of subtly diasporic dislocation is one of the sobering consequences that makes "being American . . . destructive even for the WASP" (184).[30]

As a decently well-to-do college professor rather than a famous novelist, Jack is not exactly the man that Fante's Arturo hopes to someday be, but he is close. This means that the failures of Jack's surprisingly diasporic life bode ill for the aspirational narratives of young people like Fante's protagonist and his counterparts across generations of Italian America. What remains to be seen, however, is how this critical spirit reflects more directly on the experiences of—and expresses some form of allyship with—the diasporic communities of color that encounter Jack's brand of spoiled white maleness in their American lives.

Whiteness, Wealth, and Masculinity: DeLillo's Literary Allyship

As these descriptions of Jack Gladney have already begun to suggest, DeLillo's narrator is not a particularly likable one. He is insecure and vindictive, spoiled and self-centered. He is the sort of man who will start an academic department centered on the life of Hitler without learning any German, then sheepishly hire a tutor years later to help him learn the language in secret. He is the sort of man who will attempt to kill another man for sleeping with his wife, then commend himself for having second thoughts and bringing the man to the doctor once he has been shot. In both of these details, there exist fascinating and perhaps unexpected correspondences between Jack and Arturo, with the latter's own minimization of Hitler's crimes and his misplaced sense of his own generosity and compassion in scenes of aggressive cruelty. Indeed, even if *White Noise* at large more closely resembles *Aloft* in its exploration of a pampered life, Jack is an equally fitting counterpart to Arturo in ways that suggest a trajectory of Italian American literary production from Fante's Depression-era ethnic fictions to DeLillo's much more subtly diasporic writings of the 1980s. Still, in his dealings with actual diasporic communities and in his responses to his figurative displacement from home, Jack's very unreliability and disagreeableness as DeLillo's narrator open up a space for *White Noise* to interrogate and satirize the problems of race, class, and gender symbolized by the generically white, (un)reasonably privileged American male rather than those of the scrappy, struggling immigrant. In the process, *White Noise* allies itself with those diasporic communities that have been haunted by the specter of this particular disagreeable figure, again resisting the aspirations of those in Italian America who cannot wait to lose their *italianità* and become Jack.

Who DeLillo's narrator is at home speaks volumes about his character in this way, especially as it relates to diasporic people and other racial "outsiders." Part of Jack's comfort in routines comes from the familiar obliviousness of his family as they repeat half-truths and outright misinformation about people and places that are distant from them, which they have the luxury of not being knowledgeable about because their comfortable position in the world order permits their idle self-absorption. In one noteworthy scene in the family station wagon, they repeat a series of absurdities about a girl who it seems might be a foreign exchange student living with the neighbors:

> "What do you know about Dylar?"
> "Is that the black girl who's staying with the Stovers?"
> "That's Dakar," Steffie said.
> "Dakar isn't her name, it's where she's from," Denise said.
> "It's a country on the ivory coast of Africa."
> "The capital is Lagos," Babette said. "I know that because of a surfer movie I watched once where they travel all over the world." (80–81)

Jack is conscious of what his family doesn't know, remarking wryly that "the family is the cradle of the world's misinformation," yet he also seems to enjoy these family rituals, insensitive to the more serious power dynamics that reside below their surface (81). And in his own private thoughts, the distinguished professor is just as bad himself: "More and more I heard languages I could not identify much less understand," he notes passively, without bothering to educate himself about what these languages might be or about the diasporic communities that might speak them (40). As Engles notes, it is Jack's habit by default to "revert . . . to habitual uses of racialized others, casting them as bit players within his own similar enactments of a received, white male fantasy of selfhood" (763).

Later, when Jack meets Willie Mink in person, this same casual vagueness about nonwhite, less apparently American diasporic identities will recur in a more sinister form. "His nose was flat, his skin the color of a Planter's peanut," Jack reports. "What is the geography of a spoon-shaped face? Was he Melanesian, Polynesian, Indonesian, Nepalese, Surinamese, Dutch-Chinese? Was he a composite? How many people came here for Dylar? Where was Surinam?" (292–93). So predictable in his whiteness in this scene, Jack uses a food analogy to describe Willie's physical appearance in a comment that might remind Fante's readers of Arturo's descriptions of Camilla. Before he attempts to kill the man, Jack's first conversational impulse is to attempt the dreaded *What are you?* or *Where are you really from?* conversation faced daily by immigrants across the United States. "Where are you from originally," he asks, "if I can call you Willie?" (293) Jack feels entitled to the information, the narrative implies, asking the question with a sarcastic air of deference grounded not only in his status as the injured male but also in his standing as the white, native-born American. Rather than disrupting his self-indulgent whiteness, Jack's own figurative and subjectively perceived experience of diaspora, or displacement from the familiar, only causes him to double down and makes him indignant about what he sees as being owed to him.

Jack's enjoyment and eventual rejection of objects is similarly complicated by what it says about the social milieu that he belongs to and its distance from other, less luxurious worlds. Class in *White Noise* is about economic resources, but it is also about less tangible markers of privilege that separate Jack from the working-class diasporic enclaves depicted in other parts of the narrative. As a college professor, Jack has the ability to use objects to shape-shift, becoming someone else by donning a robe and glasses so that he can feel comfortably at home.

During the airborne toxic event, Jack's initial reaction to the prospect of his family's temporary displacement heightens our sense of this distance between him and characters like Camilla, who fail to become someone else by dressing differently and who are continually physically displaced during the course of their lives. He remarks egotistically, "Society is set up in such a way that it's the poor and the uneducated who suffer the main impact of natural and man-made disasters. People in low-lying areas get the floods, people in shanties get the hurricanes and tornadoes. I'm a college professor. Did you ever see a college professor rowing a boat down his own street in one of those TV floods?" (112) Importantly, Jack seems to find this idea reassuring, not repugnant; he enjoys the feeling of security that this Othering language of "shanties" produces in him, with its connotations of diasporic refugees and other economically marginalized people.[31] Even when he is proven wrong and the family is required to evacuate, the stink of privilege follows DeLillo's narrator, since this certainty about himself and his life is as much the luxury here as any actual protection from adversity. Soon Jack will learn of Babette's indiscretion and begin throwing away objects the way a petulant child might discard a beloved toy, rejecting materialism for himself without considering other people's problems—like overflowing landfills or the people who might wish to buy his discarded items at Goodwill. By then, it does not matter that the family's station wagon "has one whole rusted door" (6). Jack is as unrepentantly spoiled in his unmoored disappointment and regret as he is in the security and comfort of his former life.[32]

Meanwhile, being displaced from Babette-as-home brings the toxic, brittle masculinity of DeLillo's protagonist to the fore, showcasing its far-reaching influence. As a spouse, Jack is painfully similar to the husband in Henrik Ibsen's *A Doll's House*, whose self-righteous response to his wife's legal indiscretions betrays his self-centeredness.[33] In his murderous encounter with Willie Mink, Jack more closely resembles the vengeful Gino in Forster's *Where Angels Fear to Tread*, who shows no hesitation and no remorse in inflicting pain on Forster's protagonist after the death of his son.[34] Capitalizing on an obscure side effect of the experimental drug, which makes it impossible for the drug's users to distinguish between words and events, he seems to enjoy emotionally torturing the confused Willie: "I recalled Babette's remarks about the side effects of the medication. I said, as a test, 'Falling plane.' He looked at me, gripping the arms of the chair, the first signs of panic building in his eyes. 'Plunging aircraft,' I said, pronouncing the words crisply, authoritatively. He kicked off his sandals, folded himself over into the recommended crash position" (295). At the end of the scene, having decided not to kill his planned victim after all, Jack calls himself "virtuous," "stately," and "generous," echoing the conspicuous consumption scene at the Mid-Village Mall as he celebrates his own supposed kindness of spirit (299). Here we might again remember Arturo's similar emotions as he resolves to take pity on a dying fellow writer by not verbally shredding his manuscript to bits. Bandini-esque in his self-satisfaction, Jack, too, sees his own identity through a distorted lens. He tells himself that he is "large and selfless" as he drags Willie into a religious hospital for potential life-saving, conveniently forgetting that Willie is close to death because of gunshot wounds that Jack has inflicted (299).[35] While no one emerges blameless from this scenario, DeLillo gives particular attention to the literally life-threatening consequences of pampered and self-righteous white male self-pity for members of diasporic communities who must come face to face with this particular social phenomenon.

If there is one single common denominator in Arturo and Jack's various forms of kinship, it is the persistence of the same toxic social expectations for American masculinity, in which men are encouraged to respond to women's lived experiences by "making it all about them," to take revenge on each other through acts of violence and destruction, and still somehow to enjoy the intoxicating illusion of their own superiority. Shaped so conventionally in these ways, men like Jack are not just a danger to other men. They are also tiring for women like Babette, who has to remind her husband that her story "is not a story about [his] disappointment at [her] silence," and they are even more bothersome for diasporic women of color like Camilla, who must put up with their egotism on all fronts: their ethnic- and class-based arrogance as well as their sense of their own masculine splendor (183). While there is no Camilla with as visible a presence in this novel, only women and girls at the very border of the narrative such as the "African" guest of the Stovers, DeLillo writes a skewering portrayal of this vexing male creature and his anatomy as it emerges in the throes of a figurative voyage from home (81).

Viewed through the lens of diaspora, *White Noise* looks a bit different than it otherwise might. The breakdown of Jack Gladney's life, from which he seems only to partially recover, becomes legible in a new way as a separation from the parts of home—the things, people, and beliefs about people—that make it feel like home to him in the first place. Even at the supermarket, where Jack once says that the products for sale bring a sense of "well-being . . . to *some snug home* in [their] souls," the novel's final scene forebodingly references "wandering" and death (20, 310; my italics). For Jack himself, the process of being separated from his former life is as painful as a real-life experience of diaspora, a violent physical displacement from a beloved and familiar homeland. Jack as narrator is unable to abstract away from the details of his existence to see how his tale of woe compares with more physical and less self-indulgent forms of displacement. However, by writing Jack's experience as though he were being cast away from a metaphorical homeland, DeLillo's satire paradoxically draws attention to the stories of actual diasporas that remain largely unwritten in the novel—the languages and histories about which Jack is so bumbling in his unfamiliarity, and the diasporic people and communities of color that he variously affronts and hurts. So it is that *White Noise* makes another literary gesture of allyship, creating a space for reflection and perhaps even for healing from these injuries.

Centering Men: Two Cautionary Tales

A few years after *Ask the Dust* was first published, Fante became involved in the production of the unfinished and unreleased Orson Welles film *It's All True*. While the film's purpose and its subject matter would change as the project progressed, it was originally intended to contain four short films celebrating the African American, Mexican, Canadian, and Italian American ethnic and national communities within the larger cultural context of the Americas.[36]

The film Fante was involved in writing for the project, titled "My Friend Bonito," was set in Mexico in 1908 and was a historically based if somewhat saccharine story of child activism, centering on a mestizo boy who had successfully advocated to save the life of a bullfighting bull. Significantly, filming for the short piece took place in Mexico, countering the persisting tendency of Hollywood to represent Othered spaces without actually locating production there. As an extension of Fante's work on *Ask the Dust*, projects like *It's All True* speak to Fante's commitment to working across diasporas despite his flawed ways of conceiving some of these endeavors.

As the inclusion of Italian America in the film project suggests, the Italian diasporic community in the United States was in the same precarious position as Arturo Bandini in the first few decades of the twentieth century. Veiled expressions of intolerance, crude slurs and hate speech, and even physical violence—both threatened and actual—created the perfect conditions for Italian Americans to buckle under the pressures of white supremacy and enact racist norms in interactions with diasporic communities of color. A careful reading of Fante's novel in light of these realities reveals the larger import of Arturo's narrative voice and its instability: how this quintessential modernism of the novel works against racist, sexist, and classist ideologies, encouraging readers to do better than Arturo does and making Fante into an ally across diasporas. *Ask the Dust* singles out anti Chicanx sentiment and stereotyping as well as class elitism and toxic masculinity as intertwined and misguided social values that desperately need to change for the United States to become better aligned with ideals that it has betrayed from the country's very founding, and for Italian America to wrestle successfully with the hypocritical legacy of anti-Italian prejudice and trauma. Meanwhile, in DeLillo's hands, the aspirations and imaginings of his narrator are translated into a fully assimilated, purportedly deracialized reality. *White Noise* looks back to a diasporic Italian America and predicts what Arturo's children or his children's children might experience if their proclivities were left unchecked: the drowning in possessions, the experiences of figurative displacement brought on by insidious ideas of gender as well as by this unchecked materialism, the unending existential dread that no amount of whiteness can neutralize. The novel also gestures toward the harms done to other actually displaced communities obliged to interface with the Gladneys of America.

Although the main focus here has been on Italian American writers' expressions of allyship with diasporic communities of color, these narrative subtleties will find echoes in novels by De Rosa and Puzo, where other diasporas take center stage whose perceived or actually ambiguous relationship to whiteness echoes the alienated experiences of Italian Americans.

Chapter 5

Off-White Allies

Writing Irish and Romani Women's Lives
from Puzo to De Rosa

Even a quick glance at the novels of Tina De Rosa and Mario Puzo reveals their importance to Italian American women's writing and to American fiction about the experiences of women of Italian descent. De Rosa today is recognized as one of Italian America's most important twentieth-century woman authors. Meanwhile, in the years prior to his death in 1999, Puzo became increasingly vocal about the importance of women—particularly his mother—to his work. In the preface to a new edition of *The Fortunate Pilgrim* in 1996, Puzo wrote that after becoming "rich and famous" from the ever-popular *Godfather* franchise, he had discovered that the Godfather and his own mother, the model for the heroine of this earlier novel, were essentially one and the same: "Whenever the Godfather opened his mouth, in my own mind I heard the voice of my mother. I heard her wisdom, her ruthlessness, and her unconquerable love for her family and for life itself, qualities not valued in women at the time. The Don's courage and loyalty came from her; his humanity came from her.... And so, I know now, without Lucia Santa [the protagonist of *The Fortunate Pilgrim*], I could not have written *The Godfather*" (x). With Puzo's own words as a guide, we can look to *The Fortunate Pilgrim* itself, alongside De Rosa's *Paper Fish*, as two of the most interesting Italian American novels of the last sixty years where gender issues are concerned. Like *Ask the Dust* and *White Noise*, these novels do interrogate problems of Italian American masculinity, yet they also unapologetically center women to a degree that neither Fante's nor DeLillo's narrative does.

Questions of diaspora remain just as important here, and between the lines of each novel's main plot, we can also see gestures of allyship across diasporas. Both of these autobiographical novels make references to other embattled diasporic communities that, like the Italian American one, have historically occupied the fringes of whiteness to varying degrees in the minds of outsiders. In *Paper Fish*, it is Romani people who play this role as representatives of a long-standing diaspora shaped by currents of anti-Romani superstition and persecution.[1] In *The Fortunate Pilgrim*, it is Irish Americans who receive Puzo's sporadic yet potent attention in this way.[2] And intriguingly, it is the figures of women—especially the older women Puzo's narrator describes as "crones"—who are the most evocative focus of both writers' attention as they reach across diasporas (16). While exploring the almost morbid fascination of the communities' children with their wizened female elders, these novels also simultaneously bear witness to how diasporic foreignness is fetishized in the minds of children, and both texts consider carefully how the three categories of difference in age, gender, and ethnicity intersect. Readers who have finished either novel would be hard-pressed to deny the complex matrix of prejudices affecting these women whose age and ethno-national identities as well as their gender mark them as Othered, but they may also be more likely to reinterrogate some of those received notions of difference as the boundaries blur between the Italian, Romani, and Irish diasporic communities—which, it seems, may not be so entirely different from each other after all if they share this set of experiences. The result is a distinct type of solidarity built on subtle expressions of unity but not on attempted erasures of difference. At the same time, *The Fortunate Pilgrim* and *Paper Fish* urge readers to focus in on other gender issues that transcend the experience of displacement from home: burdens and inequalities that are an extension of this particular problem of gender and diaspora, but that move beyond it as well. As these identity factors continually collide within the two narratives, they work reciprocally, each illuminating the other.

Puzo, Gender, and the Italian Diaspora

Puzo's novel of New York City immigrant life resonates closely with some of the perspectives on gender explored in "Italian novels" such as Alcott's or Wharton's. By his own account, Puzo was clearly intrigued by the concepts of feminine strength and masculine weakness, and this inversion of gender stereotypes is one of the more overt ideological features of his novel, which chronicles the triumphs and misfortunes of an Italian American family in the 1920s and 1930s, culminating in their successful move to a home of their own on Long Island around the time of World War II. This victory is both practical and symbolic, and the credit for it belongs to determined matriarch Lucia Santa, who scrimps and saves through one family trial after another until the victory becomes possible. One by one, in contrast, Puzo's male characters fall by the wayside. Father figure Frank Corbo develops a debilitating mental illness that stems from his feelings of alienation from those around him; stepsons Lorenzo and Vinnie crumble under social pressure in different ways—one allowing himself to become a womanizing mafioso, the other apparently dying by suicide; and it is only in the few slim final chapters of the novel, after all these tragedies, that Frank's own biological son Gino can be convinced to partly assume the mantle of family responsibility that Lucia Santa wears for life. What results is an intriguing intervention in an Italian American family structure that has traditionally afforded a woman power as the family's "symbolic center" only so long as she exhibits "unquestioned acceptance of a patriarchal view of the world" ("Broken Images" 88). Writing decades earlier, Puzo anticipates the way that contemporary writers like Louisa Ermelino would "create . . . new notions of masculinity" in novels such as *The Sisters Mallone*, "giving us a good sense of how gender lines have always been blurred" as she exposes "the mothers" as an undeniable site of power in Italian American communities ("Mafia Stories" 115–16).

Robert Anthony Orsi, in his book *The Madonna of 115th Street*, captures vividly the tension between what he refers to as the "public" and "private" images of "the good woman" in the Italian American cultural imagination. Orsi describes how, defined according to "the public definition of the good woman," her sphere was restricted and her role within it was circumscribed, yet intensely demanding:

> [S]he rose long before everyone else and was still awake when the last male drifted off to sleep at night. A good woman felt uncomfortable outside the domus; an extreme statement of this isolation was the insistence among many male immigrants that their wives not learn English and the pride among many women at not having done so after many years in the

United States. A good woman did not know how to leave the neighborhood and never learned anything about public transportation. A good woman was utterly loyal to her husband and children; she would sacrifice "everything" for them, as the popular expression put it. She overlooked and covered over her husband's faults. She was humble, submissive, obedient. And above all, she was silent. . . . (145)

Of course, as Orsi clarifies, "the private reality . . . was quite different," making women "the powers to be reckoned with in the domus, the sources of authority and tradition," even as men asserted their power in maintaining this public conception of what good femininity ought to be, and as they jockeyed to be publicly perceived as the authorities of their households (145).

Puzo's female protagonist, though she retains the traditional roles of wife and mother, nevertheless rewrites traditional gender scripts when her sheer strength of personality spills over from the private reality of the novel into its more public world, raising questions about her "acceptance" of the patriarchal values that Bona and Orsi refer to. In this way, Lucia Santa not only brings to life "the de facto matriarchy of immigrant New York" but also models something that moves beyond it (Ferraro 499).[3] She is described as a "beleaguered general" who "planned tactics, mulled strategy, counted resources, measured the loyalties of her allies," and is able to "guard . . . her daughter with her eyes" as she walks down the street from their tenement and into the world (162, 230). As this metaphorical language sporadically reappears throughout the novel, the events of the plot reinforce it: Lucia Santa never crumbles or wavers though any of the masculine-derived crises that pain her and complicate her life. Importantly, the tactical moves she makes are as often public as they are private. If her second husband must remain in the sanitarium for her to safeguard the well-being of her children, for instance, then so be it: she will make the choice decisively, not without emotion but without regret. The public obligation of an Italian American woman to "cover over her husband's faults" does not trouble Puzo's heroine. Likewise, the grief she feels at the death of her son Vinnie, a grief that is so uncharacteristically violent that it frightens her children, is finished too quickly to interfere with her management and protection of the family. Here, since the community's women in mourning were traditionally "called upon to express the grief of the domus while their husbands stood by mutely," the rapid pace of Lucia Santa's mourning and the speed at which she returns to the regular business of providing for her family become an additional challenge to Italian American conceptions of the patriarchy (Orsi 132). Lucia Santa does cry loudly and violently at her son's death, and her tears prove so intimidating that only the other women in the family are emotionally strong enough to stay by her side, "coiling and twining around each other like snakes" while her sons flee. In that moment, a mother's mourning becomes a testament to the emotional resilience of women in their expected role rather than outside of it. Still, the larger truth of Lucia Santa's character is that she is too occupied with the survival of her family to remain in this prescribed role for long. Like the men in the "Mafia tales" of Italian Harlem, she is obliged to "protect . . . the domus" in ways that run counter to established expectations for Italian American women (128).

Despite Lucia Santa's gender nonconformity, *The Fortunate Pilgrim* also anticipates the valorization of traditional "women's work" outside of second-wave white feminism, treating Lucia Santa's daughter Octavia with scorn because of the contempt that she, in turn, displays for her mother's life choices. Here is a young woman whose feminism is shortsighted, Puzo suggests, belittling what it does not understand. After all, there is far more to her mother's life than a simple story of entrapment "into dreamless slavery by children and the unknown pleasures of a marriage bed," yet Octavia does not recognize this (11). Early in the novel, Puzo's narrator calls Octavia "Judas-like" for plotting her "treason and escape," asserting a certain allegiance to Lucia Santa and her particular brand of domestic empowerment (11). There is something especially refreshing in Puzo's preemptive embrace of what would eventually become a pivotal feminist reinterpretation of empowered womanhood: one that responded to the complaints of culturally diverse feminists by recognizing the choices to marry and bear children as equally legitimate possibilities for contemporary women.[4] Octavia's responses to her mother record the difficulties confronting young Italian American women who "often resented and sometimes resisted this pressure to . . . conform to the expectations of the domus," while drawing attention to ways that the younger generation's understanding of these complexities might sometimes falter (Orsi 141).

On the other hand, male readers—whether Italian or otherwise—might be forgiven for bristling at Lucia Santa's combative inversion of gender stereotypes as she rails against male incompetence. Paradoxically, through Lucia Santa's questioning of and resistance to the patriarchy,

Puzo makes criticisms of Italian American masculinity that themselves might seem to reinforce traditional notions of gender. As she muses about the fate of her first husband, the matriarch's philosophy is laid bare in plain-spoken free indirect discourse: "The truth was simple. He had been a kind, hard-working, ignorant, pleasure-loving man. Her feeling had been the feeling of millions of women toward improvident husbands. That men should control the money in the house, have the power to make decisions that decided the fate of infants—what folly! Men were not competent. More—they were not serious" (27). In valorizing diverse forms of femininity, contemporary feminist thought also insists that men not be treated as helpless or incompetent where family responsibilities are concerned. At times, in privileging and validating Lucia Santa's perspective, *The Fortunate Pilgrim* seems to fail at this. Yet Puzo's characters and their experiences also make a strong argument for seeing the larger gendered social schema of the novel as a poisonous system that practically demands such domestic incompetence from men. In other words, if this statement of Lucia Santa's seems to hold true in the world of the novel, its veracity also seems traceable to social conditioning rather than to any innately gendered lack. Frank Corbo, for instance, is the kind of man who is tender with his children and thinks nothing of taking on supposedly womanly tasks, even wheeling a stroller around the streets outside their tenement. In his world, however, this sort of behavior is viewed as aberrant rather than being valued, for "what Italian male wheeled his baby in the summer night?" (15) Frank, being male, is also not supposed to require tenderness in return for his own, and it is not expected to bother him when he feels "the hatred of his stepdaughter" toward him, so that it becomes further proof of his strangeness when the gentle father is driven from home by the feeling that "life was a dream of beauty felt and not understood, of love twisted into cruelty" (15). As in *Ask the Dust*, toxic expectations for masculinity, which reward aggression and punish gentleness in men, are a dominant component of the social fabric that makes Frank Corbo lost and "sick" (101).[5]

Puzo's language marks these social ills as at least partly particular to Italian American life and conceptions of gender. Curiously, however, Frank prescribes himself the typical American—and typically gendered—"rest cure" that had been treated so differently from its feminine equivalent at the start of the twentieth century, when men with "nervous" complaints had been "sent out West" by doctors like the famed Silas Weir Mitchell, "to engage in prolonged periods of cattle roping, hunting, roughriding and male bonding" (Stiles 32). Frank's own plan is similar: "he would meet a farm truck and disappear without a word. . . . He would work in the brown and green fields of summer, gain peace from love, restore his strength" (15). Within the span of a few pages, Frank transitions from transgressing gender roles to accepting them to the detriment of the entire family. He will eventually lose touch with the physical reality around him, experiencing a sort of psychosis not unlike the ailment that confronts the protagonist of Charlotte Perkins Gilman's "The Yellow Wall-paper," who is subjected to the female version of the "rest cure" as Perkins Gilman herself was while under Mitchell's care. Meanwhile, Lucia Santa must confront the lack of authority her children confer to her as a matriarchal head of household in her husband's absence, lamenting that her son Lorenzo "would never have dared leave a paternal roof" (64).

Even and especially when the "cure" is quintessentially American, these sorts of gender issues are intrinsically tied not just to problems of ethnic identity but to specific challenges of diaspora as well. As Gardaphé suggests in "Italian American Masculinities," there is the sense in Puzo's works that "an Italianate sense of masculinity cannot survive transplantation to the United States" because of the conditions of life within the diaspora (558). This is as true for men who attempt to assert themselves as providers and protectors—only to be thwarted by the various prejudices and other dangers of a new homeland—as it is for men like Frank who might perhaps tend more naturally toward nonconformity with both Italian and American masculinities. And indeed, Frank is described as being driven to mental illness not simply by gendered experiences of alienation but because of the intersection of his maleness and his diasporic identity. Puzo's narrator reflects, "It was always the men who crumbled under the glories of the new land, never the women. There were many cases of Italian men who became insane and had to be committed, as if in leaving their homeland they had torn a vital root from their minds" (106). This idea adds a new layer to Stuart Hall's understanding of diaspora as the impossibility of physical return. For Frank, a return to his homeland would be physically impossible not just because it would require "pushing other people into the sea" but because the person he once was has been physically and mentally dismantled by the process of leaving (235). Once he has completed the process of severing himself from home, there is no Frank Corbo left to return; he has been consumed by this collision of gender and departure.

While men's experiences at times come to the forefront of *The Fortunate Pilgrim*, it is really women's experiences that the novel most highlights, generally by contrast. Later, when Octavia is belittled by a "mansplaining" government employee who has been extorting her mother in exchange for welfare funds, the differing intersections of gender, class, and diaspora are put into relief:

> La Fortezza spoke now of literature. "Ah, Zola, he knew how to write about the poor. A great artist, you know. A Frenchman."
>
> Octavia said quietly, "I know." But La Fortezza went on. ". . . Now there is a man whose books your daughter should read, Signora Corbo. That would be an education in itself. And it would make you understand yourself Octavia, and your environment."
>
> Octavia, itching to spit in his eye, nodded quietly. (176)

Anyone who has read Rebecca Solnit's essay "Men Explain Things to Me" is bound to read this passage with extra interest. Solnit's piece chronicles, among other encounters, a conversation in which a man describes her own book to her and recommends that she read it. Something similar happens to Octavia here, as the unfortunate, egotistical La Fortezza makes assumptions about what Octavia does and doesn't know, condescending to explain to her things with which she is already intimately familiar—including her own class status. In this scene, however, it is specifically because of Octavia's status as a poor second-generation immigrant as well as because of her gender that La Fortezza believes he is in a position to take advantage of her. By "speak[ing] politically," Octavia makes a rebuttal that acknowledges this; she protests that La Fortezza ought to "find some greenhorn girl off the boat [he] can impress and try to screw her" (Messenger 136; Puzo 178). For his own part, by engaging these complexities, Puzo weaves a tapestry of women's diasporic lives in which distinct facets of identity prove mutually constitutive, each with its own weight and influence.

Encountering Irish America

The same connections will recur in Puzo's brief, intermittent, yet potent references to Irishwomen throughout the novel, where gender and diaspora will continue to meaningfully collide—this time in ways that help the narrative function as an interdiasporic ally text. To understand exactly how this happens, it may be necessary to again step back and think a bit more particularly about *The Fortunate Pilgrim* as a diasporic novel. Spanning multiple generations, Puzo's text is in a good position to examine the unique social proposition that is so often made to participants in a diaspora once they reach their newly adopted home: they may be allowed to retain some cultural traditions from the old country, but they had better expect their children to adopt the new ways of the only homeland they have ever directly experienced. Because the novel centers on a multigenerational household, the special brand of alienation and accommodation that occurs across generations under these circumstances emerges in more vivid detail than is possible in a narrative like *Ask the Dust*, and Puzo allows readers to begin to understand alliances across diasporas in the context of this special tension. For first-generation members of the diaspora, the act of accommodation occurs largely by proxy as they allow their children this type of latitude, although in the world of *The Fortunate Pilgrim*, the prospect of parents letting their children decide is itself a gesture of adaptation to American norms—as, in some cases, is their own decision to rebel against parental authority in leaving Italy in the first place. Puzo's narrator carefully considers all three of these stages of accommodation across the generations, tracing the process backward from "the corruption of the innocent by the new land" to their parents' acceptance of this corruption as "a price that must be paid" and to more distant histories in which the parents themselves, in leaving Italy, had been "liberated" by similar "audacity" (6, 7).

In his reading of *The Fortunate Pilgrim*, Thomas J. Ferraro recalls how Puzo's Italian American women see "the structure of individual self-discipline, filial obedience, and punitive parental authority . . . crumbling before their very eyes" in episodes of rebellion that "would be taken as tongue-in-cheek self-parody if the day-to-day conflicts . . . weren't still, at that time, so serious (76). One of the most marked signals of parental acquiescence to such rebellion in Puzo's novel is the ability of their children to run wild in the streets on days when they would traditionally be expected to work for their families and nights when they would be expected, just as dutifully, to keep their parents company. A touchstone of parent-child conflict in the narrative, this sometimes contested freedom of children from family responsibility becomes a handy narrative tool in that the adventures of Italian children facilitate encounters with members of other diasporic communities—encounters that sometimes inspire horror in childlike imaginations but that are likely to have another sort of effect on adult readers. In one such episode near the beginning of the novel, a young Gino runs away from home in search of fun only to be frightened by the astonishing face of "an old Irish crone" who "rested her head on a furry pillow and watched him move past her down the empty silent street" (18). Gino will eventually be berated for his insolence and told that he must obey his mother, yet in the meantime, this brief, early moment in the text establishes a queasy relationship between the Irish and Italian diasporic communities by illustrating how Othering ideas take hold, even and especially in the minds of children. In this way, as the wheels of accommodation turn, the normal workings of a diasporic community à la Clifford become an occasion for the text to reach across diasporas, documenting the intergenerational proliferation of prejudice, even as Puzo tackles another particularly thorny gender issue.

The fear that Gino feels is not unusual, especially given the uneasiness with which Italian Americans and Irish Americans related to each other during this period. This was a time when an Italian American might be lucky enough to be promoted to the job of supervisor in a factory only to find that "his mainly Irish coworkers . . . resented working for a 'guinea,'" and when similarly derogatory views of Irish Americans proliferated among members of the Italian diasporic community in their midst (Padurano 102). Anti-Irish sentiment was of course far from exclusive to Italian Americans, as is legible in the United States' history of anti-Irish employment discrimination, which remains quite famous despite recent debates about the phenomenon.[6] Meanwhile, Italian Americans and Irish Americans shared other diasporic experiences that created natural affinities and at least partial resemblances between their communities, intensifying the irony of their mutual antipathy. The Irish Potato Famine, enshrined in the American communal consciousness as a subject of popular as well as scholarly histories, spurred the migration of people from agricultural communities not unlike those of the southern Italians who would arrive in the US in the late nineteenth and early twentieth centuries.[7] Ireland's colonial relationship with England—a relationship of conquest and subordination that inspired fervent political and cultural opposition from those who wished to see Ireland attain fully independent statehood—has likewise inspired popular cultural artifacts from films to music.[8] Anti-Irish sentiment on US soil, like anti-Italian sentiment, also tended to be driven by the Catholicism of the two groups. This commonality emerged as the demographics of Italian-US immigration shifted so that more southern Catholics than northern Protestants began to arrive in the United States.

The Irish in America, then, have a diasporic history that features similar sources of social alienation from US "majority" culture, similar economic reasons for leaving home, and familiar experiences of political oppression and persecution—ones that also characterized the relationship between Northern Italy's ruling elites and its southern peasant class in the wake of unification. In fact, Puzo's narrator himself describes this intra-Italian dynamic in terms that would not be wholly inappropriate if applied to the Irish in their relationship to England: "For centuries [Italy's] government had been the most bitter enemy of their fathers and fathers' fathers before them. The rich had spat on the poor. Pimps of Rome and the north had sucked their blood" (235). Understanding the Irish in the US as a diasporic community hinges on these kinds of details, which suggest a foundation for allyship between Puzo as a writer and this ethnic enclave that is so sporadically mentioned in his novel, and which lend an ironic cast to the novel's depictions of Irish-Italian animosity.

When the older woman Gino encounters is specifically characterized as Irish, it becomes clear that her ethnicity is a factor in the fear that he feels. Nevertheless, Puzo paints a fuller and more intersectional picture as three elements of the woman's personhood—her age, her ethnicity, and her gender—become discernable in the boy's Othering vision of her identity: "In that weak yellow light her head was bony with age, her thin, whiskered mouth bloody with the light of a holy red candle. Behind that feral face, faintly visible in the shadows of her room, a vase, a lamp, and a graven image gleamed like old bones. Gino stared at her. The teeth bared in greeting. Gino ran" (18). Here, Puzo vividly illustrates how that combination of "veneration and revulsion" that is so typical of fetishism can infect the minds of children as well as adults (Dobie 148). The "feral face" and "bared" teeth that Gino perceives—for here Puzo makes liberal use of free indirect discourse—show how little humanness he finds in the Irishwoman. What we really see in this description, however, is Gino's fixation not just on the woman as "Irish" but on the grim signs and trappings of her age and femininity: her "bony" aged face as well as the vase and lamp, with their subtly, stereotypically domestic associations. Then there is the term *crone*, which labels the stranger as a woman in a highly specific way. This person is past the time when she can bear children of her own, though as Gino's response proves, she can certainly still frighten them. Foreign to the boy in these three ways—neither young nor Italian nor male—the woman cannot possibly inspire any other feelings than fear and even horror. Or so it seems.

The unfairness of the boy's judgments is not explicitly highlighted by Puzo's narrator. Still, as adult readers who are likely to have a more intimate knowledge of at least one of these identity categories than Gino does (since who among us is not aging?), we may feel rather keenly the injustice of a world that teaches young boys to see women who can no longer bear children as alien and as a threat. One of the most noxious pillars of the patriarchy is the persisting view that women of child-bearing age should be treated as delicate, pleasurable objects of the male gaze while "crones," no longer biologically useful or sexually desirable to men, transform into creatures to be mistrusted or even feared. Although it has been a long-standing Western tradition to associate strong women past their childbearing years with witchcraft and other fearsome things, specific rhetoric took hold in the 1960s, the historical moment when Puzo was writing, that uniquely intensified and shifted this negative view of the changes to women's biological identities in their later years of life.[9] As Lynn Hankinson Nelson notes, it was then that "concepts and metaphors related to 'production'" led menopause to be scientifically framed as a negative development for women, a signal of female bodies' corruption or degeneration rather than a natural and productive experience in itself: "Beginning in the 1960s, menopause was taken to signal the start of a stage of life in which a woman's reproductive organs 'failed to produce' sufficient estrogens, a failure that was assumed to be detrimental to her health," and the World Health Organization eventually "defined menopause as 'an estrogen-deficiency *disease*'" (158, my italics).[10] Without any personal knowledge of this medical terminology, Gino nevertheless embodies this negative vision of women's aging bodies as "diseased," and he also exemplifies the wariness that it engenders, particularly among boys and men. The fearful lens through which Gino views the woman, projecting stereotypes onto her physical body based on that body's perceived failures, brings these cultural attitudes into sharp relief. Even if the boy himself is unlikely to have more than a passing, almost subconscious familiarity with this discourse of aging womanhood, this arguably makes the scene more powerful, as if suggesting that such cultural ideas are so strongly rooted that they can overtake and color children's perceptions almost by osmosis.

For readers who might wonder if ethnic sameness could be sufficient to protect the novel's Italian American women from eventually being viewed this way themselves, it is important to note that Puzo suggests the opposite. The brand of ageism and sexism confronting the old Irishwoman, while colored by ethnicity, is not limited to non-Italian outsiders. Instead, in *The Fortunate Pilgrim*, some of the most potent ideas about Irish and Italian American women's experiences of diaspora come from the similar responses that their age and gender inspire among the community's future men. A parallel scene early in the narrative illustrates this just before Gino's initial flight from home, as the very thing he wishes to escape is the "circle of old women's faces, some hairy and mustached," that includes his mother and her friend Zia Louche that night (16). Zia Louche herself is described as an "old crone" with a "withered claw" that holds him "like a fly" (16). With these words, the Italian American woman is consigned to the same group as the old Irishwoman—sexless, animalistic, and genderless, or perhaps even frighteningly masculinized. Here, Gino seems to embody a generally more American way of thinking about age and gender: something quite different from "the position of great respect" that young Italian Americans have reported assigning to their grandmothers and more akin to the American expectation that "it is the young who rule" (qtd. in Orsi 131, 107). By exploring a youthful, seemingly instinctual manifestation of this toxic ideology, Puzo expresses solidarity with women like his own mother just as he does in the introduction to the novel, when he remembers not having properly appreciated his mother for her strength. After all, while Lucia Santa has recently had a baby, even she will someday be old enough to be looked on as a "crone" by a new crop of young neighborhood boys. More to the point, however, this parallelism poses an important interdiasporic question: if these women are so alike in the imaginations of the boys and men who look on them, and if they must variously confront and tolerate the same prejudiced ideas flung in their direction, can their differences be so very great after all? Without erasing cultural difference to the point of bland and generic multiculturalism, *The Fortunate Pilgrim*'s quick references to Irish and Italian American crones make a gesture of solidarity that both records instances of prejudice and suggests that perhaps such prejudice ought not to exist in the first place.

This appealing idea emerges despite the words of the adults in the narrative, including adult women, who show that they are willing to degrade other women across the boundaries of diaspora. Lucia Santa makes crude jokes repeatedly at the expense of women she identifies as Irish: "All the girls are off the street except those little Irish tramps on Ninth Avenue," she says at one point with "mock fervor," continuing on to express her relief that her son Lorenzo "only ruins good, decent Italian girls" (26). The phrase "Irish tramp" will repeat later on, along with memorable moments like the one when Lucia Santa, through the voice of Puzo's narrator, muses that her son "could have married a whore, or a slattern, or even one of the Irish" (227, 143). There is an obvious note of humor in this use of "even," and perhaps a sense of friendly or playful interethnic rivalry, but neither cancels out the more serious historical current of prejudice that these comments evoke, especially when they recur throughout. Lucia Santa's comments make it clear that Gino's response to the "Irish crone" is not just an instinctual reaction to a seemingly frightening image—it is also a learned response to adult examples. A genealogy of prejudice emerges from these textual wrinkles, as do suggestions for how to root it out. Such efforts, the novel implies, would have to begin with adults, and particularly with adult women working across diasporas, who would need to resist the impulse to turn on each other or to replicate the species of misogyny and sexual objectification Lucia Santa describes her own son exemplifying. The fact that Lucia Santa is otherwise the unambiguous heroine of the novel drives the point home further: strong, admirable women fall into these ethnic traps, too.

The Fortunate Pilgrim also furthers this line of thinking by showcasing additional historically rich parallels between the Irish and Italian diasporic experiences in the US, which emerge in moments when the alienation of the novel's Italians is laid bare. Italian-descended children may fear Irish-descended ones and may view them as the Other, but those children and their parents are similarly derided by other Americans, creating a layer of hypocrisy not unlike what we saw in *Ask the Dust*, with diasporic communities turning on each other within the world of the text despite the shared experiences that should bring them together. Ethnic slurs are casually reproduced in the novel in ways that intimate their ubiquity, especially when they are pitilessly flung at characters as young as Gino, who is called a "little black guinea bastard" (53).[11] Puzo also plumbs Italian emigration-as-diaspora in exploring a diversity of reasons for the displacement of his characters from home, all of them violent in some sense, and all of them paralleling the Irish diasporic experience. Lucia Santa is threatened with economic violence that may inhibit her from living a full life in tangible ways: too poor to marry, she will never have children or a family of her own, her father tells her—and so home for her represents the death of a crucial ambition and arguably a human right, making her lose "all respect for her father, for her home, for her country" (8). Lucia Santa's backstory thus creates a thematic link between the economic history of Ireland and that of Italy as they relate to experiences of diaspora. Meanwhile, the introduction of the Coluccis, "whose family had emigrated to America for religious reasons instead of poverty," creates an opportunity for the narrative to examine additional issues of religious discrimination in Italy itself as well as in the US—issues that have their own inverted echoes in British-Irish history given the tensions between Irish Catholics and the Church of England (92).[12] Dennis Barone reminds us that at the end of the nineteenth century, Italian Protestants still "struggled against the vigorous and at times violent residual strength of the Catholic Church and its pervasive influence on the populace at large" (39). Brief references to such issues help Puzo's novel to show that its Italians have earned the title of "diasporic community" in much the same way as the narrative's Irish Americans, not just through the discrimination against southern Italian Catholics that occurred on American shores but also, paradoxically, through distinct patterns of persecution that Italian Protestants had endured at home.

Acts of disloyalty across diasporas in *The Fortunate Pilgrim* have added resonance in moments when the narrative's Italians "eat their own," forcing each other to feel hopelessly alienated within the community itself. In one episode early in the novel, Lucia Santa discovers that her neighbors and friends have conspired to pressure her to give up her youngest son for adoption after her husband's death. The novel uses blunt language to describe its heroine's feelings of estrangement from her community in the wake of this betrayal: "She screamed in Italian, 'Fiends. Whores. Murderers of children.' She ran up and down the stairs, and out of her mouth came a filth she had never known she knew, that the invisible listeners would eat the tripe of their parents, that they committed the foulest acts of animals" (40). Taken within this larger context, Lucia Santa's lack of co-conspiratorial or even sympathetic feeling toward the Irish American women adjacent to her community takes on additional layers of meaning. It becomes symptomatic of a larger lack of community feeling and support both within and across Lucia Santa's diasporic enclave, where the neighbor women will help a young widow to find a new husband only because they are afraid that otherwise, she will seduce their own spouses. In this way, if Fante locates the origin of interethnic failures of solidarity in the Anglo-American discrimination against Italians and Italian Americans, Puzo suggests a different genealogy of these failures that originates within the community itself.

What Puzo interestingly does not do is bring his Irish American characters into the light by drawing them, like Octavia's Jewish poet-husband, into the family's inner circle. Although there are relatively few pages devoted to Octavia's spouse, an intellectual who horrifies Lucia Santa by carrying around a stack of books in a way that supposedly does not befit a grown man, it is clear that the character of Norman Bergeron defies ethnic stereotypes in a gesture of allyship across diasporas. In Lucia Santa's complaint that Octavia has "picked for a husband the only Jew who does not know how to make money," and in Puzo's narrator's wry description of the man as knowing "only one thing thoroughly: Yiddish literature—a talent he himself said was less in demand than any other on earth," we can hear the narrative voice gently poking fun at and (if modestly) rewriting caricatures of Jewish identity (203–204). In counterpoint to these stale ideas, Octavia's husband is simply allowed to be himself, or at worst, is made to fit a fresher and more finely tuned stereotype: that of the politically and socially liberal New Yorker, the unabashed Jewish American intellectual—a very particular brand of diasporic figure.[13] Still, even as its characters of Irish descent remain incompletely formed figures at the margins of the narrative, their placement there serves its own function, pointing out to readers how these barely known caricatures can become the targets of ethnic animus. In other words, by *not* bringing the Irish diaspora into the center of the narrative, Puzo deepens his genealogy of prejudice, locating other roots of that animus in the reality of diasporic families living side by side on the same city blocks but simply not knowing each other.

The arc of Puzo's novel ultimately allows it to eke out a subtle argument about interdiasporic relationships, even as it makes a much more direct and constant argument about issues of gender more broadly. Italian America has long indulged intergenerational currents of prejudice against diasporic communities like the Irish one, yet these communities have shared experiences, including experiences of gender discrimination and ageism, that destabilize assumptions of Otherness projected onto Irish Americans by their Italian counterparts. This is in many ways an old story, but *The Fortunate Pilgrim* retells it in vivid and urgent language in these short scenes. While also making a wider-ranging exploration of diverse issues of gender, Puzo interweaves these delicate thematic strands into a novel that is thus more occupied with questions of solidarity across diasporas than it may initially seem to be.

Writing Romani Lives: The Other Side of "Off-White"

There are a few important details that separate De Rosa's *Paper Fish* from *The Fortunate Pilgrim*. Set half a country away from New York City and two decades after the start of the Great Depression, De Rosa's stylistically distinctive novel examines Italian American womanhood from the perspective of a woman writer, and the book's persisting marginalization in larger literary and academic circles speaks to the double disadvantage of being Italian American and a woman in the US literary landscape.[14] Still, critics like Bona have eloquently located shared elements across the two texts, such as the way that "family cohesion . . . takes precedence over the legal system" in both narratives (*By the Breath* 28). Although *Paper Fish* can certainly be read as focusing on an "enclosed enclave of immigrant Italians," intriguing additional parallels emerge when we bring De Rosa's quite peripheral Romani characters into the center of the reading process like Puzo's Irish ones (29–30). In fact, De Rosa's sometimes disorienting modernist prose features a vision of Romani identity that eerily echoes Puzo's depictions of the Irishwomen at the outskirts of *The Fortunate Pilgrim* and its fictional world.

In this painful coming-of-age story centered on the young Carmolina, Romani women—especially older ones—become a target of fascination for multiple generations of Italian and Italian American girl children, who are simultaneously terrified of and entranced by them. Several conclusions can be and have been drawn from this element of the novel; for instance, Bona sees the intergenerational proliferation of storytelling about the "gypsies" in the narrative as a testament to the "significance of telling tales" as a pastime across the narrative's generations of Italian-descended girls and women ("Broken Images" 97). For my own part, more than considering what the Romani characters in *Paper Fish* demonstrate about the novel's Italian characters in isolation, I am interested in interrogating what they say about the particular interdiasporic relationship between the Romani and Italian American communities in the novel's sociocultural milieu, and about the possibility of literary allyship across those diasporic boundaries. As the girls vacillate between fear and admiration, De Rosa's novel interrogates the social position of the Romani community in mid-century Chicago, especially their Othering at the hands of diasporic communities outside their own, which the novel deservedly censures for their anti-Romani attitudes and fetishization of Romani culture. De Rosa lets us see Romani women through the eyes of girls rather than those of boys, but the women's gendered position remains palpable, as does its intersectional influence on issues of ethnic identity and ageism confronting the community.

Like the Irish and the Italians in America, Roma have at times been viewed by non-Roma as ambiguously racialized, though their perceived difference has led to much graver consequences in many contexts. Romani feminist scholar Ethel C. Brooks catalogs the long history in which "Romani people throughout the world have been subject to enslavement, forced displacement and exile, violence, and death . . . treated as subhuman and persecuted and exploited accordingly," including in the twentieth century, when Roma "experienced near-annihilation in the Holocaust," and the current period, when Romani people continue to "face neofascist and centrist state violence, including murders, pogroms, forced expulsions, forced sterilization, and manifold other violences throughout Europe and beyond" (3). In the United States, as early as 1885, Roma began to be excluded under US immigration policy in a signal of their perceived separation from white Europeans.[15] Ronald Lee, a Romani writer and activist, has referred to Roma in Canada as an "off-white minority group," reflecting the liminal status of Roma in North America as they have been perceived by both government actors and other non-Romani people (qtd. in Sutherland 3). These vague racial impressions have been accompanied by the usual assumptions about Romani identities as less "civilized" than white Western identities, which have been used in attempts to justify this long history of persecution and discrimination. Contemporary knowledge of Romani people in their own diversity and "difference across [the] diaspora" tells a more precise story of Romani migration; for instance, "Romologists mainly concur that people speaking proto-Romani . . . left northwest India around 1000 A.D.," even if "in the United States, this knowledge remains esoteric" (Lemon 84–86). Such information situates Roma in the United States more definitively in relation to white Western Europe. Yet in the twentieth century in the minds of Anglo-American whites, the Romani diasporic community tended to be viewed more nebulously: through a cloud of mystery, as an indefinable and suspicious Other.

This perception of the Romani diasporic community as ineffably foreign was shared by many Italian Americans; as Kenneth Scambray phrases it in his reading of *Paper Fish*, Roma were understood as "mythological figures" in "the folklore of their Italian neighbors" (61). It is to this familiar version of Romani identity and experience that De Rosa seems to be responding in *Paper Fish*. At the same time, De Rosa's narrative establishes a degree of kinship between Roma and Italians in this historical moment, when the Italian diasporic community in the US also continued to be viewed with suspicion by other white Americans due to factors ranging from "the negative feelings generated toward Italian immigrants by Italy's status as an enemy in World War II" to the persistent appeal of shadowy mafia stereotypes (Candeloro 77).[16] De Rosa was vocal about wanting to resist the way the Italian American neighborhood where she had grown up in Chicago was "denigrated" by outsiders who "were afraid to come" there (qtd. in Giunta 227). As we know, some Italians on US soil, particularly "the ranks of the urban working class" in the 1950s, responded to this continuing current of suspicion by taking extra pains to assert both their whiteness and their Americanness in postwar America, with their *italianità* becoming useful more "as a synonym for not being 'Black,' 'Puerto Rican,' 'Jewish,' or 'Irish'" (Cinotto 15). De Rosa takes a different approach, however. In rejecting "the notion of a monolithic 'white ethnicity' and bring[ing] to the forefront the marginalization suffered by a particular group of white ethnics," Italian Americans themselves, *Paper Fish* achieves a special degree of complexity by also excavating the experiences of a diasporic enclave that was only adjacent to De Rosa's own lived experience and community memberships, and one that Italian Americans often targeted for its perceived difference (Giunta 227).

Roma reappear throughout De Rosa's novel, not just in scenes where they are physically present but also in moments when they become a topic of conversation, a target of gossip or blame, or the subject of a cautionary tale told repeatedly to Italian and Italian American youngsters, whose parents warn them that they may be stolen by "gypsies" at any time. When Carmolina disappears, there are adults in the community who "know the gypsies have taken" her (33). When the pipe that brings the holy water into the neighborhood's Catholic church malfunctions, Romani characters are blamed again: "The gypsies have stolen the holy water, the women say, and bless themselves with parched hands. But the water is pumping out of the fire hydrant onto the children who play in it" (119).[17] Carmolina herself is warned directly: "They like to steal little ones, especially if they pretty, like you," the grocer tells her (57). In all of these permutations, De Rosa's Roma seem to exist in a narrow space between the reality of who they are—a diasporic people not so unlike the novel's Italians, except in the degree to which they have been persecuted—and the ghoulish, mystical caricature projected onto them by the children and adults who have witnessed them in their neighborhoods.

Carmolina's family relationship with these ideas about Romani people begins, chronologically speaking, with her grandmother Doria, who first encounters them not in the United States but in Italy during her own childhood. This narrative detail is historically grounded in the facts of Romani migration into Italy, which was already occurring as early as the fifteenth century and has continued into the 2000s, when more than a hundred thousand Roma with "legal status . . . as foreigners" were documented to "live apart and resist assimilation" on Italian soil (Renouard 123; Rossi 96). In sociological circles, this dynamic seems to inspire descriptions that emphasize the diasporic character of the community, sometimes sympathetically and sometimes pejoratively. De Rosa's rendering of Romani figures on Italian shores similarly emphasizes the stigmatization of Romani identity by outsiders to the community and illuminates the ways that this prejudice has fueled the community's experiences of social alienation:

> Doria had seen them, the black eyes and black souls of them. The breasts of the women were large, like the udders of cows; they swung under bright red dresses. Their bodies were dressed in golden jewelry; they wore silver combs in their hair. They were beautiful; they were terrifying. They frightened goats in the night so that their milk turned sour; they terrified the chickens so that they went barren. . . . The gypsies ride black horses, Doria said, and Sabatina [her sister] heard the singing of the gypsies, heard the cry of the dulcimers and the strangled chatter of bells. . . . (20)

This passage is remarkably clear in describing the Italians' fetishistic vision of Romani identity, with its classically contradictory mix of admiration and terror.[18] Viewed from this exoticizing vantage-point, the brightly colored clothing, shiny jewelry, and beautiful singing of "the gypsies" make them the focus of young Doria's awe. Even so, the community lore about the dangers supposedly posed by these outsiders colors Doria's perception so that in the relative innocence of her childhood, she already dehumanizes these seemingly strange women ("like the udders of cows") and imagines them as vaguely murderous ("the strangled chatter of bells").

Written in a modernist, almost feverish style, this snapshot of Doria's encounters with Romani women reflects far more on her own community's collective consciousness than it does on the identities of the women themselves. It also reveals the tricky intersection of gender and ethnicity as Doria fixates on the women's dresses, hair, and breasts. This is a young girl who has been specifically taught to fear others who, despite their foreignness, are shaped much like larger versions of herself—as though their womanhood makes them more fearsome even though it is a quality that she will someday share with them. Doria's view of these Roma is specifically colored by her mother's words; her sister Sabatina, who does not like to work, is deemed "the child of royalty . . . kidnapped by gypsies who wore golden earrings and stole children" (20). And it is Doria who passes on this family lore to Carmolina during her early childhood, leaving her susceptible to similarly feverish visions of Romani people infiltrating the Italian American neighborhood where she lives on Chicago's West Side. So it is that Doria and Puzo's Gino come to occupy two sides of the same coin, examining Romani and Irish American women in the world around them and finding in them something strange enough to inspire horror, not because of what is there but because of what they have been taught to see.[19]

Carmolina takes things a step further, though, first attempting to dress up as a Romani woman and eventually imitating their migrations on her own smaller scale when she runs away from home, fearing that her parents are about to send her away as they have threatened with her sister Doriana. This is not to say that the Romani figures around her are not also a potential source of misplaced fear for Doria's granddaughter, who sees a Romani woman in her neighborhood and is captivated and terrified by the woman's "old hands shrunken together in her lap like dead flowers" as well as her "black old mouth" (66). But in Carmolina's responses, it becomes easier to see what De Rosa herself has commented on: that she is "fascinated" by her "exotic" neighbors—that she even "has a gypsy soul" and cannot help but want to be like them (Meyer 197). Carmolina embodies this equally problematic desire when she takes a pair of her mother's hoop earrings and clips them onto her own ears, proclaiming that she is "playing gypsy" and raising questions of cultural appropriation as it relates to fetishism (60). What does it mean for a community to discriminate against a diasporic people, as the Italian American adults of the novel discriminate against Chicago's Roma ("they were like cats," Augie the grocer muses), only to have their children fetishize and cannibalize the culture they have rejected (56)? As a Romani communications intern at the National Organization for Women wrote in a recent blog post for NOW, referring to herself semi-anonymously as Naomi P., "[w]hen folks unknowingly or knowingly profit off of the word 'gypsy,' claim they have a 'gypsy soul,' or use 'gypsy aesthetic' for a day at Coachella, they are reinforcing racist stereotypes of Romani women and dehumanizing" them ("The 'G' Word"). *Paper Fish* raises and reraises this objection as De Rosa's characters continue to alternately insult and emulate the Romani people who live alongside them, until it is clear that imitation here is not simply a form of flattery, however innocent it may be on Carmolina's part. Even in proclaiming that "gypsies . . . are a brave strong people," Carmolina emphasizes the purported difference of her neighbors and rewrites their identities based on an essentializing vision imposed on them from outside (79).

This essentializing discourse doesn't necessarily reflect poorly on Carmolina as a child who is simply emulating her surroundings, and De Rosa's own comments about the young girl describe her fascination with the Romani community from a perspective that is distanced or even sympathetic more than it is critical, recalling how "the beauty of them" and their "mystery" make Romani women appealing to child and grandmother alike (Meyer 79). Nevertheless, perhaps more than De Rosa intended, the novel also becomes an invitation to critique the insidious ways that prejudice is passed down, sometimes through seemingly flattering caricatures rather than through outright expressions of intolerance. Like *Ask the Dust, Paper Fish* calls out for us to read it as having a textual life of its own, with meanings that complicate and enhance its sociopolitical importance as an ally text. Such sociopolitically rigorous readings remain possible and important even if we admire the novel for what interviewer Lisa Meyer, echoing De Rosa in a review of the text, refers to as its own ineffable "beauty" and "mystery" ("She's Making Sense").

As the narrative progresses, these gestures of literary solidarity come to rely meaningfully on now-familiar questions of age and ageism that emerge from Carmolina's observations of Romani women. The woman Carmolina sees first in the passage above is specifically marked as older in ways that recall similar moments in *The Fortunate Pilgrim*: "Carmolina could see the pink patches of her skull gleaming like the insides of a shell. Her eyes and mouth were enormous. The mouth was as black as the eyes, like a hole in her face. Carmolina saw that she was laughing, but no sound came out" (66). The facts of this description are simple: the woman has become partly bald and has lost her teeth. Like her "shrunken" hands, these are simple realities of aging, yet they are described in a half-fanciful, half-horrifying style, with images that threaten to haunt readers long after the scene has passed. Not only is this woman foreign, but she has lost the things that were supposed to make her beautiful—that would have defined her in the eyes of a society in which conventional femininity is as much about hair, teeth, and skin as it is about the ability to give birth to and raise children. As all of these unfamiliar elements captivate Carmolina's attention, what results is an act of witnessing on De Rosa's part in which her narrative, like Puzo's, points to the intersection of age, gender, and ethnic and diasporic identity in determining what is perceived as difference from inside an Italian American community looking outward. This self-reflexive bent of the narrative in examining the anatomy of fetishism and prejudice within the community makes it another example of literary allyship à la Puzo and even Fante, though nearly fifty years separate *Paper Fish* from *Ask the Dust*. The same concerns continue to recur, almost obsessively, as De Rosa records the tendency to stereotype aging Romani women as "old witches" (Brooks 3). While there are other extremely pressing and intersectional gender issues facing Romani people that De Rosa's narrative does not even begin to address, such as the European history of forced sterilization of Romani women, this confrontation with stereotypes and recognition of Italian American complicity in upholding them is essential.

Beyond these distinct histories of persecution, the truth is that the Romani women in *Paper Fish* are not so dissimilar from the novel's Italians, who seem to resemble them in sometimes unexpected ways. This is something that readers can see, even if the young Doria and Carmolina sometimes miss these similarities in their rush either to fear or to emulate the foreigners in their midst. Carmolina may wish to look like the Romani women around her when she puts on her mother's hoop earrings, but what she fails to recognize is that this approach to "playing gypsy" also makes her look like her mother.[20] The hoop earrings that Carmolina wears, in connecting her both to her mother and to the Romani women she idolizes, come to symbolize what is shared between the two communities of women rather than what separates them. Like Carmolina gazing at her mother through one of the earrings after she has unclipped it from her ear, we can perceive Carmolina's entire family differently through the lens of this small, unspoken connection. More globally, the vivid and impressionistic images that populate the narrative create compelling implied connections between Italian and Romani women, particularly the elderly ones. These images include descriptions of Grandma Doria herself as "the only member of the family who has little whiskers on her chin, like a goat," as though the hormonal vicissitudes of menopause have somehow made her, too, appear less human and more animal (23). In a particularly gruesome scene, Carmolina witnesses the Italian butcher's wife beheading a chicken, mesmerized by the woman's toothless mouth: "Her face turned towards Carmolina; her mouth was a black slit, smiling. There were no teeth in the slit, only slick thin gums" (58). The recurrence of this imagery of blackness not only recalls Pardini's concept of Italian Americans' "invisible blackness" as it has been periodically rendered visible by African American literary artists; it also creates a kinship between Mrs. Schiavone and the elderly woman from the diaspora next door. With these poetic correspondences, *Paper Fish* dethrones the Othering of Romani people from its default position of acceptance in Italian America and beyond, making it difficult for readers standing outside the text to continue to buy into these stereotypes. Instead, we witness two diasporic communities needlessly at odds because of the same animus that the novel's Italians have experienced from mainstream America, with women—and especially older women—as its most vulnerable targets.

The implied kinship between Roma and Italian Americans deepens in moments colored by the realities of anti-Italian prejudice, so that in a similar manner to *Ask the Dust* and *The Fortunate Pilgrim*, the novel also achieves allyship with other diasporas indirectly, by first recognizing the suffering of Italian America. Carmolina's wanderings through Chicago after she leaves her home expose her to the same kind of responses that her own neighbors express on encountering Romani people. Repeatedly called a "dago kid" by adults, including one who expels her from a restaurant, she is also robbed and beaten by other children (27, 77). It would be difficult not to hear the echoes of Fante here, as *Paper Fish*, like Fante's earlier novel, paints red-blooded American adults and their children as equally complicit in perpetuating anti-Italian sentiment. These prejudices and abuses demand a revised understanding of the Romani community as Italian American readers compare the Roma's treatment by Italian-descended people to the latter's treatment by Anglo-Americans. Perhaps, De Rosa implies, Romani people are not so foreign after all. Indeed, their historically "off-white" status and its discontents are largely what binds De Rosa's Italian and Romani characters to each other, despite so many Italian Americans' anxiety to deny this affinity, and despite the very real differences in their histories—which De Rosa evokes, for instance, by meticulously depicting how cultural outsiders have used discourses of theft to render Romani people suspect in the eyes of their neighbors. Following in the wake of Puzo and Fante, De Rosa collapses the distance between diasporas and sympathetically records Anglo-American rejections of *italianità* while looking on Italian America with a deservedly critical eye.

In a way, Carmolina's flight itself—the tangible reality of her child's body wandering the streets—puts this Italian-Romani sympathy most sharply into relief. Carmolina is emulating the movements of the Romani diaspora when she leaves her home, but she is also treading a path that symbolically invokes her people's diasporic movement, a painful history that is retreaded in intermittent but profound detail throughout the narrative. More than any other Italian American novel discussed in this section of the book, *Paper Fish* dwells on the physicality of "the long voyage to America," for which Carmolina's journey becomes a microcosm (*By the Breath* 92). Doria's memories form one example as she recalls how in "the sea crossing, there was confusion. The sea coughed and spit and screamed at the boat that carried her, it spit up cruel black waves. The sea rankled; it could stop nothing. A young man was tossed over the side and churned down to dust on the floor of the sea" (16). De Rosa's narrator rounds out this pained story of dislocation from home by pairing this depiction of a vengeful, thwarted sea with descriptions of the human fear it could produce. Carmolina's Italian neighbors, she learns, "crossed the ocean together and tossed in the ship's belly with the kerosene lamp above them. Terrified of fire, of one flame turning the ship of immigrants into a holocaust on the sea, they held each other's shoulders and with their eyes closed prayed one hundred and nine novenas" (74). As Carmolina wanders, so has her own diasporic community, and so have her not-so-unfamiliar Romani neighbors with their brightly colored clothing and glistening jewelry, though their journeys are not described in such detail.[21] Yet the Italian women's clannishness has long separated them from those who could have been their friends, overdeveloping the boundaries between diasporas. By admitting both of these realities, De Rosa allies herself multidimensionally with Romani people in the United States and beyond.

The history of De Rosa's family is a history of reaching across cultures. Like Carmolina herself, De Rosa was the child of a Lithuanian mother and an Italian father. *Paper Fish* capitalizes on this personal knowledge in shaping the figure of Sarah, Carmolina's mother, who vivifies the experience of becoming submerged in a new family with a distinctly different heritage. The struggles of this experience are something that the text confronts in stark terms: Sarah "could never quite catch up" to her new family's foreign tongue, and she struggles to eat enough pastina to satisfy her mother-in-law during her pregnancy, just as she struggles to accept the neighborhood's received wisdom about the treatment of childhood fevers, which seems to leave her baby Doriana with a developmental disability after they place her in cold water instead of calling a doctor who can treat her illness (50).[22] Yet there is much more here in terms of cross-cultural commentary, written between the lines of the novel's "gypsy" episodes.[23] *Paper Fish* does not pretend that the Romani and Italian diasporas are identical, and neither should we, for to do so would be to erase the extraordinary extent of the modern and contemporary violence against Romani people, among other differences. Nevertheless, bolstered especially by its explorations of gender and age, De Rosa's narrative of interdiasporic encounter and its failures does testify to and deconstruct the exaggerative discourses of difference that have fueled the displacement and ongoing persecution of the Romani diasporic community.

De Rosa's (Other) Gender Dilemmas

Because the women of *Paper Fish* are both the greatest targets and the greatest purveyors of anti-Romani prejudice, it seems natural that this species of intolerance would be central to the narrative's larger exploration of gender in 1940s and 1950s America—Italian and otherwise. Diaspora and its conflicts function to illuminate problems of gender that, more broadly conceived, range from masculine vulnerability to collisions of girlhood and disability in a world that is often kind to neither. At the same time, the opposite also remains true: tracing these larger gendered phenomena as they appear in De Rosa's novel often works to illuminate additional, granular details of the complex interrelationships between two distinct diasporic worlds.

De Rosa's writing is uniquely evocative in capturing the drab drudgery of everyday "women's work" in diasporic contexts. Carmolina's mother does the same repetitive tasks every day as a girl working in her family's restaurant, taking orders and scrubbing dishes in her white uniform. De Rosa writes Marco into her narrative of Sarah's history in a way that suggests that he might disrupt the ever-consistent rhythm of her working life:

Always she gently pulled the white stuff of the waitress apron over her full breasts and cast shyly her black eyes down while they ordered steak and eggs. Like a mouse she ran into the kitchen with their orders written down. . . . At night she walked the three blocks home past small quiet houses behind the hollyhocks, the lights already out in the living rooms and the bedroom lights hissing soft and blue. Then she would stop and remove her shoes. . . . When the young policeman walked into the restaurant one morning and ordered breakfast she had been aware of little other than her tooth, which hurt, and of his skin, which was darker than hers." (48–49)

Artful as any other moment in the novel, this passage brings to life the repetitive habits of Sarah's young existence, punctuated by Marco's sudden appearance in a place where nothing otherwise has tended to change from day to day. Sarah herself remembers something similar, how they "all worked so hard" at the restaurant and how after work she "would fall asleep thinking . . . it would have to change someday" (95). As she recalls, it is when she sees her future husband's eyes and his smile for the first time that she does see "[her] life changing" (95). For Sarah, however, marriage ultimately means the same work in a different permutation. Instead of washing dishes in the back of her parents' restaurant, she plucks chicken whiskers from their skin with tweezers for the family's dinner. As De Rosa's narrator reports, this "was something she did every day of her life, something she would do every day for longer into the future than she dare imagine" (9). Sarah trades the kitchen of her old family's restaurant for the kitchen of her new family's flat, always knowing that directly across the street, her mother-in-law is doing the same thing in her own cramped apartment, where far too many bodies—and mouths to feed—are housed under one roof.

It is worth noting that De Rosa partly diverges from Puzo in her manner of presenting these realities of immigrant kitchens and bedrooms. At times, the narrative voice almost seems to resemble Puzo's Octavia, with her arguments about "enslaved" women, making it more difficult to read *Paper Fish* as moving beyond reductively second-wave arguments about feminine servitude in the domestic sphere—the same arguments of "well-meaning social workers who wanted to 'save'" Italian American women "from what they viewed as an undemocratic patriarchal system without recognizing that in that very system [they] had found validation"

(Barolini 17). Is Sarah oppressed by domestic labor in a way that Puzo never encourages us to see Lucia Santa as being? Her life certainly offers her little choice and little power to determine the direction of the events around her; she cannot even have a cigarette once her husband returns home from work.[24] Still, domestic work in the narrative's world is often depicted as beautiful and certainly as essential, as when Doria cooks for her granddaughter; as Edvige Giunta comments, she finds "the sacred in the mundane" (220). And De Rosa's genealogy of interdiasporic prejudice is helpfully fleshed out in the novel's more damning descriptions of domestic labor, which suggest another point of origin for the animosity between Italian and Romani women, one that recalls the tense relationships between Lucia Santa and her neighbors. Romani people are obsessively accused of domestic crimes, crimes that involve interruptions to family food supplies or that otherwise disrupt the life of the "good" Italian home, whether in rural Italy or Chicago. It is not just the holy water or Carmolina herself that they are accused of stealing; instead, they are assigned the blame for sour milk and "barren" chickens as well. Rather than demonizing her Romani characters as these comments themselves do, De Rosa's emphasis on these snippets of gossip reveals the scarcity consciousness of Italian women eking out a fragile domestic life against twin backdrops of rural and urban poverty, just as it illustrates the ways in which their Romani neighbors are resultantly scapegoated. De Rosa, then, joins Puzo in exploring larger issues of gender and class through diasporic identities and conflicts.

De Rosa also doesn't shy away from examining how men's experiences add to this tapestry of gendered identities. In one scene, after young Carmolina's unexplained disappearance from the house, her father Marco finds himself sitting at his desk at work, bewildered by his own tears: "He ran his hands across his eyes, the hands to him seemed helpless, lifeless, without power. They got wet when they touched his face. He looked at them, confused. . . . His hands were wet; he was confused" (83). Marco is not just resistant to the experience of crying—instead, it is as though he cannot fully understand it. For him, the physical reality of his tears does not compute, perhaps because it does not square with the gendered expectations for his responses to grief. In another moment, De Rosa's narrator follows Sarah through her memories of her wedding night, revealing how tentatively her new husband approaches her body. Again, tears figure prominently in this scene; Marco "wanted to weep" on seeing his wife's body, and in fact, he does (8). At every turn, Marco's sensitivity and his tenderness push the boundaries of what Western masculinity—Italian or otherwise—is supposed to look like, resisting the received wisdom surrounding aggression and emotionality that threatened to dominate men's lives in the mid-century United States and that still permeates so much of American culture today.

Written in this way, Marco's character is less unflatteringly shaded than the men who populate *The Fortunate Pilgrim*, but he still displays a kind of brotherhood with beleaguered husbands like Frank Corbo. And when Marco snaps in a more typically toxic way after Carmolina's return, trading tears for aggression, the picture darkens:

> Daddy sat her down on the bed. He slammed her down hard.
> This, he said, is your bed.
> He twisted her around by the neck to look at the room.
> This, he said, is your bedroom.
> This, he said, is where you live, and you are never going to leave us again.
> She looked at him. When I grow up, she said, I'm going to go away forever.
> Over my dead body, Daddy said. (107)

Carmolina bears the brunt of her father's inability to communicate what he really feels: that his life has almost come to pieces while she has been gone—that he cannot survive another separation from her. Carmolina remains deeply attached to her father, so that when he dies, her mother has to hold her "as though she were a child" (48). Still, the social cause and effects are clear: when gender roles are overly rigid, men, women, and children suffer. Neither Puzo nor De Rosa lets readers avoid this. Meanwhile, it is Carmolina's interdiasporic collision with the Romani community that forces this potentially uncomfortable realization on readers. By giving Carmolina inspiration to wander, the Romani women around her create conditions in which the smooth machinery of conventional masculinity breaks down, revealing the fissures in its facade of social control. In this way, diaspora and gender continue to intermingle and inform each other.

Paper Fish has other complexities that reflect uniquely on the gendered universe of its characters. Bona's early study of the novel has opened up the critical conversation about *Paper Fish* to questions of disability and illness, identifying another identity factor that intersects with gender in shaping the lives of the novel's women and girls. The character of Doriana, Carmolina's older sister, makes this turn in the conversation urgently necessary. As Bona rightly notes, "the journey motif" becomes a way for the girls' family, particularly Grandma Doria, to conceptualize Doriana's experience of disability: she is "lost in the forest" and has not been able to find her way home ("Broken Images" 96, 111). The parallel with diaspora as a concept is striking, giving the girl a new, metaphorical layer of kinship with her own diasporic community as well as with her Romani neighbors—yet the novel, with its understated way of expressing this idea, stops short of melodramatically instrumentalizing or objectifying Romani people as poetic objects of comparison. It also refuses to Other or fetishize Doriana herself as a child with a disability. De Rosa's narrator records the wanderings of Doriana's attention, mental travels that give her agency and challenge others' attempts to control and define her:

> Doriana was, as a child, particularly impossible to hold in any one place. She seemed always to be moving towards another place, different from this. She was impatient of the glass bottles which held milk for her, of the toys colored especially to make her smile. She was impatient of it all, the little yellow duck was wrong. Sarah remarked it often, it startled her when she approached the crib, to find the child so taken elsewhere. (7)

The challenge continues as Doriana proceeds into womanhood in one of the novel's final scenes, still clutching a doll to her lap, with "the perfect skin of a baby" and eyes "locked into themselves" (113). The adult Doriana continues to traverse her own mental world, violating gendered and ableist expectations for women both inside and outside of Italian America, even as she enacts a quintessential caretaking ritual that serves to socialize young girls across the United States. Like the old Romani woman with her bald head and toothless mouth, Doriana discomfits observers who, in their bigotry, find her as unsettlingly childlike as the old woman is unsettlingly aged, disturbed that she must still be taken care of instead of taking care of others. Neither of them conforms to the version of womanhood that would put their families' and their neighbors' minds at ease. As De Rosa explores the contours of Doriana's mind, *Paper Fish* knits a quiet, implicit story of disability as diaspora, where being "lost" or displaced means encountering new constellations of prejudice.

Allyship Two Ways

In the end, gender issues occupy these two novels as palpably as they are molded by painful separations from home. The gendered peculiarities of Italian American households from the Depression through the postwar era come vividly to life in parallel with broader problems of gender that are deeply embedded in the American social fabric, and which both shape and are shaped by stories of diaspora. What is subtler here is the twinned acts of witnessing through which Puzo and De Rosa vivify currents of prejudice against other diasporic communities than their own, scrutinizing their intersection with gendered expectations, disappointments, and intermittent, muted triumphs. *The Fortunate Pilgrim* is not primarily a novel about Irish America any more than *Paper Fish* is primarily a novel about the Romani community in Chicago. Yet the two narratives are painfully aware of the playful rivalries, fetishistic admiration, and straightforward expressions of intolerance that marked Italian America's response to these other communities. Children's fictional interactions with older women, their fear and fascination, become a flashpoint for these complexities and a quiet way of expressing solidarity across diasporas by acknowledging, yet again, where it has failed or faltered. Two-dimensional images of the Irish and Romani diasporas are unlikely to survive a reading of these novels, which destabilize stereotypes even as they draw attention to them.

Conclusion

The Limits of Allyship

Returning to Italy with *A Ciambra*

While we may sometimes be tempted to think of the Italian diaspora as something that is fully finished, emigration from Italy continues today just as flows of migration onto Italian shores continue to be a factor in the growth of the Italian population. In the midst of these migratory movements, successive generations of Italian American writers and artists continue to think through issues of allyship across diasporas as they reinterrogate the meaning of *italianità*. We can see this not just in contemporary fiction but in cinema, for instance, with recent works like Jonas Carpignano's 2017 film *A Ciambra* gesturing toward these dynamics as they persist in the United States and in Italy itself.

Unlike the majority of the narratives in this book, *A Ciambra* is actually set in Italy, in Calabria more specifically, where the film's teen protagonist, Pio Amato, works to navigate the complexities of life in the Romani diasporic community in which he lives. At his side are a cast of family and friends who include the "African" Ayiva, who has emigrated from Burkina Faso. The relationship between the two young men has prompted critics to recognize the film as concerned with alliances or allyship, though the concept of diaspora tends not to figure as explicitly in these conversations. Beyond the solidarity of friendship, there is also the "tentative alliance" between the Romani community and the mafia in the film, a more uneasy and unsettling type of partnership that Carpignano has described as naturally developing when "immigrants have to make use of the underground economy" and thus "rub shoulders with the people who run the underground economy" (Jerkins; Aftab). Here again, in other words, ethno-nationality and socioeconomic status are inextricably linked. The Romani-Italian and Romani-Burkinabe alliances emerge as opposing forces as the film progresses, since the Amato family's dealings with the mafia ultimately lead to a situation in which Pio becomes complicit in betraying Ayiva, signaling what Carpignano has termed "the limits of the relationship between these two groups," the Romani people on the one hand and the Burkinabe on the other, together with the larger community of Ghanaian and Nigerian migrants who share the space of the refugee camp with Ayiva (Saito).

Both of these diasporic communities face challenges in the film that directly result from the intolerance they experience at the hands of other Italians. This pattern of prejudice is a reality that has been thoroughly documented by groups such as Human Rights Watch, which in the last decade has increasingly drawn attention to hate crimes in Italy that have targeted individuals based on race, ethnicity, and national origin, including acts of violence and aggression that have specifically singled out Romani and Burkinabe residents, as well as the targeting of these communities by police. Families like Pio's, who live in isolated settlements that are emphatically separated from the more privileged echelons of Italian society, face these alienating expressions of anti-Romani animosity while also struggling with feelings of disconnection from cultural traditions that have long been central to Romani society. The latter is something that Alexian Santino Spinelli, the Romani Italian musician and poet, has poignantly recorded in verse, contrasting a life in which "a tent was [the speaker's] home" with the "prison with bars" that the speaker encounters in living within "walls / so well-built" (41). Meanwhile, emigrants from Burkina Faso face even more dramatically articulated forms of discrimination than the Romani families in *A Ciambra*, not only from "mainstream" Italian society but from other marginalized communities like the Romani one itself, which in the film aggressively spouts racist ideas about "Africans." Again, the film's rendering of anti-African sentiment is grounded in contemporary realities in Italy, where "experiences of violence, social erasure, and social marginalization" have encouraged the development of "a pan-African Black consciousness across ethnic, linguistic, and religious differences," which *A Ciambra* also captures in the transnational union of refugee camp residents who hail not just from Burkina Faso but from Ghana and Nigeria as well (Merrill 99). Despite their substantial differences, then, both groups embody the kind of alienation in a new place, painful estrangement from home and tradition, enduring emotional connections to a remembered land, and forging of diasporic community enclaves that serve as hallmarks of diaspora.

The parallels between the Romani and African experiences on Italian soil have tempted some viewers of *A Ciambra* to indulge false equivalences between them, much as some Italian Americans have been tempted to make false equivalences between the experiences of Italians on US shores and those of diasporic communities of color. Stephen Saito, in his introduction to an interview with Carpignano, describes the Burkinabe diasporic community as "a group as diminished and displaced in [the] larger society as [Romani people] are." Yet Carpignano himself has a different, rather more nuanced vision of the relationship between the two groups, describing how in "many ways, the African community feels like what the Gypsy community must've felt like when it just arrived" in Italy (Saito). In other words, despite their persisting marginalization, Roma in Italy today operate from a position of relative advantage in interfacing with Burkinabe or Ghanaian refugees. Pio's family also exemplifies the racial prejudice directed at the community's Burkinabe, Nigerian, and Ghanaian residents, describing them as "drunks" and suggesting that stealing from them, given their race, is far from objectionable. Like Fante's Italian American and Chicanx characters, Pio, Ayiva, and the communities they represent are enmeshed in a dynamic in which earlier migrants abuse later ones, with racial identity as well as national origin coloring the lens of identification or disidentification through which each group views its counterparts.

Pio, of course, is the exception to this rule during the bulk of the film. Just fourteen years old, he seems to idolize Ayiva much in the way he does his own older brother, and their relationship, if anything, is more functional and emotionally open than the relationship between the two Amato sons. During some of the happiest moments in what is sometimes an emotionally challenging viewing experience, *A Ciambra* basks in the understated contentment of Pio and Ayiva's interactions, which testify to the possibility of a healing sort of allyship between them across the boundaries of diaspora. Ayiva supports Pio's efforts to earn a living for his family while his father and older brother are in prison, while Pio offers emotional support to Ayiva when he reveals, after a cryptic Skype call, that his family consists of just his sister and his daughter, with his wife inexplicably absent. These moments of solidarity make it all the more painful when Pio's older brother and the rest of his family pressure him into betraying Ayiva, assisting them in stealing a storage unit full of items that he has been planning to bring home to Burkina Faso and sell. In Ayiva's mind, this plan represents a way to ensure his financial security upon his desired return home; correspondingly, Pio's betrayal specifically undermines Ayiva's ambitions as a diasporic individual and counters the acts of support and allyship that pass between them in the film's earlier scenes, giving the film a painful awareness of the pitfalls and failures of solidarity as well as its potentialities.

Carpignano himself is both Black and Italian American. The son of an Italian father and a Barbadian American mother, he was born in the Bronx but lived in both Italy and New York during his youth. Carpignano's own complexly diasporic identity seems to have generated substantial rewards in his treatment of the film's subject matter: not only the diasporic experiences of its characters but the ways they reach across the gaps between those diverse experiences to forge authentic bonds, and the ways those bonds are tested, as in so many of the narratives we have seen elsewhere in this book. Remarking on his family background and childhood experiences, Carpignano has commented,

> I've always been very sensitive to race issues in Italy. My mother's African American and my father's Italian, so growing up in Italy, I was always very conscious of the fact that there were no other black people in our circle. And once the immigrant wave started to come, I looked at it with a lot of interest because you could feel even from the beginning that in some way this was going to alter the social fabric of our town and of our society. (Saito)

As an Italian American with African diasporic roots, Carpignano also does not hesitate to criticize nondiasporic Italy's dysfunctional treatment of the diasporic communities within its national borders, which *A Ciambra* vividly captures. After all, it is not just Roma who are cruelly racist in the words and actions that they direct toward refugees like Ayiva. Instead, as the film makes plain, institutional or structural factors such as the bias in the Italian criminal justice system and the mafia's emphatic hold on the "underground economy" disadvantage Romani and Burkinabe migrants alike, though not necessarily to the same extent, and the film forges a clear critique of the class inequality and uneven distribution of resources that shape so much of the diasporic experience on contemporary Italian shores. In the process of laying these facts bare, *A Ciambra* plays its own part in deconstructing received notions of *italianità*, not only by flipping the script and casting the Italian mafia and police presence as authorities that forcefully Other more marginalized people, but also by expanding viewers' notions of who and what culturally qualifies as Italian in the first place. In other words, Carpignano argues, the "fact that a film where there are very few white Italian characters is representing Italy [in film festivals like the Oscars] is very important. It goes a long way towards a more diverse dialogue or representation of *what it means to be Italian*, if this is the film that represents Italian cinema" (Saita, my italics). In a moment when nationalism and xenophobia are on the rise in Italy, threatening the acceptance of this multiethnic vision of *italianità*, these types of conversations spurred by Italian American emigrants and their children have a vital place in the landscape of allyship across diasporas. In taking on the responsibility for this species of witnessing, Carpignano becomes an ally of multiple diasporic communities in the country of his father's birth, while also grappling with ideas—for instance, about socioeconomic injustice—that have an expansive resonance beyond these diasporic worlds.

The embattled whiteness of Italians in the United States has given way to a multiplicity of Italian Americas. One has actively participated in and capitalized on American racism, while another has testified to Italians' role in upholding structures of white supremacy and has aimed to disrupt and dismantle those structures. These diverse identities have produced richly varied literary responses. Writing from outside the Italian diaspora, authors from other diasporas have resisted essentialist notions of *italianità* while calling many Italian Americans to account for their aspirational attitude toward elements of American culture that are subtly or overtly racist, as well as for accompanying class ambitions and toxic visions of gender and sexuality. Both of these approaches have been expressions of allyship. Meanwhile, Italian-descended writers in the United States have plumbed their own communities' failings and suggested different aspirations for Italian America, working in solidarity with diasporic communities that have been targets of Italian American racism in intersectional permutations—while reenvisioning those communities in counterpoint to prevailing stereotypes. As part of a larger conversation about the social justice issues that continue to shape the fabric of the United States, which these narratives eagerly engage in as they scrutinize the broader implications of problems of gender, sexuality, and class outside the diaspora(s), these literary interventions in interdiasporic understanding have the potential to produce revolutionary social consequences, forging meaningful alliances and creating spaces for healing and rebuilding through alternative modes of representation. Films like *A Ciambra* gesture toward the role of other media in expanding this literary dialogue and remind us of the need to look transnationally back to Italy itself to continue the conversation.

Notes

Chapter 1

1. Lawrence's travel narrative muses on the supposed importance of the phallus to the Italian as "the symbol of individual creative immortality," cloaking unsubstantiated claims in a tone of objective authority that reveals more about Anglo-American ideals of gender identity than it does about Italy—although this is not to say that Italy itself has never suffered from similar problems (56).

2. Not only did *Daisy Miller* sell 20,000 copies in a matter of weeks, but it was also quickly pirated, meaning that this official sales figure does not capture the extent of its rapid reach. See Horne.

3. Lawrence's essay "On the Lago di Garda," part of his longer travel narrative *Twilight in Italy*, actually tells of his travels in the north of the country, not far from Verona. Still, in both Italy and abroad, ideas like his would be increasingly applied to southerners as a way of distinguishing them from northern Italians.

4. Even if James can be understood as a member of the queer diaspora abroad, this membership is one he would acquire slowly as the years passed. Eric Haralson reminds us that in the 1880s and 1890s, "James's manner of engaging the social and personal fact of same-sex passion (by no means a rare manner) was furtive and intermittent, vacillating between detection and deflection, flirtation and flight" (61).

5. As Susan Cheever remarks, this aspect of Alcott's upbringing has been subject to the whims of biographers, each viewing the famous father-daughter relationship through their own lens: "Yet in spite of . . . the facts, every biography has a story imposed on the facts by the biographer: Bronson Alcott was a genius who loved his girls but couldn't manage to make a living, or Bronson Alcott was a punitive father who traumatized his daughters. Both are true according to the facts" (62).

6. Names have a bewitching power in terms of what they reveal about social class and social mobility. Gregory Clark's recent book *The Son Also Rises* is one recent

study of what surnames and their representation in various professions can tell us about social mobility in the US and globally. While Clark's focus in the US is the early twentieth century and beyond, readers have used a similar lens to examine Daisy and to consider the importance of James's chosen name for his heroine.

7. See Higley. Daisy herself is from the more pedestrian Schenectady, which only adds to the novella's class tensions. While she claims to have had access to a great deal of "society" in New York City, we sense that these experiences have been among the nouveau riche rather than the old money elite.

8. Interestingly, this is a recurrent trope in Forster's "Italian novels." I am thinking particularly of *Where Angels Fear to Tread* and of Philip's delight at his on-again, off-again friendship with the Italian Gino, although George's momentary intimacy with Reverend Beebe in *A Room with a View* is also a good example.

9. Despite this overtly stereotyping discourse, *Twilight in Italy* tends to be interpreted more as a classically objective portrait of Italian life and landscapes, as in the summary on the book jacket for the Penguin edition of the text, which describes it as "a vibrant account" that "brings to life the vigorous spontaneity of a society as yet untouched by the deadening effect of industrialization."

10. Here there is a kinship between Alcott's text and nineteenth-century English novels like *Jane Eyre*, with its "poor and plain" protagonist who is unafraid to stand up for herself, where the angelically self-sacrificing Helen Burns remains a secondary character rather than ever becoming its main focus.

11. In one moment, the payments from Jo's writing cause her to take "great comfort in the knowledge that she could supply her own wants, and need ask no one for a penny"—which feels both like a feminist statement and uncomfortably like a romantic ode to capitalist self-reliance (424).

12. See Baily.

13. As Maddalena Tirabassi notes, Italian American families tended to see a woman's marriage in much the same way, with dowry items from home filling immigrant women's trunks to support their transfer from one household to another.

14. We have known about these comments of Alcott's for some time. They were anthologized, for instance, in an 1890 collection of Alcott's letters and journals. Still, letters like this one have not necessarily received the attention that they deserve.

15. "Roman Fever" was originally published in 1934 and revised for republication in 1936.

16. This is not to say that premarital sex was not also happening earlier than this and in smaller, more provincial towns. One study of church records in Groton, Connecticut revealed that in that particular congregation, nearly a third of those baptized between 1761 and 1775 admitted to having sex before marriage. See Mandelker.

17. In one 2013 example, Häagen Dazs hawked its new gelato in the US using a commercial named "Arguments," filmed in Italian and subtitled in English. The commercial featured a young Italian couple loudly arguing, spontaneously

making up over a spoonful of the tasty dessert, and then breaking just as unpredictably into a second iteration of the dispute. The stereotypical takeaway was that Italians are lovers: loud, emotionally volatile, passionate lovers.

18. Building on its earlier innovations in the nineteenth century, Italy's per capita electricity consumption in the 1930s was high enough to distinguish it as an increasingly modernizing landscape, with 14.8 billion kilowatt hours total consumption by 1937. See M. Clark.

19. One contradiction that seems to have kept some readers from acknowledging this primitivist bent in writings like Wharton's is the tension between these attitudes and the typically adoring Anglo-American responses to Renaissance Italian art, architecture, and culture more broadly. Here, it is critical to understand that two things can be true at the same time: that twentieth-century Italy can be looked on as backward even as the Italy of Michelangelo is prized as a pillar of Western civilization in a systemically racist culture. See Brodhead.

20. Minghella's father emigrated from Frosinone, and his mother's family is from Valvori.

21. Minghella himself did not prove entirely impervious to these ideas. In writing about Italy, he mentions the country's "more primitive mores" in the years leading up to *il boom* (82). Significantly given that his mother's and father's families were both from central Italy, he also once commented that "to [him] Italy, *and particularly the south*, is hugely pagan" rather than the offering the "civilized European culture" of Henry James's *The Ambassadors* (79, my italics).

22. It is commonly understood that the comment Dickie Greenleaf's father makes to Tom about "a certain book by Henry James" is meant as a reference to *The Ambassadors*, whose plot in this respect is similar to that of Highsmith's novel (28).

23. Highsmith's stance on others' future knowledge of her own sexuality is quite clear; at one point she commented in her journal that this topic had a rightful place in her biography, saying that "everyone must know I am queer, or gay" (qtd. in Wilson 9).

24. There is by no means a consensus about Minghella's rendering in this respect. Some did feel strongly when the film was released that it perpetuated negative stereotypes of queerness, as critics' reviews and even letters to the editor of *The Advocate* demonstrated. Many of those comments echo Trask's feelings about the novel. See Benshoff.

25. Chester Himes's *If He Hollers Let Him Go* and James Baldwin's *Notes of a Native Son* come to mind, as do *Ask the Dust* and *Giovanni's Room*.

26. Here I depart from Žižek, whose position is that "real for Minghella means humanly comprehensible, whereas what is real about Highsmith's Ripley is some inhuman core that does not answer to the moral categories Minghella wrestles to make sense of Highsmith's world" (Goldberg 117–18).

27. Regarding the bathing scene, see Haralson's article "'Thinking about Homosex' in Forster and James." As Robert K. Martin suggests, the unsuccessful

marriage proposal that ends *Where Angels Fear to Tread* is motivated by the male protagonist's wish to "achieve his goals, indirectly, as part of a homosocial triangle of desire ... embracing Gino *through* Caroline" (256, italics in the original).

Chapter 2

1. See Armengol; Leeming.

2. Hall points out that both David and Giovanni "are capable of maintaining physical, sexual relationships with both men and women, at different times in their lives and with different degrees of emotional satisfaction" (157).

3. Although Yasmin Y. Degout is right that David's "inner conflict" centers on "his fear of not meeting the heterosexual values of his society," I believe she misreads the novel in suggesting that "Baldwin ... creates a psychological history that can be used to explain *homoerotic love as behavior that is produced by diagnosable circumstances* within a society" (430, my italics). Instead, the "history" in *Giovanni's Room* functions to explain why sexual self-denial and the suppression of queerness persist in postwar US culture while capturing the destruction of lives and relationships that results.

4. Bryan R. Washington makes a similar argument in suggesting that "the novel struggles to get us to see ... the brainwashing power of American bourgeois morality" (77).

5. This aspect of the text is interesting in light of Baldwin's statements about "whether or not homosexuality is natural," a question that he suggests is "pointless" because "the answer never can be Yes," since "it would rob the normal—who are simply the many—of their necessary sense of security and order" (qtd. in Degout 426).

6. Buchen makes an eloquent case for Fidelman's maturation, commenting that "Fidelman spiritually travels ... from a self-centered, grasping, often obsessive son of a bitch to a lover of men and women" (64).

7. Later, Baldwin further extended his geographic trajectory by living for a time in Turkey.

8. This is an important distinction. Critics like Valerie Rohy miss the mark somewhat in suggesting that "the text conspicuously compares David as American with Giovanni as European," rather than seeing Giovanni's character as representative of a specific ethno-national culture (222).

9. Even when we consider other novels of Baldwin's such as *Another Country*, this typology of European identities remains at play. Although Paris and the French Mediterranean also function as sites of homoerotic fulfillment for an American expatriate in *Another Country*, that fulfillment comes after a painstaking, slow courtship process—perhaps because the American's lover is a cautious, reserved Frenchman rather than an impulsive Italian.

10. Painter cites *The Fire Next Time* rather than "On Being 'White'... and Other Lies," but both texts are essential to this facet of whiteness studies.

11. Imagine how differently a novel like *Where Angels Fear to Tread* might read if it were instead titled *Gino* or *Gino's Place*.

12. In *A Room with a View*, shocked and disturbed by the death of the Italian in the Florentine piazza, George exclaims, "I shall want to live, I say" (46).

13. In fact, Woolf's Russians in *Orlando* are quite similar to Malamud's Italians in *Pictures of Fidelman*, facilitating a humorous and trenchant critique of English nationalism in another novel centered on mutable and complex queer identities. Regarding the latter, see Donald Hall.

14. See Gordon.

15. In *Seize the Day*, Wilhelm Adler is initially characterized as driftless and disempowered by his wife.

16. As Levis Sullam illustrates, the role of Italians themselves in the deportations has previously been obscured and minimized.

Chapter 3

1. For one helpful explanation of Korean migration as diasporic, see Choi.

2. See Baily.

3. Throughout this chapter, I use the name and pronoun for Leda/Dante that most closely correspond to those used in whatever part of the book I am referencing. While other characters see Dante as a man and refer to (and think of) her as "him" in the early years of her passing, it is many years before Dante begins to think of himself in this way. For most of the novel, Dante uses the name but not, privately, the accompanying pronoun, and the novel's narrator follows suit. As I will discuss later, the multiplicity and complexity of Leda/Dante's gender identities are elemental here, so it is vital that we talk and think about this character in ways that reflect that complexity.

4. I am appropriating this term from Marxist theory in considering not just how the working class within the novel understands the forces of class exerting pressure on them but also how the novel itself approaches issues of class.

5. Here we can see an instance where the name by which we should refer to Leda/Dante shifts as we move forward and backward in time within the world of the narrative. As a worker in the cigarette factory, Leda is passing as a man and is publicly known as Dante, though she does not yet privately see herself as Dante or use masculine pronouns to refer to herself, nor does De Robertis's narrator refer to her in that way. During the voyage across the ocean, which precedes this moment, Leda is known simply as Leda, and she publicly identifies as a woman. This slipperiness gestures toward the necessity of making

Leda/Dante the authority on these questions of gender and listening carefully as Leda/Dante's gender identity evolves over the course of the novel.

6. Although Dante is the overt target of the attack by musician Joaquín, Joaquín's history of calling Santiago his nickname "Negro" in a way that sounds less like a term of endearment and more like a "slithering attack" makes it clear where Joaquín stands where matters of race are concerned (294–95).

7. Hall remembers how during his childhood in Jamaica in the 1940s and 1950s, he "never once heard a single person refer to themselves or to others as, in some way, or as having been at some time in the past, 'African'" (231).

8. While the name "Dante" has been passed down within the family for generations, here I am referring to the "original" Dante in the immediate world of the novel, Leda's cousin and husband.

9. The novel was awarded the Stonewall Book Award for LGBTQ literature in 2016.

10. This is also an issue that is addressed in *Aloft*, when the narrator's son and his wife employ a nanny and housekeeper who "stays six nights a week, only leaving on Sunday morning to spend a day and night with her husband and two children and mother" (69). For one nonfictional reference text, see Barbara Ehrenreich and Arlie Russell Hochschild's *Global Woman: Nannies, Maids, and Sex Workers in the New Economy*.

11. See Millward, Dodd, et al.

12. This is a refrain that will repeat in Fante.

13. This comment of Jerry's painfully foreshadows the ending of the novel, in which Theresa's death will be caused partly by a storm that escalates while she and her father are flying home from Maine to Long Island—but even then, it is Theresa who convinces her father to fly.

14. While Forster's novels are not common points of comparison for Lee's work, in a review for *The Guardian*, Ursula Le Guin does put Lee's newer novel *On Such a Full Sea* in conversation with Forster's "The Machine Stops" as an early example of dystopian literature.

15. In one interview, Lee mused, "I feel like one of the things I like about writing about an Italian-American guy [is] having thoughts that sounded like his and kind of go against the grain of what people expect of him, an Italian-American landscaper on Long Island. Some people will read the book and think, 'I've never had an Italian-American landscaper who talks like this and thinks like this.' They always just want Tony Soprano or some 'goomba' who's kind of an idiot—that bugs me" (Quan).

16. Lawrence also uses these terms in *Twilight in Italy* alongside his references to Italy as a "Latin" space. In the American novels, the rhetoric is not quite so explicit, but the attitude remains the same.

17. As Sohn suggests, Jerry "knows precisely what to say to appease certain parties but does not comprehend why he must say it" (40).

18. His wife's nipples during her pregnancy are "the color of dark caramels," while his girlfriend Rita's skin is "a summertime cocoa" (58). Incidentally, this is also not the first time that a reader has brought DeLillo and Lee into conversation. In her study of *Aloft* as a "post-traumatic" novel of 9/11, Kathy Knapp reflects on how DeLillo and Lee have both taken that event as a focus in their writing, though in strikingly different ways (196).

19. Here I am thinking, for instance, of Arthur Miller's *Death of a Salesman*.

20. David Cowart makes a similar argument about Lee's *A Gesture Life*, suggesting that "Lee focuses on the complicity of [the] immigrant in acts of victimization in another life" (106).

21. Regarding this division among readers of the novel, see Sohn.

Chapter 4

1. While Arturo Bandini's birthplace is Colorado, diaspora theory would suggest that the United States remains his adopted home, something that can continue to be true for migrants of the second generation and beyond who experience social alienation, selective accommodation, and other hallmarks of diaspora.

2. Matthew Elliott makes a similar point in arguing that "Arturo Bandini remains an unreliable narrator even at the end of the novel" (531). Yet it is critical to understand the consequences of this unreliability: that Arturo serves as a negative or cautionary example for readers.

3. This is a critical distinction because it corrects the common distortion of the concept of toxic masculinity into a vilification of men or a way of stereotyping men and masculinity. See Salter.

4. See Gardaphé's commentary on DeLillo in *Italian Signs, American Streets*, which has been central to pushing readers in this direction.

5. While the Mexican Revolution was certainly also a factor in establishing the flow of migration from Mexico to the United States, it has been all too easy for Americans to abdicate responsibility for the displacement of Mexican citizens from their country of birth by ignoring the effects of the United States' own actions.

6. As Carey McWilliams wrote in *Factories in the Field*, his 1935 exposé of the abuse of migrant farm workers in California, "the same army . . . has followed the crops [in California] since 1870," though it has variously included "cheap labor" from "China, Japan, the Philippine Islands, Puerto Rico, Mexico, the Deep South, and Europe" (8, 7). Interestingly, Fante and McWilliams developed a friendship in the 1930s.

7. The term *Chicanx diaspora* typically refers to the scattering of Mexican individuals and families into a range of US communities specifically. Although earlier conceptions of diaspora demanded that groups have scattered into several

distinct nations to be considered diasporic, theorists like Boyce Davies have done important work to move us beyond this obsession with nation-states and toward a more transnational vision that admits the types of historical complexities at play in the relationship between the United States and Mexico. See Boyce Davies's commentary on Caribbean migration in *Black Women, Writing, and Identity: Migrations of the Subject*.

8. Fante's letters are full of this misogynist bluster. While some of these sentiments are directed at white women, both sexism and racism are clearly, intersectionally at work in his responses to women of Mexican descent.

9. Gardaphé recognizes this same treatment of Filipinx characters by Arturo in *The Road to Los Angeles*.

10. See *Italian Signs, American Streets*.

11. As Alexandra Délano notes, there is no consensus within the Mexican government regarding whether the term *diaspora* should be applied to Chicanx residents of the United States. However, a former Mexican ambassador to the US, Arturo Sarukhan, has made an eloquent case for using the term to describe Chicanx experiences, and Chicanx community organizers such as Gabriel Rincón have argued that the term should indeed be applied to the "forced migration" of Mexican citizens from home (qtd. in Délano 1).

12. Kordich argues that Arturo "does not seek out the embrace of Southern California's Italian community" but also does not "search for complete assimilation into the WASP mainstream" (17). Likewise, Ryan notes that "[e]ven as he reflects a defining American anxiety," Arturo "is excluded from full participation in Americanness" (205). In these earlier studies, the focus has been somewhat different than in later articles like Matthew Elliot's, which more baldly name Arturo's racism and more persistently focus on it.

13. As David A. Hollinger notes, "Prior to 1960, if you were in charge of something big and had opportunities to influence the direction of society, chances are you grew up in a white Protestant milieu" (ix). Interestingly, however, this pressure to conform came not just from the Anglo-Saxon majority in this period but even from other Catholics with a different orientation toward their faith. A great deal, for instance, has been written on the tense relationship between Irish and Italian Catholics, as well as on the general criticisms of Italian Catholics by non-Italians. In an essay titled "Utterly Faithless Specimens," Peter R. D'Agostino reminds us that "[m]any historians have pointed out, and many Italian Americans themselves can recount, how their particular 'style' of religiosity met with harsh criticism from fellow Catholics in the United States," which included disapproval of their "strong devotion to the cult of saints" and "absence of sacramental regularity in favor of familial and lay religious practices such as home alters" (36). There and in his book *Rome in America*, D'Agostino adds that other Catholics also "lamented Italian immigrants' unwillingness to finance parishes" and "their

lack of respect for clergy," in addition to their "aberrant devotional styles" (59). D'Agostino points out that anti-Italian sentiment more broadly made Italian Catholics a more intense target of scrutiny than other groups with potentially eyebrow-raising practices; thus, "the orthodoxy of Irish wakes," for instance, was not subjected to the same critiques ("Utterly Faithless" 37).

14. Lombard can be used as an Anglicization of the Italian name Lombardi or Lombardo, and Lombard is also not unheard of as an Irish surname, though it can instead be English or French. Camilla's selection suggests that in her view, it is perhaps more advantageous to be viewed as an assimilationist Italian or Irish American than as a Mexican American. This commentary reflects her awareness (and, by extension, the novel's awareness) of the privilege of Italian Americans relative to diasporic people of color in the US.

15. The singer El Vez, known as "The Mexican Elvis," sings of "blue suede huaraches" rather than "blue suede shoes," connecting huaraches as a cultural symbol of Mexico with Elvis as a cultural symbol of the United States (qtd. in Saldívar xiii). Florencio Sánchez Cámara tells similar stories of Chicanx characters, including a man named Pedro Vidales, the "first Chicano to loaf around the streets of Chicago with his huaraches" (107).

16. Elliott makes a similar point in chronicling Arturo's "racial romanticism" (539).

17. While Chicanx nationalism's own embrace of pre-Columbian indigenous history as a cultural inheritance of Mexican Americans was key to the movement, Arturo invokes these vague references without any sense of the history behind them and as a way of disavowing the Chicanx diaspora's very real modernity.

18. See Tompkins on "the representation of African Americans as food" (103).

19. Again, see *Twilight in Italy* and Lawrence's descriptions of "the Italian," which combine animalistic language with comparative judgments about southern indolence and "Northern purposive industry" (44).

20. Gardaphé identifies this as well, suggesting that although Arturo's poor treatment of other immigrant communities "has been read as racism, readers must realize the irony created through such depictions" (*Leaving Little Italy* 164).

21. See Kordich.

22. Gender was essential to Kimberlé Crenshaw's original formulation when she introduced the concept of intersectionality, examining intersecting and mutually constitutive forms of gender and racial discrimination. Nevertheless, the concept is also relevant to other forms of inequality, including (as here) the intersection of class and ethnic inequality.

23. This becomes particularly interesting if we consider the racist history of tipping in the United States. By using her tips in this way, Camilla subversively appropriates this legacy and uses it to tackle another facet of American social inequality. See Jayaraman.

24. See Hall.

25. As Barone notes, Fante's views on Italy shifted over time and during the course of his travels there; see Barone's article "Rome If You Want To." Fante's desired and executed return trips to Italy speak to that other familiar quality of diasporic communities, the determination to return home "when conditions are appropriate" (Safran 83–84).

26. Veblen writes that "property now becomes the most easily recognised evidence of a reputable degree of success as distinguished from heroic or signal achievement. It therefore becomes the conventional basis of esteem. Its possession in some amount becomes necessary in order to [have] any reputable standing in the community. It becomes indispensable to accumulate, to acquire property, in order to retain one's good name. . . . So soon as the possession of property becomes the basis of popular esteem, therefore, it becomes also a requisite *to the complacency which we call self-respect*" (28–29, 31; my italics).

27. Like so many moments in *White Noise*, the mall scene is rich in the sort of exaggerated detail that encourages us to ridicule Jack rather than sympathizing with him. The mall, for instance, is described as "a ten-story building arranged around a center court of waterfalls, promenades, and gardens" (83). The sheer height of the generically named complex, dubbed the Mid-Village Mall, gives a surrealist cast to the scene; even the famous Minnesotan Mall of America is only four stories tall.

28. It is difficult to read this passage and not think again of modernist masterworks like Woolf's *Orlando*, which uses exaggeration to similarly satirical effect.

29. Take, for example, the Los Angeles–based band that named itself the Airborne Toxic Event in an homage to *White Noise*.

30. As both Safran and Clifford note, and as I have mentioned elsewhere in this book, this shared quality of the experience is part of what defines diaspora (and distinguishes it from exile).

31. Making a similar argument about this scene, Engles refers to this as "a class-based mode of self-assertion" (765).

32. Given the traditional mistrust of academia in many working-class Italian American families, DeLillo's decision to focus his entire narrative on the figure of a college professor is somewhat daring. At the same time, the critical eye that DeLillo turns on the trappings of the academic world, not just robes and glasses but diplomas and galley proofs of articles, too, betrays the narrative's roundabout, satirical indebtedness to this traditional attitude of suspicion.

33. Late in Ibsen's play, husband Torvald Helmer learns that his wife has saved his life by forging her father's signature on a loan document that allows the family to provide Torvald with life-saving medical care. Rather than expressing gratitude for his wife's sacrifice, Torvald is indignant at the scandal that her actions might cause in his workplace if her crime were discovered.

34. This is one of the scenes from Forster's novel that makes it so unrepentantly fetishistic, as it paints a mesmerizing and horrifying picture of *italianità*.

35. There are more than traces of the white savior complex here as well, as Jack's faulty self-perception echoes the false sense of superiority of white colonizers who convinced themselves that they were benevolent leaders delivering the colonized from an uncivilized fate.

36. Duke Ellington was also under contract to work on a different film for the project, "The Story of Jazz." The plan had been for Louis Armstrong to play himself in that film.

Chapter 5

1. As I will discuss in greater depth later in this chapter, Roma have traditionally been understood as ethno-racially ambiguous by outside observers, especially American ones, though anthropological insights clarify that the Romani diaspora has its origins in India.

2. There are also some interesting references in *The Fortunate Pilgrim* to the Jewish diasporic community in New York City, and I will explore these references as a partial counterpoint to Puzo's way of representing Irishness.

3. As Ferraro notes, *The Godfather* deepens this vision of gender by colliding it with religion, as "the southern Italian worship of the matriarch" cedes "to an imaginative reinscription of the southern Italian feminine propensity to worship . . . smack in the midst of this half-century's most markedly patriarchal fantasy" (515).

4. In fact, Puzo interestingly echoes the complaints that some Chicana feminists would later make about the second wave, suggesting that the women's movement was "too focused on men as the oppressors" and that the extended families that "represented both economic and cultural survival" for Chicanas could not be excluded from the quest for women's liberation as part of a larger battle for human rights (Freedman 89). *The Fortunate Pilgrim* suggests that Italian American feminism requires similar culturally specific accommodations, especially to account for the traditional centrality of the family in Italian American life and for women's ways of subversively challenging the patriarchy from within this system.

5. The toxic masculinity that specifically disadvantages men who do not conform to stereotypical notions of aggressive, even violent manhood, creating "hierarchies favoring some and victimizing others," has always been an American problem more broadly rather than an Italian American problem exclusively (Keith 2).

6. See Richard Jensen's 2002 article "No Irish Need Apply: A Myth of Victimization" and the now-famous 2015 rebuttal by teenage scholar Rebecca A. Fried, both published in Oxford University Press's *Journal of Social History*.

7. Recent books written for a wider nonacademic audience about the Great Famine include John Kelly's *The Graves are Walking* and the juvenile nonfiction title *Black Potatoes*, by Susan Campbell Bartoletti. Books for children on the subject are incredibly common.

8. It is important to remember that Ireland did not receive full independence and international recognition as an independent republic until the middle of the twentieth century, having originally attained the status of a "dominion" in 1922 after the Irish War of Independence, and that Northern Ireland remains under English control to this day. As Bernard Beck has said of similar representations of Scottish rebels, these popular songs and films about England's oppression of Ireland have generated a current of sympathy that has not been extended to "contemporary peoples of color" living under similar conditions (31).

9. Orsi points out that some older Italian American women "were respected for their skill in healing with traditional cures and for their knowledge of southern Italian magical rituals"; in other words, the association of age and gender with uncommon powers that some might deem the stuff of "witchcraft" is specifically present in the Italian diaspora as well, but perhaps with different (more positive) undertones (132).

10. Puzo has also suggested that *The Fortunate Pilgrim* may have become more popular over time due to the women's movement, more specifically "the change in women's roles"—and perhaps, correspondingly, its resistance to such ideas about older women's bodies (x).

11. That the term *guinea* has sometimes been self-reflexively used within the community when Italian Americans refer to each other or themselves does not make the term any less offensive when used by Anglo-Americans. Regarding Italian Americans' "invisible blackness," again see Pardini, who writes at length about Italian Americans' "composite, fuzzed, and unstable mixture of racial status . . . , that at once baffled, repulsed, and attracted white and black Americans alike" (79).

12. In this way, Puzo's novel considers the experiences of Protestants who would have been marginalized in Italy as well as those of Italian Catholics marginalized in the United States. However, the portrayal of Italian Protestantism in the narrative is arguably unflattering and thus perhaps not characteristically an act of allyship.

13. Here we might also think of the character of Louis in Pietro di Donato's *Christ in Concrete*.

14. See the 1986 afterword to the novel written by Edvige Giunta. Giunta remarks that if "Italian/American male authors have been struggling to achieve recognition, the problems of invisibility and legitimization are magnified for Italian/American women" (139). In the preface to her anthology of Italian American women's writing, titled *The Dream Book*, Helen Barolini similarly comments that "being Italian American, being female, and being a writer was being thrice an outsider," so that "an Italian American woman with literary aspirations . . . seems

to stand alone, unconnected to any body of literature or group of writers—an anomaly, a freak occurrence, a frequent non-repeater, ephemeral" (xii).

15. See Morikawa.

16. Candeloro also points out that in what he calls the "Italian American Trend" of this period, cultural icons like Frank Sinatra and Joe DiMaggio made Italian American culture uniquely visible in the "mass media" of the United States (77). Nevertheless, as the experiences of people of color in the US demonstrate even more dramatically, the acceptance of entertainment and sports icons from a marginalized community should not in any way be confused with the elimination of prejudice against that community.

17. This is a fraught detail, especially given the history of Catholic antagonism of Romani people, including in Italy, where, for instance, the Council of Trent announced in 1563 that Roma could not be priests.

18. Again, see Dobie.

19. While scholars like Bona and Scambray also comment on the multigenerational fascination with Romani people that permeates *Paper Fish*, my more specific focus here is the way that this portrayal can be read as exposing and criticizing anti-Romani sentiment and stereotypes of Romani culture.

20. Italian American women, like women of color though certainly not to the same degree, have at times received negative attention for wearing hoop earrings. In *Italian American Women, Food, and Identity*, the authors relate a story of one Italian American woman who had "a colleague (a middle-aged professor)" tell her that "'hoop earrings are unprofessional' and assume . . . she was from New Jersey" when she wore them (171).

21. De Rosa has also commented on Italian America's bright colors as a signal of its difference, although as Giunta notes, the older women in her novel are distinguished for their persistently black wardrobe.

22. The family members cannot come to an agreement about exactly what causes Doriana's condition, but Sarah believes that the fever is the cause.

23. Because *Paper Fish* is not commonly taught or studied, it is unsurprising that there has been little critical commentary on these tenuous relationships between Italian and Romani women. The fact that De Rosa wrote only one novel may also be a factor in her relative marginalization. Nevertheless, this gap in the scholarship recalls the same intersectional inequalities that seem to have kept De Rosa's writing from reaching as wide an audience as that of some of her male peers in Italian America.

24. Sarah's experience is also complicated by the fact that she is not the Italian American matriarch but the Lithuanian American daughter-in-law. As such, her position confers similar responsibilities to Lucia Santa's or Doria's without, arguably, allowing her the same potential advantages. She is not the "symbolic center" of the Italian American family but a mere satellite—and an imported one at that.

Bibliography

Aftab, Kaleem. "Diff 2017: 'A Ciambra' Tells the Stories of Daily Lives in Mafia Country." *The National*, https://www.thenational.ae/arts-culture/film/diff-2017-a-ciambra-tells-the-untold-stories-of-daily-lives-in-mafia-country-1.683140, 10 Dec. 2017.

Alberghene, Janice M. "Autobiography and the Boundaries of Interpretation: On Reading *Little Women* and *The Living Is Easy*." *Little Women and the Feminist Imagination: Criticism, Controversy, Personal Essays*, edited by Janice M. Alberghene and Beverly Lyon Clark. Routledge, 2013.

Alcott, Louisa May. *Little Women*. 1868. Puffin, 2014.

———. *Louisa May Alcott: Her Life, Letters, and Journals*. Edited by Ednah D. Cheney. Roberts Brothers, 1890.

"*Aloft* from Chang-rae Lee." *NPR*, www.npr.org/templates/story/story.php?storyId=1841682, 18 April 2004.

Ardis, Ann. "Hellenism and the Lure of Italy." *The Cambridge Companion to E. M. Forster*. Cambridge UP, 2007, pp. 62–76.

Armengol, Josep M. "In the Dark Room: Homosexuality and/as Blackness in James Baldwin's Giovanni's Room." *Signs: Journal of Women in Culture and Society*, vol. 37, no. 3, 2012, pp. 671–93.

Arthurs, Joshua. *Excavating Modernity: The Roman Past in Fascist Italy*. Cornell UP, 2012.

Baily, Samuel L. *Immigrants in the Lands of Promise: Italians in Buenos Aires and New York City, 1870–1914*. Cornell UP, 1999.

Balderrama, Francisco E., and Raymond Rodríguez. *Decade of Betrayal: Mexican Repatriation in the 1930s*. U of New Mexico P, 2006.

Baldwin, James. *Another Country*. 1960. Vintage, 1993.

———. *Giovanni's Room: A Novel*. Delta Trade Paperbacks, 1956.

———. *Go Tell It on the Mountain*. 1953. Vintage, 2013.

———. *Notes of a Native Son*. 1955. Beacon Press, 2012.

———. "On Being White . . . and Other Lies." *Black on White: Black Writers on What It Means to Be White*, edited by David R. Roediger. Schocken, 1998.

Barolini, Helen, editor. Introduction. *The Dream Book: An Anthology of Writing by Italian American Women*, Syracuse UP, 1985.
Barone, Dennis. *Beyond Memory: Italian Protestants in Italy and America*. SUNY P, 2016.
Bartoletti, Susan Campbell. *Black Potatoes: The Story of the Great Irish Famine, 1845–1850*. Houghton Mifflin, 2001.
Beck, Bernard. "White Natives: Braveheart and Rob Roy as Colonial Victims." *Multicultural Education*, vol. 3, no. 1, 1995, pp. 31–33.
Bellow, Saul. *Seize the Day*. Penguin, 2003.
Belluck, Pam. "Being of Two Cultures and Belonging to Neither: After an Acclaimed Novel, a Korean-American Writer Searches for His Roots." *New York Times*, www.nytimes.com/1995/07/10/nyregion/being-two-cultures-belonging-neither-after-acclaimed-novel-korean-american.html, 10 July 1995.
Benshoff, Harry M. "Reception of a Queer Mainstream Film." *New Queer Cinema: A Critical Reader*, edited by Michele Aaron, Rutgers UP, 2004.
Berman, Jessica. *Modernist Commitments: Ethics, Politics, and Transnational Modernism*. Columbia UP, 2011.
Berry, Faith. *Langston Hughes: Before and Beyond Harlem*. Citadel, 1983.
Blackburn, William. "'Moral Pap for the Young'?: A New Look at Louisa May Alcott's *Little Men*." *Children's Literature Association Quarterly*, 1980 Proceedings, pp. 98–106.
Bona, Mary Jo. "Broken Images, Broken Lives: Carmolina's Journey in Tina De Rosa's *Paper Fish*." *MELUS: Multi-Ethnic Literature of the United States*, vol. 14, no. 3–4, 1987, pp. 87–106.
———. *By the Breath of Their Mouths: Narratives of Resistance in Italian America*. SUNY P, 2010.
Boyce Davies, Carole. *Black Women, Writing and Identity: Migrations of the Subject*. Routledge, 1994.
Bourdieu, Pierre. *Acts of Resistance: Against the Tyranny of the Market*. New Press, 1998.
Brim, Matt. "After Queer Baldwin." *After Queer Studies: Literature, Theory, and Sexuality in the 21st Century*, edited by Tyler Bradway and E. L. McCallum. Cambridge UP, 2019.
Broder, Sherri. *Tramps, Unfit Mothers, and Neglected Children: Negotiating the Family in Late Nineteenth-Century Philadelphia*. U of Pennsylvania P, 2002.
Brodhead, Richard H. "Strangers on a Train: The Double Dram of Italy in the American Gilded Age." *Modernism/modernity*, vol. 1, no. 2, 1994, pp. 1–19.
Bronte, Charlotte. *Jane Eyre*. 1847. Penguin, 2006.
Brooks, Ethel C. "The Possibilities of Romani Feminism." *Signs*, vol. 38, no. 1, 2012, pp. 1–11.
Buchen, Irving H. "Malamud's Italian Progress: Art and Bisexuality." *Modern Language Studies*, vol. 20, no. 2, 1990, pp. 64–78.

Candeloro, Dominic L. "What Luigi Basco Taught America about Italian Americans." *Anti-Italianism: Essays on a Prejudice*, edited by William J. Connell and Fred Gardaphé. Palgrave Macmillan, 2010.
Carpignano, Jonas, director. *A Ciambra*. Academy Two, 2017.
Casillo, Robert. *Gangster Priest: The Italian American Cinema of Martin Scorsese*. U of Toronto P, 2006.
Chbosky, Stephen. *The Perks of Being a Wallflower*. Gallery Books, 1999.
Cheever, Susan. *Louisa May Alcott: A Personal Biography*. Simon & Schuster, 2010.
Chesnutt, Charles W. *The House Behind the Cedars*. 1900. Penguin, 1993.
Choi, Inbom. "Korean Diaspora in the Making: Its Current Status and Impact on the Korean Economy." *The Korean Diaspora in the World Economy: Special Report 15*, edited by C. Fred Bergsten and Inbom Choi, Peterson Institute for International Economics, pp. 9-29.
Cinotto, Simone, editor. Introduction. *Making Italian America: Consumer Culture and the Production of Ethnic Identities*. Fordham UP, 2014.
Clark, Gregory. *The Son Also Rises: Surnames and the History of Social Mobility*. Princeton UP, 2014.
Clark, Martin. *Modern Italy: 1871 to the Present*. 1984. Routledge, 2014.
Clements, Paul. *Charles Bukowski, Outsider Literature, and the Beat Movement*. Routledge, 2013.
Clifford, James. "Diasporas." *Cultural Anthropology*, vol. 9, no. 3, 1994, pp. 302-38.
Collins, Richard. *John Fante: A Literary Portrait*. Guernica, 2000.
Connell, R. W., and James W. Messerschmidt. "Hegemonic Masculinity: Rethinking the Concept." *Gender and Society*, vol. 19, no. 6, 2005, pp. 829-59.
Cooper, Stephen. *Full of Life: A Biography of John Fante*. North Point, 2000.
Cooper, Stephen, and David Fine, editors. *John Fante: A Critical Gathering*. Fairleigh Dickinson UP, 1999.
Cosco, Joseph P. *Imagining Italians: The Clash of Romance and Race in American Perceptions, 1880–1910*. SUNY P, 2003.
Cowart, David. *Don DeLillo: The Physics of Language*. U of Georgia P, 2003.
———. *Trailing Clouds: Immigrant Fiction in Contemporary America*. Cornell UP, 2006.
Crenshaw, Kimberlé. "Demarginalizing the Intersection of Race and Sex: A Black Feminist Critique of Antidiscrimination Doctrine, Feminist Theory, and Antiracist Politics." *University of Chicago Legal Forum* 1989, pp. 139–67.
Cutter, Martha J. *Lost and Found in Translation: Contemporary Ethnic American Writing and the Politics of Language Diversity*. U of North Carolina P, 2005.
D'Agostino, Peter R. *Rome in America: Transnational Catholic Ideology from the Risorgimento to Fascism*. U of North Carolina P, 2004.
———. "'Utterly Faithless Specimens': Italians in the Catholic Church in America." *Anti-Italianism: Essays on a Prejudice*, edited by William J. Connell and Fred Gardaphé, Palgrave Macmillan, 2010.

Degout, Yasmin Y. "Dividing the Mind: Contradictory Portraits of Homoerotic Love in *Giovanni's Room*." *African American Review*, vol. 26, no. 3, 1992, pp. 425–35.

Délano, Alexandra. *Mexico and Its Diaspora in the United States: Policies of Emigration Since 1848*. Cambridge UP, 2011.

DeLillo, Don. *White Noise*. Penguin, 1985.

De Robertis, Carolina. *The Gods of Tango*. Vintage Books, 2016.

———. "Uruguay, Little Trailblazer That Could." *Huffington Post*, https://www.huffpost.com/entry/uruguay-little-trailblazer-that-could_b_4490748, 22 Dec. 2013.

De Rosa, Tina. *Paper Fish*. 1980. The Feminist Press, 2003.

Dick, Bruce. Interview with Luis Rodríguez. *A Poet's Truth: Conversations with Latino/Latina Poets*. U of A P, 2003.

Di Donato, Pietro. *Christ in Concrete*. 1939. Signet, 1993.

Dobie, Madeleine. *Foreign Bodies: Gender, Language, and Culture in French Orientalism*. Stanford UP, 2001.

Dottolo, Andrea L., and Carol Dottolo. *Italian American Women, Food, and Identity: Stories at the Table*. Palgrave Macmillan, 2018.

Dreiser, Theodore. *Sister Carrie*. 1900. Penguin, 1994.

Ehrenreich, Barbara, and Arlie Russell Hochschild. *Global Woman: Nannies, Maids, and Sex Workers in the New Economy*. Henry Holt, 2002.

Elgrably, Jordan, and George Plimpton. "The Art of Fiction LXXVIII: James Baldwin." *The Paris Review*, vol. 26, 1984, pp. 49–82.

Ellerby, Janet Mason. *Embroidering the Scarlet A: Unwed Mothers and Illegitimate Children in American Fiction and Film*. U of Michigan P, 2015.

Elliott, Matthew. "John Fante's *Ask the Dust* and Fictions of Whiteness." *Twentieth Century Literature*, vol. 56, no. 4, 2010, pp. 530–44.

Elsden, Annamaria Formichella. *Roman Fever: Domesticity and Nationalism in Nineteenth Century American Women's Writing*. Ohio State UP, 2004.

Engles, Tim. "Who Are You, Really? Fantasies of the White Self in *White Noise*." *Modern Fiction Studies*, vol. 45, no. 3, 1999, pp. 755–87.

Ennis, José Antonio. "Italian-Spanish Contact in Early 20th Century Argentina." *Journal of Language Contact*, vol. 8, no. 1, 2015.

Fante, John. *Ask the Dust*. 1939. New York: Harper Perennial, 1980.

———. Letter to Jo Campiglia. 29 Nov. 1938. "P.S," *Ask the Dust*, 1939, Harper, 1980.

———. *Prologue to* Ask the Dust. Black Sparrow, 1990.

———. *The Road to Los Angeles*. 1985. Ecco, 2002.

———. *Selected Letters 1932–1981*. Edited by Seamus Cooney, Harper Collins, 2010.

Fermaglich, Kirsten. *American Dreams and Nazi Nightmares: Early Holocaust Consciousness and Liberal America, 1957–1965*. Brandeis UP, 2006.

Ferraro, Thomas J. *Feeling Italian: The Art of Ethnicity in America.* New York UP, 2005.

———. "'My Way' in 'Our America': Art, Ethnicity, Profession." *American Literary History*, vol. 12, no. 3, 2000, pp. 499–522.

Forster, E. M. *Maurice.* 1971. Norton, 2005.

———. *A Room with a View.* 1908. Barnes and Noble, 2005.

———. "The Story of a Panic." *The Machine Stops and Other Stories*, edited by Rod Mengham. Edward Arnold, 1977.

———. *Where Angels Fear to Tread.* 1905. Barnes and Noble, 2006.

Fortier, Anne-Marie. "Queer Diaspora." *Handbook of Lesbian and Gay Studies*, edited by Diane Richardson and Steven Seidman, Sage, 2002, pp. 183–98.

Freedman, Estelle B. *No Turning Back: The History of Feminism and the Future of Women.* Ballantine, 2002.

Fried, Rebecca A. "No Irish Need Deny: Evidence for the Historicity of NINA Restrictions in Advertisements and Signs." *Journal of Social History*, vol. 49, no. 4, 2016, pp. 829–54.

Gabaccia, Donna. *Italy's Many Diasporas.* U of Washington P, 2000.

———. "Race, Nation, Hyphen: Italian-Americans and American Multiculturalism in Comparative Perspective." *Are Italians White?: How Race Is Made in America*, edited by Jennifer Guglielmo and Salvatore Salerno. Routledge, 2003, pp. 44–59.

Gallo, Patrick J. *Ethnic Alienation: The Italian Americans.* Fairleigh Dickinson UP, 1974.

Gardaphé, Fred L. "Italian American Masculinities." *The Routledge History of Italian Americans.* Routledge, 2018.

———. *Italian Signs, American Streets: The Evolution of Italian American Narrative.* Duke UP, 1996.

———. *Leaving Little Italy: Essaying Italian American Culture.* SUNY P, 2003.

———. "Mafia Stories and the American Gangster." *The Cambridge Companion to American Crime Fiction*, edited by Catherine Ross Nickerson. Cambridge UP, 2010.

Giunta, Edvige. Afterword. *Paper Fish.* By Tina De Rosa. 1980. The Feminist Press, 2003.

———. "A Song from the Ghetto." *Beyond* The Godfather: *Italian American Writers on the Real Italian American Experience*, edited by A. Kenneth Ciongoli and Jay Parini. UP of New England, 1997.

Goldberg, Jonathan. *Melodrama: An Aesthetics of Impossibility.* Duke UP, 2016.

Goldstone, Claire. *The Struggle for America's Promise: Equal Opportunity at the Dawn of Corporate Capital.* UP of Mississippi, 2014.

Gonzalez, Gilbert G., and Raul A. Fernandez. *A Century of Chicano History: Empire, Nations, and Migration.* Routledge, 2003.

Goodlad, Lauren M. E. "Where Liberals Fear to Tread: E. M. Forster's Queer Internationalism and the Ethics of Care." *NOVEL: A Forum on Fiction*, vol. 39, no. 3, 2006, pp. 307–36.

Gordon, Andrew. "When in Rome: Philip Roth's *Portnoy's Complaint* and Bernard Malamud's *Pictures of Fidelman*." *Philip Roth Studies*, vol. 4, no. 1, 2008, pp. 39–46.

Goscilo, Margaret. "Forster's Italian Comedies: Que[e]rying Heterosexuality Abroad." *Seeing Double: Revisioning Edwardian and Modernist Literature*. St. Martin's, 1996, pp. 193–214.

Grasso, Linda. "Louisa May Alcott's 'Magic Inkstand': Little Women, Feminism, and the Myth of Regeneration." *Frontiers: A Journal of Women Studies*, vol. 19, no. 1, 1998, pp. 177–92.

Greven, David. "Queer Ripley: Minghella, Highsmith, and the Antisocial." *Patricia Highsmith on Screen*, edited by Wieland Schwanebeck and Douglas McFarland. Palgrave Macmillan, 2018.

Guglielmo, Jennifer. "Introduction: White Lies, Dark Truths." *Are Italians White?: How Race Is Made in America*, edited by Jennifer Guglielmo and Salvatore Salerno. Routledge, 2003, pp. 1–14.

Guglielmo, Jennifer, and Salvatore Salerno. *Are Italians White?: How Race Is Made in America*. Routledge, 2003.

Guglielmo, Thomas A. "'No Color Barrier': Italians, Race, and Power in the United States." *Are Italians White?: How Race Is Made in America*, edited by Jennifer Guglielmo and Salvatore Salerno. Routledge, 2003, pp. 29–43.

Guida, George. "In Imagination of the Past: John Fante's *Ask the Dust* as Italian American Modernism." *John Fante: A Critical Gathering*, edited by Stephen Cooper and David Fine. Fairleigh Dickinson UP, 1999, pp. 131–44.

Hall, Donald. *Queer Theories*. New York: Palgrave Macmillan, 2003.

Hall, Stuart. "Cultural Identity and Diaspora." *Identity: Community, Culture, Difference*, edited by Jonathan Rutherford. Lawrence & Wishart, 1990.

Halse Anderson, Laurie. *Speak*. Farrar, Straus and Giroux, 1999.

Hamilton Buckley, Jerome. *Season of Youth: The Bildungsroman from Dickens to Golding*. Harvard UP, 1974.

Hankinson Nelson, Lynne. *Biology and Feminism: A Philosophical Introduction*. Cambridge UP, 2017.

Haralson, Eric. *Henry James and Queer Morality*. Cambridge UP: 2003.

———. "'Thinking about Homosex' in Forster and James." *Queer Forster*, edited by Robert K. Martin and George Piggford. U of Chicago P, 1997, pp. 59–73.

Harrison, Russell. *Against the American Dream: Essays on Charles Bukowski*. Black Sparrow Press, 1994.

Hawthorne, Nathaniel. *The Marble Faun*. 1860. Penguin, 1990.

Henderson, Mae G. "James Baldwin's *Giovanni's Room*: Expatriation, 'Racial Drag,' and Homosexual Panic." *Black Queer Studies: A Critical Anthology*, edited by E. Patrick Johnson and Mae G. Henderson. Duke UP, 2005, pp. 298–322.

Hicks, Granville. "Tormented Triangle." *The New York Times*. 14 Oct. 1956.
Highsmith, Patricia. *The Talented Mr. Ripley*.1955. Norton, 2008.
———. *The Price of Salt*. 1952. Norton, 2004.
Higley, Stephen Richard. *Privilege, Power, and Place: The Geography of the American Upper Class*. Rowman and Littlefield, 1995.
Himes, Chester. *If He Hollers Let Him Go*. 1945. Thunder's Mouth Press, 2002.
Hinojosa, Lynne Walhout. "Religion and Puritan Typology in E. M. Forster's *A Room with a View*." *Journal of Modern Literature*, vol. 33, no. 4, 2010, pp. 72–94.
Hoffman, Beatrix. *Health Care for Some: Rights and Rationing in the United States since 1930*. U of Chicago P, 2012.
Hollinger, David A. *After Cloven Tongues of Fire: Protestant Liberalism in Modern American History*. Princeton UP, 2013.
Horne, Philip. "Henry James at Work." *The Cambridge Companion to Henry James*, edited by Jonathan Freedman, Cambridge UP, 1998.
Horsley, Katharine, and Lee Horsley. "Learning Italian: Serial Killers Abroad in the Novels of Highsmith and Harris." *Differences, Deceits and Desires: Murder and Mayhem in Italian Crime Fiction*, edited by Mirna Cicioni and Nicoletta Di Ciolla. U of Delaware P, 2008, pp. 191–205.
Human Rights Watch. *Everyday Intolerance: Racist and Xenophobic Violence in Italy*. 2011.
Ibsen, Henrik. *A Doll's House*. 1879. *A Doll's House and Other Plays*, Penguin, 2016.
Ickes, William. *Everyday Mind-Reading*. Prometheus Books, 2003.
Indigenous Action Media. *Accomplices Not Allies: Abolishing the Ally Industrial Complex*. www.indigenousaction.org/accomplices-not-allies-abolishing-the-ally-industrial-complex/, 4 May 2014.
Jacobsen, Douglas. *The World's Christians: Who They Are, Where They Are, and How They Got There*. Wiley-Blackwell, 2011.
Jacobson, Matthew Frye. *Whiteness of a Different Color: European Immigrants and the Alchemy of Race*. Harvard UP, 1999.
James, Henry. *The Ambassadors*. 1903. Barnes and Noble, 2007.
———. "Americans Abroad." *Collected Travel Writings: Great Britain and America*. Library of America, 1993.
———. *Daisy Miller*. 1878. *Daisy Miller and Other Stories*. Oxford World's Classics, 2009.
———. *Henry James Letters: 1875–1883*. Harvard UP, 1975.
———. *Roderick Hudson*. 1875. Penguin, 1986.
James, Nick. "My Bloody Valentine." *Anthony Minghella: Interviews*, edited by Mario Falsetto, UP of Mississippi, 2013.
Jayaraman, Saru. *Forked: A New Standard for American Dining*, Oxford UP, 2016.
Jarrett, Gene Andrew. *African American Literature Beyond Race: An Alternative Reader*, New York UP, 2006.

Jenkins, Mark. "In Gritty 'A Ciambra,' A Romani Teen Must Choose: His Friend, or His Community?" *NPR*, https://www.npr.org/2018/01/25/579711983/in-gritty-a-ciambra-a-romani-teen-must-choose-his-friend-or-his-community, 25 Jan. 2018.

Jensen, Richard. "No Irish Need Apply: A Myth of Victimization." *Journal of Social History*, vol. 36, no. 2, 2002, pp. 405–29.

Jerng, Mark C. "Nowhere in Particular: Perceiving Race, Chang-rae Lee's *Aloft*, and the Question of Asian American Fiction." *Modern Fiction Studies*, vol. 56, no. 1, 2010, pp. 183–204.

Johnson, Lisa. "Daisy Miller: Cowboy Feminist." *Henry James Review*, vol. 22, no. 1, 2001, pp. 41–58.

———. "'If this is improper . . . then I am all improper, and you must give me up': Daisy Miller and Other Uppity White Women as Resistant Emblems of America." *Women as Sites of Culture: Women's Roles in Cultural Formation from the Renaissance to the Twentieth Century*, edited by Susan Shifrin, Routledge, 2017.

Johnson-Roullier, Cyraina E. "(An)Other Modernism: James Baldwin, Giovanni's Room, and the Rhetoric of Flight." *Modern Fiction Studies*, vol. 45, no. 4, 1999, pp. 932–56.

"Jhumpa Lahiri: By the Book." *New York Times*, 8 Sept. 2013, p. BR8.

Kane, Gregory. "Ethnic Jabs Leave the Jabber with a Bad Bruise." *Baltimore Sun*, www.baltimoresun.com/news/bs-xpm-2006-01-25-0601250074-story.html, 25 Jan. 2006.

Katz, Brigit. "New Orleans Apologizes for 1891 Lynching of Italian-Americans." *Smithsonian Magazine*, www.smithsonianmag.com/smart-news/new-orleans-apologizes-1891-lynching-italian-americans-180971959/, 15 Apr. 2019.

Keith, Thomas. *Masculinities in Contemporary American Culture: An Intersectional Approach to the Complexities and Challenges of Male Identity*. Routledge, 2017.

Kelly, Hillary. "We Regret to Inform You That *Little Women* Is Not a Feminist Novel." *Vulture*, www.vulture.com/2018/09/were-sorry-to-say-that-little-women-is-not-a-feminist-novel.html, 28 Sept. 2018.

Kertzer, David I. Foreword. *The Italian Executioners: The Genocide of the Jews of Italy*, by Simon Levis Sullam. Princeton UP, 2018.

Knapp, Kathy. "The Business of Forgetting: Postwar Living Memorials and the Post-Traumatic Suburb in Chang-rae Lee's *Aloft*." *Twentieth-Century Literature*, vol. 59, no. 2, 2013, pp. 196–231.

Kordich, Catherine J. "John Fante's *Ask the Dust*: A Border Reading." *MELUS: Multi-Ethnic Literature of the United States*, vol. 20, no. 4, 1995, pp. 17–27.

LaGumina, Salvatore J. "Discrimination, Prejudice and Italian American History." *The Routledge History of Italian Americans*, edited by William J. Connell and Stanislao G. Pugliese. Routledge, 2018.

Lamont, Amélie. *Guide to Allyship*. www.guidetoallyship.com/, 12 May 2019.

Larsen, Nella. *Passing.* 1929. Penguin, 1997.
Laurila, Mark. "The Los Angeles Booster Myth, the Anti-Myth, and John Fante's *Ask the Dust.*" *John Fante: A Critical Gathering*, edited by Stephen Cooper and David Fine. Fairleigh Dickinson UP, 1999, pp. 112-30.
Lawrence, D. H. *Aaron's Rod.* 1922. Penguin, 1996.
———. *Twilight in Italy.* 1916. Viking, 1958.
Lee, Hermione. *Edith Wharton.* Vintage Books, 2008.
Lee, A. Robert. *Multicultural American Literature: Comparative Black, Native, Latino/a and Asian American Fictions.* UP of Mississippi, 2003.
Lee, Chang-rae. *Aloft.* Riverhead Books, 2004.
Lee, Daniel Youngwon. "A Conversation with Chang-rae Lee." *Asian American Policy Review*, www.aapr.hkspublications.org/2015/11/17/a-conversation-with-chang-rae/, 17 Nov. 2015.
Lee, James Kyung-Jin. *Urban Triage: Race and the Fictions of Multiculturalism.* U of Minnesota P, 2004.
Le Guin, Ursula. "*On Such a Full Sea* by Chang-rae Lee: Review." *The Guardian*, www.theguardian.com/books/2014/jan/30/on-such-full-sea-chang-rae-lee-review, 30 Jan. 2014.
Leeming, David. *James Baldwin: A Biography.* 1994. New York: Arcade, 2015.
Lemon, Alaina. *Between Two Fires: Gypsy Performance and Romani Memory from Pushkin to Post-Socialism.* Duke UP, 2000.
Lentricchia, Frank, ed. Introduction. *New Essays on* White Noise. Cambridge UP, 1991, 1-14.
Li, Stephanie. *Playing in the White: Black Writers, White Subjects.* Oxford UP, 2015.
Luconi, Stefano. "Italian Immigrants' Political Adjustment in the Americas: The Case of the United States and Argentina." *IdeAs: Idées d'Amériques*, www.journals.openedition.org/ideas/1259.
Mandelker, Ira L. *Religion, Society, and Utopia in Nineteenth-Century America.* U of Massachusetts P, 1984.
Malamud, Bernard. *The Assistant.* 1957. Farrar, Straus & Giroux, 2003.
———. *Pictures of Fidelman.* Farrar, Straus & Giroux, 1969.
Malouf, Michael. *Transatlantic Solidarities: Irish Nationalism and Caribbean Poetics.* U of Virginia P, 2009.
Maril, Robert. "Breaking: The Airborne Toxic Event." *Rolling Stone*, www.rollingstone.com/music/music-news/breaking-the-airborne-toxic-event-2-100189/, 8 Apr. 2009.
Martin, Robert K. "'It Must Have Been the Umbrella': Forster's Queer Begetting." *Queer Forster*, edited by Robert K. Martin and George Piggford. U of Chicago P, 1997, pp. 255-273.
Martínez, Elizabeth. *De Colores Means All of Us: Latina Views for a Multi-Colored Century.* South End, 1998.

May, Jill P. "Feminism and Children's Literature: Fitting 'Little Women' into the American Literary Canon." *CEA Critic*, vol. 56, no. 3, 1994, pp. 19-27.
Mayall, David. *Gypsy-Travellers in Nineteenth-Century Society*. Cambridge UP, 1988.
McWilliams, Carey. *Factories in the Field: The Story of Migratory Farm Labor in California*. 1935. U of California P, 1999.
Messenger, Chris. The *Godfather and American Culture: How the Corleones Became "Our Gang."* SUNY P, 2002.
Meyer, Lisa A. "Breaking the Silence: An Interview with Tina De Rosa." *American Woman, Italian Style: Italian Americana's Best Writings on Women*, edited by Carol Bonomo Albright and Christine Palamidessi Moore. Fordham UP, 2011.
———. "She's Making Sense of a New Life." *Los Angeles Times*, www.latimes.com/archives/la-xpm-1997-03-27-ls-42419-story.html, 27 Mar. 1997.
Meyers, Jeffrey. *Homosexuality and Literature, 1890–1930*. Queens UP, 1977.
Miller, Arthur. *Death of a Salesman*. 1949. Penguin, 1976.
Millward, Dodd, et al. *Killing Off the Lesbians: A Symbolic Annihilation on Film and Television*. McFarland, 2017.
Minghella, Anthony. "Italy: The Director's Cut." *Anthony Minghella: Interviews*, edited by Mario Falsetto. UP of Mississippi, 2013.
Mitchell, Don. *They Saved the Crops: Labor, Landscape, and the Struggle over Industrial Farming in Bracero-Era California*. U of Georgia P, 2012.
Morikawa, Suzuko. "Dynamics, Intricacy, and Multiplicity of Romani Identity in the United States." *Emerging Voices: Experiences of Underrepresented Asian Americans*, edited by Huping Ling., Rutgers UP, 2008.
Mossman, James. "Race, Hate, Sex, and Color: A Conversation with James Baldwin and Colin Macinnes." 1965. *Conversations with James Baldwin*, edited by Fred L. Standley and Louis H. Pratt. UP of Mississippi, 1989.
Muscio, Giuliana, and Joseph Sciorra, et al. *Mediated Ethnicity: New Italian-American Cinema*. Calandra Italian American Institute, 2010.
Musel-Gilley, Oné. "Author Interview: Carolina De Robertis." *Las Comadres*, www.lascomadres.com/latinolit/author-interview-carolina-de-robertis/, 21 Dec. 2012.
Myers, Tony. *Slavoj Žižek*. Routledge, 2003.
Oliver-Rotger, Maria Antònia, editor. Introduction. *Identity, Diaspora and Return in American Literature*. Routledge, 2015.
Orsi, Robert Anthony. *The Madonna of 115th Street: Faith and Community in Italian Harlem, 1880–1950*. 1985. Yale UP, 2010.
Ortego, Philip D. "Fables of Identity: Stereotype and Caricature of Chicanos in Steinbeck's *Tortilla Flat*." *Journal of Ethnic Studies*, vol. 1, 1973, pp. 39-43.
P., Naomi. "The 'G' Word Isn't for You: How 'Gypsy' Erases Romani Women." *National Organization for Women*, www.now.org/blog/the-g-word-isnt-for-you-how-gypsy-erases-romani-women/, 2 Oct. 2017.

Padurano, Dominique. "Consuming *La Bella Figura*: Charles Atlas and American Masculinity, 1910-1940." *Making Italian America: Consumer Culture and the Production of Ethnic Identities*, edited by Simone Cinotto, Fordham UP, 2014.
Pahl, Dennis. "'Going Down' with Henry James's Uptown Girl: Genteel Anxiety and the Promiscuous World of *Daisy Miller*." *LIT: Literature, Interpretation, Theory*, vol. 12, 2001, pp. 129-64.
Painter, Nell Irvin. *The History of White People*. Norton, 2010.
Pardini, Samuele F. S. *In the Name of the Mother: Italian Americans, African Americans, and Modernity from Booker T. Washington to Bruce Springsteen*. Dartmouth College Press, 2017.
Pepper, Andrew. "Postwar American Noir: Confronting Fordism." *Crime Culture: Figuring Criminality in Fiction and Film*, edited by Bran Nicol, Eugene McNulty, and Patricia Pulham. Continuum, 2011.
Perkins Gilman, Charlotte. "The Yellow Wall-Paper." 1892. *The Yellow Wall-Paper and Other Stories*. Oxford UP, 2009.
Phillips, Caryl. *A New World Order: Essays*. Vintage, 2009.
Pifer, Ellen. *Saul Bellow Against the Grain*. U of Pennsylvania P, 1990.
Puzo, Mario. *The Fortunate Pilgrim*. 1964. Ballantine, 1997.
———. *The Godfather*. 1969. Signet, 1978.
Quan, Kenneth. Interview with Chang-rae Lee. *Asia Pacific Arts*, www.asiapacificarts. usc.edu/article@apa-chang-rae_lee_voice_for_a_new_identity_9233.aspx.html, 12 Apr. 2004.
Rampersad, Arnold. *The Life of Langston Hughes, Volume II: 1941-1967, I Dream a World*. Oxford UP, 2002.
Renouard, Anne-Cécile. "Constructing a Roma Cause in Contemporary Finland and Italy: The Social and Cultural Significance of Roma and Pro-Roma Mobilizations." *From Silence to Protest: International Perspectives on Weakly Resourced Groups*, edited by Didier Chabanet and Frédéric Royall. Routledge, 2016.
Roediger, David R. *Black on White: Black Writers on What It Means to Be White*. Schocken, 1998.
———. *Working Toward Whiteness: How America's Immigrants Became White—The Strange Journey from Ellis Island to the Suburbs*. Basic Books, 2005.
Rohy, Valerie. "Displacing Desire: Passing, Nostalgia, and *Giovanni's Room*." *Passing and the Fictions of Identity*, edited by Elaine K. Ginsberg. Duke UP, 1996, pp. 218-33.
Rossi, Ernest E. "Italians and Mexicans: A Comparison." *Italian Americans: Bridges to Italy, Bonds to America*, edited by Luciano J. Iorizzo and Ernest E. Rossi. Teneo Press, 2010.
Rossini, Daniela. *Woodrow Wilson and the American Myth in Italy: Culture, Diplomacy, and War Propaganda*, translated by Anthony Shugaar. Harvard UP, 2008.

Roszak, Suzanne. "Conformist Culture and the Failures of Empathy: Reading James Baldwin and Patricia Highsmith." *Rethinking Empathy through Literature*, edited by Meghan Marie Hammond and Sue J. Kim. Routledge, 2014.

———. "Social Non-Conformists in Forster's Italy: Otherness and the Enlightened English Tourist." *ARIEL: A Review of International English Literature*, vol. 45, no. 1-2, 2014, pp. 167-94.

Roth, Philip. *Portnoy's Complaint*. 1969. Vintage, 1994.

Rowe, John Carlos. *Literary Culture and U.S. Imperialism: From the Revolution to World War II*. Oxford UP, 2000.

Ryan, Melissa. "At Home in America: John Fante and the Imaginative American Self." *Studies in American Fiction*, vol. 32, no. 2, 2004, pp. 185-212.

Safran, William. "Diasporas in Modern Societies: Myths of Homeland and Return." *Diaspora: A Journal of Transnational Studies*, vol. 1, no. 1, 1991, pp. 83-99.

Saito, Stephen. "Interview: Jonas Carpignano on Capturing Life in 'A Ciambra.'" *The Moveable Fest*, http://moveablefest.com/jonas-carpignano-a-ciambra/, 1 Feb. 2018.

Saldívar, José David. *Border Matters: Remapping American Cultural Studies*. U of California P, 1997.

Salerno, Salvatore. "*I Delitti della Razza Bianca* (Crimes of the White Race): Italian Anarchists' Racial Discourse as Crime." *Are Italians White?: How Race Is Made in America*, edited by Jennifer Guglielmo and Salvatore Salerno. Routledge, 2003, pp. 111-23.

Salter, Michael. "The Problem with a Fight against Toxic Masculinity." *The Atlantic*, www.theatlantic.com/health/archive/2019/02/toxic-masculinity-history/583411/, 27 Feb. 2019.

Sánchez Cámara, Florencio. *El notata y las mujeres mágicas*. Editorial Joaquín Mortiz, 1980.

Scambray, Kenneth. *The North American Italian Renaissance: Italian Writing in America and Canada*. Guernica, 2000.

Schenkar, Joan. *The Talented Miss Highsmith: The Secret Life and Serious Art of Patricia Highsmith*. St. Martin's Press, 2009.

Schiel, Natassja. "A Conversation with Carolina De Robertis on Immigration, Sexuality, and the True Origins of the Tango." *Los Angeles Review of Books*, www.lareviewofbooks.org/article/conversation-carolina-de-robertis-immigration-sexuality-true-origins-tango/, 20 Apr. 2016.

Schimel, Lawrence. "Diaspora, Sweet Diaspora: Queer Culture in Post-Zionist Jewish Identity." *PoMoSexuals: Challenging Assumptions about Gender and Sexuality*, edited by Carol Queen and Lawrence Schimel. Cleiss Press, pp. 163-73.

Scorsese, Martin. *Gangs of New York*. Miramax, 2002.

Scruggs, Charles. "'Oh for a Mexican Girl!': The Limits of Literature in John Fante's *Ask the Dust*." *Western American Literature*, vol. 38, no. 3, 2003, pp. 228-45.

SLJ's Top 100 Must-Have YA Books. School Library Journal, 2017.
Sohn, Stephen Hong. *Racial Asymmetries: Asian American Fictional Worlds*. NYU P, 2014.
Solnit, Rebecca. "Men Explain Things to Me." 2008. *Guernica*, www.guernicamag.com/rebecca-solnit-men-explain-things-to-me/20 Aug. 2012.
Spinelli, Alexian Santino. "Son of the Wind." *The Roads of the Roma: A PEN Anthology of Gypsy Writers*, edited by Siobhan Dowd, Ian Hancock, and Rajko Djurić. U of Hertfordshire P, 2004.
Squires, Michael, and Lynn K. Talbot. *Living at the Edge: a Biography of D. H. Lawrence and Frieda Von Richthofen*. U of Wisconsin P, 2002.
Starr, Kevin. *Endangered Dreams: The Great Depression in California*. Oxford UP, 1996.
Steinbeck, John. *Tortilla Flat*. 1935. Penguin, 1977.
Stiles, Anne. "Go Rest, Young Man." *Monitor on Psychology*, vol. 43, no. 1, 2012.
Sullam, Simon Levis. *The Italian Executioners: The Genocide of the Jews of Italy*. Princeton UP, 2018.
Susina, Jan. "Men and *Little Women*: Notes of a (Resisting) Male Reader." *Little Women and the Feminist Imagination: Criticism, Controversy, Personal Essays*, edited by Janice M. Alberghene and Beverly Lyon Clark. Routledge, 2013.
Sutherland, Anne. *Gypsies: The Hidden Americans*. Waveland Press, 1975.
Tamburri, Anthony Julian, Paolo A. Giordano, and Fred L. Gardaphé, editors. Introduction. *From the Margin: Writings in Italian Americana*. Purdue UP, 2000.
Theroux, Alexander. "The Misfit and Her Muses." *Wall Street Journal*, Dec. 8, 2009, p. A19.
Tirabassi, Maddalena. "Making Space for Domesticity: Household Goods in Working-Class Italian Homes, 1900-1940." *Making Italian America: Consumer Culture and the Production of Ethnic Identities*, edited by Simone Cinotto. Fordham UP, 2014.
Tompkins, Kyla Wazana. *Racial Indigestion: Eating Bodies in the Nineteenth Century*. NYU P, 2012.
Tracey, Janey. "The Conflicted Feminism of *Little Women*." *The Ploughshares Blog*, www.blog.pshares.org/index.php/the-conflicted-feminism-of-little-women/27, May 2018.
Trask, Michael. *Cruising Modernism: Class and Sexuality in American Literature and Social Thought*. Cornell UP, 2003.
———. "Patricia Highsmith's Method." *American Literary History*, vol. 22, no. 3, 2010, pp. 584-614.
Tricarico, Donald. *Guido Culture and Italian American Youth: From Bensonhurst to Jersey Shore*. Palgrave Macmillan, 2019.
Vance, William L. "Edith Wharton's Italian Mask: *The Valley of Decision*." *The Cambridge Companion to Edith Wharton*, edited by Millicent Bell. Cambridge UP, 1995.

Veblen, Thorstein. *The Theory of the Leisure Class: An Economic Study of Institutions.* 1899. Macmillan, 1912.

Vecoli, Rudolph J. "The Italian Diaspora, 1876–1976." *The Cambridge Survey of World Migration,* edited by Robin Cohen, Cambridge UP, 1995.

Verdicchio, Pasquale. *Devils in Paradise: Writings on Post-Emigrant Cultures.* Guernica, 1997.

Washington, Bryan R. *The Politics of Exile: Ideology in Henry James, F. Scott Fitzgerald, and James Baldwin.* Northeastern UP, 1995.

Webb, Clive. "The Lynching of Sicilian Immigrants in the American South, 1880–1910." *Lynching Reconsidered: New Perspectives in the Study of Mob Violence.* Routledge, 2014.

Wegelin, Christof. "The American Schlemiel Abroad: Malamud's Italian Stories and the End of American Innocence." *Twentieth Century Literature,* vol. 19, no. 2, 1973, pp. 77–88.

Wharton, Edith. 1920. *The Age of Innocence.* Penguin, 1996.

———. *The House of Mirth.* 1905. Penguin, 1993.

———. *Italian Backgrounds.* 1905. Outlook, 2018.

———. *The Valley of Decision.* Scribner's, 1902.

———. "Roman Fever." 1934. *Roman Fever and Other Stories.* Scribner, 1997.

Williams, Andreá N. *Dividing Lines: Class Anxiety and Postbellum Black Fiction.* U of Michigan P, 2013.

Wilson, Andrew. 2003. *Beautiful Shadow: A Life of Patricia Highsmith.* Bloomsbury, 2010.

Woloch, Alex. *The One vs. the Many: Characters and the Space of the Protagonist in the Novel.* Princeton UP, 2003.

Woolf, Virginia. *Orlando.* 1928. Mariner Books, 1973.

Zanoni, Elizabeth. *Migrant Marketplaces: Food and Italians in North and South America.* U of Illinois P, 2018.

Index

accommodation, selective, 3, 79–80, 117, 131, 153–54
accomplices, 3–4
"Accomplices Not Allies: Abolishing the Ally Industrial Complex" (Indigenous Action Media), 3
African Americans, 7–10, 13, 64, 71, 168, 180, 191n18; in *Little Women*, 31–32; racial violence against, 1, 10, 113
African American writers: expected to address "Negro problem," 49–50, 65; passing novel, 14, 51, 71–72. *See also* Baldwin, James
African diaspora, 12, 60, 178–79
age and ageism, 161, 166–67, 194n9; "crones," 16, 146, 154–58
Alberghene, Janice M., 31–32
Alcott, Louisa May, 20, 21, 26–33, 68, 85, 184n14; blurred boundary with Marches, 26–27, 32; family influence on, 32, 183n5; marriage, resistance to, 40. See also *Little Women* (Alcott)
alienation, across generations, 153; of self, 53–54; social, 3, 59, 71, 95, 112, 116–18, 127, 144, 164, 189n1
Alito, Samuel, 93
alliances, 4, 45, 86, 111, 114, 126–28, 182; tentative, 177–78

allyship, 1–2; in *A Ciambra*, 177–82; Black-Italian, 9, 14, 50–51, 71, 89; Chicanx-Italian, 15, 113–14, 119, 129–31; failures of, 15, 119, 121–22, 126–29, 157–59, 180; Irish-Italian, 10–11, 16, 145–46, 152–53, 157–59; Jewish-Italian, 14, 51; Korean-Italian, 15, 76–77; literary, 13–14, 16, 72, 94, 101, 138–43, 161, 167; reciprocal, 1, 4, 10, 68, 105, 114, 146; Romani-Italian, 16; 161–70; in shared community, 86, 135, 146; as term, 3–4; truth-telling, 99; Uruguyan-Italian, 75–76, 81; witnessing as, 78, 88–89, 101, 119, 123, 146, 167, 175, 181
ally texts, 10; *Aloft* as, 78; *Ask the Dust* as, 113, 119; *The Fortunate Pilgrim* as, 152–53; *Giovanni's Room* as, 50, 70–73; *The Gods of Tango* as, 77–78, 81; *Paper Fish* as, 166; *Pictures of Fidelman* as, 70–73; *White Noise* as, 111, 138–43
Aloft (Lee), 15, 70, 94–101, 139, 188n10; allyship as "tough love" in, 70, 78, 94, 101; anti-Italian prejudice in, 95–96, 101; Battaglia/Battle family in, 94–96, 101–2; consumerism critiqued in, 103–5;

Aloft (Lee) *(continued)*
narrative self-determination in, 98–99; patriarchal values in, 100–103; reviews of, 78, 98. *See also* Lee, Chang-rae; *specific characters*
Americans abroad, Italy as deadly backdrop for, 26, 39, 43
anarchists, 9, 82
Anglo-Americans, 185n19; as category, 10, 24; nondiasporic, 14. *See also* "Italian novel," Anglo-American
Another Country (Baldwin), 60, 71
anti-Black racism, 15, 60, 66, 71–72, 93–94
anti-colonial struggles, 3–4
anti-Italian prejudice, 4, 93–96, 101
antiqueerness, 2, 14, 40–43, 51–53, 57, 60, 185n24
anti-Semitism, 71, 72, 94
Argentina: Black Argentines, 88–89; class issues, 77, 82, 89; Italian immigration to, 76–77, 79; "Latin race," bonds of, 79; slavery, history of, 88. *See also The Gods of Tango* (De Robertis)
Asian Americans, 11, 14, 78, 99–100
Ask the Dust (Fante), 15, 109–10, 169; as ally text, 113, 119; assimilation in, 115–19, 190n12; cognitive empathy in, 128; consumerism in, 125–29; diasporic identity in, 114–18, 190n12; historic backstory, 112–14; *It's All True* (film) and, 143–44; misreadings of, 130; primitivism attributed to Chicanx identity in, 113, 120, 130; toxic masculinity addressed in, 113–14, 119–31, 142, 144. *See also* Fante, John; DeLillo, Don
assimilation, 80–81; in *Aloft*, 95; in *Ask the Dust*, 115–19, 190n12; desire for, 118; expected by host country, 153; identity loss due to, 1; in James, 26; masculinity and, 121–22; resistance to, 77; Romani resistance to, 164; in *White Noise*, 111
The Assistant (Malamud), 50, 60
Atlantic Monthly, 27
Austen, Jane, 83

Baily, Samuel L., 79, 80
Baldwin, James, 2, 13, 129, 186n5; as accomplice, 3; expected to write about blackness, 49–50, 65; in Paris, 60; Works: *Another Country*, 60, 71, 186n9; *Giovanni's Room*, 14, 44; *Go Tell It on the Mountain*, 49; *Notes of a Native Son*, 60; "On Being 'White' . . . and Other Lies," 65–66. *See also Giovanni's Room* (Baldwin)
Barolini, Helen, 194–95n14
Barone, Dennis, 159, 192n25
Before Columbus Foundation, 11
Bellow, Saul, 72, 187n15
Benshoff, Harry M., 40
Berman, Jessica, 124
bicultural identities, 11; in *Little Women*, 26–27, 32
bildung (coming of age), 58
Black Argentines, 88–89
Black-Italian allyship, 9, 14, 50–51, 71, 89
Black Women, Writing and Identity (Davies), 12
Bona, Mary Jo, 11, 148, 161, 173–74
Boyce Davies, Carole, 12, 190n7
Brim, Matt, 53
Brooks, Ethel C., 162
Buchen, Irving H., 56, 186n6
Buckley, Jerome Hamilton, 58
Buenos Aires, Argentina: Italian fears of as dangerous, 84–86; Italian immigration to, 76–79; yellow fever,

87–88, 90. See also *The Gods of Tango*
Burkinabe diaspora, 177–78
Burkina Faso, 177, 178
Byrd, James, 93
By the Breath of Their Mouths (Bona), 11

California: commercial agriculture, 112, 189n6
Campiglia, Jo, 113
Cantrell, LaToya (Mayor of New Orleans), 1
capitalism, 42, 125–29, 184n11
Carpignano, Jonas, 177–82
Catholicism, 79, 117–18, 154–55, 190n13; Irish and Italian parallels and differences, 159, 190–91n13
CEA Critic, 27
A Century of Chicano History (Gonzalez and Fernandez), 129
Chesnutt, Charles W., 71
Chicanx, as term, 118
Chicanx diaspora, 2, 112–13, 118–19, 123, 127, 189–90n7, 190n11, 191n17
Chicanx-Italian allyship, 15, 113–14, 119, 129–31
A Ciambra (film), 177–82
citizenship, 5–6, 31, 82
Clark, Gregory, 183–84n6
class: in Argentina, 77, 82, 89; diaspora, intersection with, 87–88; disasters, inequality of, 141; failure of solidarity in favor of competition, 16, 126–29; intersectionality of gender and diasporic identities with, 172–73; intersection of gender and sexuality with, 22, 24, 39, 60, 90–92; markers of, 140–41; white-collar and blue-collar work, 102
class critique, 109; in *A Ciambra*, 180; in *Aloft*, 102–5; in *Ask the Dust*, 110, 125–27; in *Daisy Miller*, 22, 38, 184n7; in *The Gods of Tango*, 82–84, 87–92; in *Little Women*, 28–29; in "Roman Fever," 35; in *The Talented Mr. Ripley*, 39, 41–42; in *White Noise*, 139–43, 192n32
Clifford, James, 2–3, 80, 114, 117, 135, 154
Cocoliche (Spanish-Italian hybrid dialect), 79–80, 81
Cocoliche (stock literary character), 80
cognitive empathy, 41–42, 53, 55, 56, 128
conformity, 10, 78, 97, 126–28, 190n13
Connell, Raewyn, 110
consumerism: in *Aloft*, 103–5; in *Ask the Dust*, 125–29; in *White Noise*, 132–33, 144
Cosco, Joseph P., 12, 25–26
Cowart, David, 137, 189n20
Crenshaw, Kimberlé, 191n22
"crones," 16, 146, 154–58
Cruising Modernism (Trask), 13–14
"Cultural Identity and Diaspora" (Hall), 3
Cutter, Martha J., 10–11

Daisy Miller: A Study (James), 14, 19, 20, 21–27, 35, 37–38, 44, 66, 67, 98, 183–84n6, 183n2; class critique in, 22, 38, 184n7; Italians denigrated in, 24–25; masculine self-centeredness in, 23–24; protest elements in, 21–22; regulatory categories of womanhood in, 21–22, 24–25
Degout, Yasmin Y., 186n3
dehumanization, 99, 121–22, 164, 166
DeLillo, Don, 10, 15, 109, 131–38
De Robertis, Carolina, 2, 13, 72, 97, 187–88n5, 187n3; Latina and

De Robertis, Carolina *(continued)*
Uruguayan identity of, 15, 75–76, 81. See also *The Gods of Tango* (De Robertis)
De Rosa, Tina, 2, 13, 15–16, 144, 145, 161–70; as accomplice, 3; family history, 169–70. See also *Paper Fish* (De Rosa)
diaspora: class, intersection with, 87–88; as community experience, 3, 55; competition among groups, 110, 119, 126; definitions of, 2, 55, 116, 137–38; disability as, 174–75; double displacement, 51, 60, 69–70; dualist identity, 118; first-generation, 59, 153; geographic triangles, 59–60; hegemonic attempts to disrupt transnational communities of, 11–12; "ideal type," 2; immigration distinguished from, 80–81; as impossibility of return to homeland, 3, 12, 55, 81, 138, 151; interdiasporic relations, 3, 10, 45, 86, 132, 152–53, 157, 160–61, 170, 172–73, 181–82; intersection of, 109–10, 113, 119; lack of interethnic solidarity, 15, 119, 121–22, 126–29, 157–59, 180; men, effects on, 151; multigenerational history of, 3, 88, 96, 97, 104, 153; private, 137; queer, 50–51, 55, 183n4; rethinking sex through, 51–60; second-generation, 59–60, 65–66, 152–53, 189n1; social alienation, 3, 112, 116–18, 127, 144, 155, 164, 189n1; spirituality and, 117–18; transnational, 9–12, 55, 67–68, 95–96, 178–79, 182, 190n7; violence as cause of, 12, 20, 112, 114–15, 131, 158, 162; waves of, 67–68, 76; women's lack of interethnic solidarity, 157–58

"Diasporas in Modern Societies: Myths of Homeland and Return" (Safran), 2–3
diaspora studies, 5
dimensionality: in *Aloft*, 99; in *The Fortunate Pilgrim*, 175; in *Giovanni's Room*, 51, 61, 72; in *The Gods of Tango*, 75, 81, 83; in *Paper Fish*, 169, 175; in *Pictures of Fidelman*, 51, 61, 72; three-dimensional characters, 14, 27, 51; two-dimensional/flat characters, 16, 27, 29, 33, 35, 72, 75, 83, 96
disasters, class inequalities, 141
A Doll's House (Ibsen), 141, 192n33
Dreiser, Theodore, 28

"Edith Wharton's Italian Mask" (Vance), 33
Ellerby, Janet Mason, 35
Elsden, Annamaria Formichella, 37
emigration, as choice 20–21
Engles, Tim, 131, 140
English literature, 12, 36, 43–44, 61, 67, 101, 184n10. See also *specific authors*
Ermelino, Louisa, 147
ethnic studies, 5, 10–11
Europe, Americans as outsiders in, 24
"exalting" and "debasing" love affairs, 58

Factories in the Field (McWilliams), 189n6
false equivalences between diasporas, 4, 71–72, 88, 93, 179
Fante, John, 2, 10, 13, 109–10, 159, 168; letters of, 113, 117, 130–31, 190n8; "My Friend Bonito," 143. See also *Ask the Dust* (Fante)
feminism, 22, 27–29, 31, 44, 184n11; intersectional turn, 90–91, 149–50;

second-wave concerns, 28, 149, 171–72, 193n4
Fermaglich, Kirsten, 72
Fernandez, Raul E., 112, 129
Ferraro, Thomas J., 153, 193n3
fetishization, 84; of Black identity, 120; of Chicanx identity, 110, 120, 123; by children, 146, 155; cultural appropriation and, 165–66; of Italy, 38; of Italian identity, 27, 36, 38, 83; of nonwhite women's bodies, 120–21, 123; of Romani identity, 164–65
Filipinx diaspora, 15, 114, 122–23, 190n9
Forster, E. M., 85, 98, 188n14; *Works: Maurice*, 43; *A Room with a View*, 37, 43, 67, 69, 184n8; *Where Angels Fear to Tread* (Forster), 36, 43, 64, 99, 141, 184n8, 185–86n27, 187n11
The Fortunate Pilgrim (Puzo), 15–16, 145, 146–52, 171, 190n10; aging and gender, views of, 156–57; Colucci family, 159; fetishization in, 146, 155; gender role reversal in, 147; Irish Americans and anti-Irish prejudice in, 10, 146, 152–60; multigenerational focus of, 153–54; parallels between Irish and Italian immigrants in, 154–59; patriarchal values in, 147–50, 156; "women's work" valorized in, 149. *See also* Puzo, Mario
From the Margin: Writings in Italian Americana (Tamburri, Giordano, and Gardaphé), 4–5

Gardaphé, Fred, 4–5, 114, 117, 138, 189n4, 191n20; "Italian American Masculinities," 151
Garside, E. B., 130

gender, 14–15, 28, 31, 34–35; ableist assumptions for women, 174; aging, views of, 146, 156–57, 161, 166, 194n9; challenges to Italian American women's expected roles, 147–49; "crones," 16, 146, 154–58; feminine servitude, 170–72; "good woman" images, 147–48; intersection with class and sexuality, 22, 24, 39, 60, 90–92; intersection with diaspora, ethnicity, and race, 100, 121, 146–52, 167
gender identities, 77, 85–86, 90–91, 187–88n5, 187n3
GI Bill, 102
Giordano, Paolo A, 4–5
Giovanni's Room (Baldwin), 14, 44, 49–56, 81, 129, 186n3; as about Black identities, 49–50; as ally text, 50, 70–73; cognitive empathy in, 53, 55, 56; as critique of whiteness, 64–65; diaspora in, 50–51, 55, 60, 66–67; ending of, 55–56; naturalness of relationship in, 53–54; opening of, 51–52; passing in, 51, 52, 71–72; self-denial in, 52–53, 61; sexual identity, rethinking of, 41, 51–60, 71; southern Italian stereotype in, 61–63; as "white life novel," 50, 64. *See also* Baldwin, James
Giunta, Edvige, 172, 194n14, 195n21
Godfather franchise (Puzo), 145, 193n3
The Gods of Tango (De Robertis), 15, 75–78, 97; activist possibility in, 86, 89, 101; as ally text, 77–78, 81; cabaret scenes, 89–90; class stratification in, 82–84, 87–92; dimensionality of, 75, 81, 82; gender identies in, 77, 85–86, 90–91, 187–88n5, 187n3; hybridity

The Gods of Tango (De Robertis) *(continiued)*
in, 80, 86; scrutinizing diaspora and remaking *italianità* in, 79–86; sex workers in, 90–92; silence, ethical consideration of, 83. *See also* De Robertis, Carolina
Gonzalez, Gilbert G., 112, 129
Goscilo, Margaret, 44
Go Tell It on the Mountain (Baldwin), 49
Grasso, Linda, 28, 32
Greven, David, 41
Griffith, Michael, 10
Guglielmo, Jennifer, 7–8, 123
Guglielmo, Thomas A., 5, 63
Guide to Allyship (Lamont), 3
Guido Culture and Italian American Youth: From Bensonhurst to Jersey Shore (Tricarico), 93–94
"guido" subculture, 94

Hall, Donald E., 52
Hall, Stuart, 3, 81, 89, 151, 186n2, 188n7
Hawkins, Yusef, 10, 93
Henderson, Mae, 61
The Henry James Review, 21–22
heteronormativity, 50–53; cognitive empathy, failure of, 53; postwar, 14, 16, 50, 52, 57, 61, 64, 72; in *Giovanni's Room*, 52, 53; in *Pictures of Fidelman*, 56–59; in *The Talented Mr. Ripley*, 42–43
Hicks, Granville, 49
Highsmith, Patricia, 14, 20, 26, 285n23; Works: *The Price of Salt*, 40; *Ripley* series, 41; *The Talented Mr. Ripley*, 14, 38–44, 53
historical context, 5–10; Othering of Italian Americans, 7–8; unification of Italy and, 6–7; white privilege and citizenship, 5–6

The History of White People (Painter), 65–66
Hitler, Adolf, 139
Holocaust, 162
homeland: adopted, 3, 4, 6; imagined, 5; impossibility of return to, 3, 12, 55, 81, 138, 151; longing for, 55, 111, 192n25; longing for by Italians in Argentina, 79, 80–81; positive return to, 58–59; within self, 59–60
The House Behind the Cedars (Chesnutt), 71
Hughes, Langston, 49
Human Rights Watch, 178
hybridity, 6, 86, 118

Ibsen, Henrik, 141, 192n33
Ickes, William, 41
"I Delitti della Razza Bianca" ("Crimes of the White Race") (Salerno), 9
identity, 1; deracialized, self-indulgent, 15, 109, 111, 128, 139–40, 143, 144; diasporic, 15, 55, 66–67, 70, 78, 89, 111, 151, 167, 180; dualist, 118; gender identities, 77, 85–86, 90–91, 187–88n5, 187n3; sexual, 41–43, 51–60, 71; whiteness as fictionalized shared, 65
Identity, Diaspora and Return in American Literature (ed. Oliver-Rotger), 11
immigration, 4–7, 10; alternative focus on diaspora, 12; American literary production and, 12–13; to Argentina and Uruguay, 76–79; Chicanx, 2, 112–13, 118–19, 123, 127, 189–90n7, 190n11, 191n17; diaspora distinguished from, 20–21, 80–81; Italy's unification as cause of, 114, 116; naturalization and whiteness, 6; Roma excluded

under US policy, 162; of Italians to United States, 4, 6, 62, 67–68, 71; U.S. Immigration Commission, 63; waves of, 67–68, 76; white on arrival (WOA), 6, 71

Indigenous Action Media, 3

Industrial Revolution, 22

International Ladies' Garment Workers' Union, Italian American branch, 9

intersectionality: of age, gender, and ethnicity, 146; of class, gender, and diasporic identities, 172–73; of class, gender, and sexuality, 22, 24, 39, 60, 90–92; of racism and sexism, 118

In the Name of the Mother (Pardini), 11

"invisible blackness," 64–65, 168, 194n11

Ireland, 154, 158–59, 194n8

Irish Americans: anti-Irish sentiment against, 154–55; employment discrimination against, 154; in *The Fortunate Pilgrim*, 10, 146, 152–60

Irish diaspora, 16, 32, 154–59; Catholicism and, 159, 190–91n13

Irish Potato Famine, 154

ironic stance, 124

Italian Americans: ambiguous racialization of, 64–65; anti-Black racism and, 71; anti-Semitism among, 71, 94; between marginalized and oppressor, 5; ethno-religious prejudices, 50; exhortations to remember, 4; "good woman" images, 147–48; "invisible blackness," 64–65, 168, 194n11; in oppressor role, 4; Othering of, 7–8, 12–13; as racial traitors, 9; twenty-first century prejudice encountered by, 92–93; white privilege and, 5–6, 11–12, 15, 38, 65–66, 87, 93. *See also* Italian diasporic community

Italian American studies, 2, 5

Irish-Italian allyship, 10–11, 16, 145–46, 152–53, 157–59

Italian Backgrounds (Wharton), 33, 36–37

Italian diasporic community, 1, 4, 7, 9, 13, 16, 77, 113, 116, 144, 163. *See also* Italian Americans; *italianità*; Italians; southern Italians

italianità: in *Aloft*, 94, 96, 99; Argentine vision of, 79; conformist species of, 78; defining, 4–6; distortions of by Anglo-American writers, 12–14, 27, 30, 35, 38, 43, 68; in *Giovanni's Room*, 67; in *The Gods of Tango*, 79–86; multiethnic version of, 181; not central concern in non-Italian writings, 19–20; in *Pictures of Fidelman*, 69, 72; reinterrogation/rewriting of, 16, 50–51, 60, 68, 75, 81, 99, 105, 146, 177; vis-a-vis other diasporic communities, 86

"Italian novel," Anglo-American, 16, 21, 45, 51, 61–70, 146–47; effect on audience, 20, 70–71; masculinist bent, 19; in twenty-first century, 72, 77–78, 105. *See also Aloft* (Lee); *Daisy Miller: A Study* (James); *Giovanni's Room* (Baldwin); *The Gods of Tango* (De Robertis); *Little Women* (Alcott); *Pictures of Fidelman* (Malamud); "Roman Fever" (Wharton); *A Room with a View* (Forster); *The Talented Mr. Ripley* (Highsmith); *Where Angels Fear to Tread* (Forster)

Italians: 79, 117–18, 154–55, 159, 190–91n13; instrumentalist view of, 35–36; as Other, 19; passionate stereotype of, 26, 35, 62, 82, 120, 124, 126, 184–85n17; Protestant, 159, 194n12; as rebellious, 22, 31;

Italians *(continued)*
  romanticized, 12; as violent, 50, 64, 68
Italy: Alcott's visit to, 32–33; anti-Semitism in, 72; as backdrop for American protagonists, 26, 35, 38, 67; Calabria, 177; as dangerous/deadly, 26, 34, 39, 43–44, 63–64; elitist impulse in, 6–7; genocide, World War II, 72; hate crimes in, 178; *il boom*, 39, 185n21; Ireland, parallels with, 154, 158–59; Italian America inseparable from, 70; mafia and underground economy, 177–78, 180; modernity of, 38–39, 68, 185n19; nationalism and xenophobia on rise, 181; Anglo-Americans' primitivist views of, 36, 185nn19, 21; Romani migration to, 164; romantic nationalists, 6–7; as site of liberation, 37–38, 42, 43, 51, 72–73; southern Italians stereotyped within, 6, 62–64, 68–69, 155; unification, 4, 6–7, 30, 84, 155; unification as cause of diaspora, 114, 116; unification trivialized, 32–33, 68
It's All True (film, Welles), 143–44

Jacobson, Matthew Frye, 6, 7, 117
James, Henry, 14, 19, 21–26, 70, 183n4; *The Ambassadors*, 185n22; on "emigration," 20–21; Italian immigrants essentialized by, 26. See also *Daisy Miller: A Study*
Jane Eyre (Brontë), 184n10
Japanese Americans, 8, 125
Jerng, Mark C., 78
Jewish American literary tropes, 51, 72
Jewish diaspora, 2, 15, 50–51, 59, 69, 71–72, 99, 123, 128, 160, 193n2; American and Israeli branches of, 59–60, 69; encounter with Italian American aggression in Chicago, 8–9
Jewish-Italian allyship, 14, 51
Johnson, Lisa, 21–22, 25
Johnson-Roullier, Cyraina E., 61
Justice Department, 9

Kane, Gregory, 93
Kelly, Hillary, 27
King, Martin Luther, Jr., 86
Korean diaspora, 15, 76–77, 96
Korean-Italian allyship, 15, 76–77

labor solidarity, 9–10, 82, 128
Labriola, Arturo, 9
LaGumina, Salvatore J., 92
Lamont, Amelie, 3
Larsen, Nella, 71
"Latin race," 79
"Latin races," 20, 26
Lawrence, D. H., 19, 20, 26; *Works:* "On the Lago di Garda," 183n3; *Twilight in Italy*, 19, 183n1, 184n9, 188n16
Lee, A. Robert, 5
Lee, Chang-rae, 2, 4, 13, 70, 72, 94–101, 188n10, 188n15; Italian American relatives, 76–77. See also *Aloft* (Lee)
Lee, Hermione, 33
Lee, James Kyung-Jin, 14
Lee, Ronald, 162
Lentricchia, Frank, 134
L'Era Nuova, 9
Li, Stephanie, 65
liberation, Italy as site of, 37–38, 42–43, 51, 72–73; southern Italian stereotype, 61–63
Little Women (Alcott), 20, 26–33, 38, 44; African Americans in, 31–32; class considerations in,

28–29; tension between social critique and social realities in, 27–28; dimensionality in secondary characters, 27, 29, 33; feminist writings about, 27–31; film version, 28, 29; Italians, treatment of, 26–33, 37–38, 44, 68. *See also* Alcott, Louisa May; *specific characters*
Los Angeles, 112–13, 125
Los Angeles Review of Books, 130
Lost and Found in Translation (Cutter), 10
Louis, Joe, 93

The Madonna of 115th Street (Orsi), 147–48
mafia stereotypes, 93, 163
Malamud, Bernard, 2, 13, 14, 44, 49, 50; *The Assistant,* 50, 60. See also *Pictures of Fidelman* (Malamud)
malaria ("Roman fever"), 23, 25–26, 34, 43, 100
The Marble Faun (Hawthorne), 26
Martin, Robert K., 185–86n27
Martínez, Elizabeth, 118
masculinity, 109–10, 113–14; encounter between Italian American and Chicano, 121–22; in *The Fortunate Pilgrim,* 149–50; "rest cures" for "nervous" complaints, 150–51; sensitivity and tenderness, 150, 172–73; toxic, 15, 109–10, 113–14, 119–31, 124, 142, 144, 189n3, 193n5
Massachusetts mill community, 9–10
Maurice (Forster), 43
May, Jill P., 27
McCarthy, Cormac, 10
McWilliams, Carey, 189n6
MELUS: Multi-Ethnic Literature of the United States, 11

"Men Explain Things to Me" (Solnit), 152
Mexican American War, 112, 129
Mexico: Mexican Revolution, 189n5; US neo-imperialist foreign policy in, 112, 115, 122, 189n6. *See also* Chicanx diaspora
Meyer, Lisa, 166
Migrant Marketplaces (Zanoni), 79
Minghella, Anthony, 38–39, 185nn19, 20, 21, 24
"minorities," white rhetoric of, 9
Mitchell, Silas Weir, 150
modernist fiction, 123–24
Monthly Summary of Events and Trends in Race Relations (Fisk University), 8
multigenerational histories, 3, 88, 96, 97, 104, 153
Mussolini, Benito, 36, 37
"My Friend Bonito" (Fante), 143

National Organization for Women (NOW), 166
naturalism, American, 28
Nelson, Lynn Hankinson, 156
New Orleans: 1891 murder of Italian Americans, 1, 7
New Queer Cinema, 40
New York Magazine, 27
New York Times, 7, 49
Notes of a Native Son (Baldwin), 60

"off-white" status, 16, 162, 168–69
Oliver-Rotger, Maria Antònia, 11
"On Being 'White' . . . and Other Lies" (Baldwin), 65–66
online discussions, 3, 27
Orlando (Woolf), 68, 192n28
Orsi, Robert Anthony, 147–48
Othering, 19, 60; by children, 154–55, 162; counterdiscourse to, 82; of

Othering *(continued)*
    disasters, 141; fetishization, 84; of Italian Americans, 7–8, 12–13; of Naples and Rome, 36; of older women, 146; by other diasporic communities, 161–62; of Romani diasporic community, 162–64
"outsider" characters, 24, 59, 78, 82, 139

Pahl, Dennis, 22, 23
Painter, Nell Irvin, 65–66
pan-African Black consciousness, 12, 178–79
Paper Fish (De Rosa), 15–16, 145, 161–70; as ally text, 16, 161–70, 175; anti-Romani prejudice in, 146, 170, 172; cross-cultural commentary in, 170; disability and illness in, 173–74; feminine servitude in, 170–72; marginalization of, 161, 195n23; textual life of, 166. *See also* De Rosa, Tina
Paraguayan War, 88
Pardini, Samuele F. S., 11, 64–65
Paris, 62; anti-Black racism in, 60; as queer "cultural homeland," 55
Passing (Larsen), 71
passing novel, 51, 52, 71–72
Perkins Gilman, Charlotte, 151
Pictures of Fidelman (Malamud), 14, 50–51, 55–60, 186n6, 1887n13; as ally text, 70–73; diaspora in, 56, 59–60; heterosexual liaisons in, 57–58; self-recognition through queer experience in, 58–59; stereotypes made fun of, 68–69. *See also* Malamud, Bernard
picturesque, the, 12, 20, 25–26, 36, 63
Ploughshares, 27
police targeting of diasporic groups, 178

Portnoy's Complaint (Roth), 72
The Price of Salt (Highsmith), 40
Pride and Prejudice (Austen), 83
primitivism: Anglo-American views of Italy, 36, 185nn19, 21; attributed to Chicanx people, 113, 120, 130; attributed to Romani people, 162
Proclamation of Apology (New Orleans), 1
progressivism, 118–19; literary, 60
Puzo, Mario, 10, 13, 144, 146–52, 190n10; *Godfather* franchise, 145, 193n3; mother's influence on, 145. *See also* *The Fortunate Pilgrim* (Puzo)

queer diaspora, 50–51, 55, 59, 183n4

racial traitors, 9, 25–26
racism: anti-Black, 15, 60, 66, 71–72, 93–94; Italian American participation in, 2, 8–9, 16, 94, 110, 115, 122–23, 181; against Italian Americans, 9, 95–96, 110; fallacy of "reverse racism," 93; as replication of trauma, 122–23; structural, 8, 11, 78, 93–94
rape culture, 124
reciprocal representations, 1, 4, 10, 16, 68, 105, 109, 114, 146
Reed, Ishmael, 11
Rodríguez, Luis J., 129
Roediger, David R., 7
Rohy, Valerie, 186n8
"Roman Fever" (Wharton), 14, 20, 33–38, 44, 68, 100; "Campolieri boy," 35–36, 68, 83
romantic nationalists, 6–7
Romani diaspora, 16, 146, 161–62, 170; in *A Ciambra*, 177–82; fetishization of, 164–65; Italian American Othering of, 162–64; in Italy, 164; origins of, 193n1;

perceived as "off-white," 16, 162, 168–69
Romani-Italian allyship, 16, 161–70
Rome: as dangerous/deadly, 26, 34; fetishization of, 36, 38; modernity of, 36–37; Otherness of, 36; primitivist views of, 36, 185nn19, 21; social experiment permitted in, 37–38; Wharton's descriptions of, 36–37
A Room with a View (Forster), 37, 43, 67, 69, 183n8
Ross, Edward, 64
Rossi, Dino, 92–93
Rossini, Daniela, 20
Roth, Philip, 69–70, 72

Safran, William, 2–3, 55, 79, 95, 137–38
Saito, Stephen, 179–80, 181
Scambray, Kenneth, 162–63
Schenkar, Joan, 40
Seize the Day (Bellow), 72, 187n15
selective accommodation, 3, 79–80, 131, 189n1
sexuality: intersection with class and gender, 90–92; Italians as passionate, sensuous lovers, 35, 184–85n17; premarital sex in early twentieth-century novels, 34–35, 184n16; sexual identity, rethinking of, 39–43, 51–60, 71, 185n23
Sister Carrie (Dreiser), 28
The Sisters Mallone (Ermelino), 147
social alienation, 3, 59, 71, 95, 112, 116–18, 127, 144, 164, 189n1
social Darwinism, 6–7, 42
social mobility, 16, 22, 125–29, 183–84n6
social protest, 2, 10, 14–15, 21–22, 28, 45, 82, 91, 95, 110, 129
socioeconomic injustice, 2, 78, 41, 90–92, 94, 114–15, 126–28, 181

socioeconomic status, 14–15, 24, 78, 181; in *Aloft*, 105, 109–10; in *Ask the Dust*, 125–28; in *The Gods of Tango*, 90–94; New York elite, 35; in *The Talented Mr. Ripley*, 41–43
Sohn, Stephen Hong, 98, 99, 188n17
solidarity, 1–3, 9–12, 61, 71, 77, 86, 99, 105, 114, 131, 135, 146, 166, 179–81
Solnit, Rebecca, 152
The Son Also Rises (Clark), 183–84n6
southern Italians, 4–5, 20, 154–55; Anglo-American liberation and stereotypes of, 61–63; pseudoscientific attitudes toward, 6–7, 64; stereotyped within Italy, 6, 62–64, 68–69, 155
Spinelli, Alexian Santino, 178
status fixity, 13–14
Sternberg, Rob, 130
structural inequalities: Italy, 180–81; United States, 78, 93, 115
Sullam, Levis, 187n16
Susina, Jan, 30–31

Tagliabue, Paul, 93
The Talented Mr. Ripley (Highsmith), 14, 20, 38–45; antiqueerness and homophobia addressed in, 40–43; class critique in, 39, 41–42; deceptively complex plot, 39; film adaptation of, 38–39, 40, 185n24; "mind-reading"/cognitive empathy in, 41–42, 53; Naples and Rome depicted in, 26
Tamburri, Anthony Julian, 4–5
The Theory of the Leisure Class (Veblen), 125–26, 192n26
Tirabassi, Maddalena, 184n13
"tough love," allyship as 4, 15, 93–94; in *Aloft*, 70, 78, 94, 101; in *Ask the Dust*, 131; in *Pictures of Fidelman*, 70

Tracey, Janey, 27
translation, 10–11
Trask, Michael, 13–14, 40, 185n24
travel narratives, 12, 20; *Italian Backgrounds* (Wharton), 33, 36–37; picturesque in, 25; *Twilight in Italy* (Lawrence), 19, 183nn1, 3, 184n9, 188n16
Tricarico, Donald, 93–94
Twilight in Italy (Lawrence), 19, 183nn1, 3, 184n9, 188n16

United States: anti-Black racism in, 15, 60, 66, 71–72, 93–94; anti-Catholic sentiment in, 79; anti-Chicanx sentiment in, 113; anti-Italian prejudice in, 1, 4, 7, 12, 93–96, 101, 114, 144, 154, 191n13; anti-Semitism in, 71, 72, 94; fallacy of "reverse racism," 93; heteronormativity of, 52; Immigration Commission report (1911), 63; Japanese Americans in, 8, 125; Mexico, neo-imperialist foreign policy in, 112, 115, 122; postmodern America, 131–34; Roma excluded under immigration policy, 162; social hierarchy, 22–23; social mobility, narrative of, 22–23; structural inequalities, 78, 93, 115; white on arrival (WOA), 6, 71; youth as rulers, 157
unreliability, narrative, 62, 123–24, 128, 139, 189n2
Uruguyan-Italian allyship, 75–76, 81
U.S. Immigration Commission, 63

The Valley of Decision (Wharton), 33
Vance, William L., 33
Veblen, Thorstein, 125–26, 192n26
Verdicchio, Pasquale, 121

victimization, historicized experience of, 72
violence: against African Americans, 1, 10, 112–13, 131, 158, 162; against Black Argentines, 88; anti-Chicanx, 113; anti-Romani and anti-Burkinabe, 178; as cause of diasporas, 12, 20, 112, 114–15, 131, 158, 162; economic, by Italy, 116, 131, 158–59; economic, by United States, 112; erosion of self linked to, 41; by Italian Americans against African Americans, 10; Italians stereotypically linked with, 50, 64, 68, 82; toxic masculinity and, 110, 142
Vulture, 27

Walker, Francis Amasa, 7
Washington, Bryan R., 186n4
Welles, Orson, 143–44
"We Regret to Inform You That *Little Women* Is Not a Feminist Novel," 27
Wharton, Edith, 14, 20, 33–38, 85; Works: *Italian Backgrounds*, 33, 36–37; "Roman Fever," 14, 20, 33–38, 44, 68, 100; *The Valley of Decision*, 33
Where Angels Fear to Tread (Forster), 36, 43, 64, 141, 184n8, 185–86n27, 187n11; third-person narrator, 99
white ethnic writers, scholarly treatment of, 10–11
whiteness, 9; destabilized by "invisible blackness," 64–65; distinct European identities vs., 65–66, 94
Whiteness of a Different Color (Jacobson), 6
White Noise (DeLillo), 15, 109, 110–11, 131–38; as ally text, 138–43;

consumerism in, 132–33, 144; diasporic elements in, 111, 133–43; "expert" concept in, 133–34, 136; fear of death in, 111, 135–36; mall scene, 133, 142, 192n27; plot of, 135–36; routine/ritual in, 131–32, 136–37, 140; satirization of race, class, and gender, 139–43, 192n32; toxic cloud episode, 134–36; toxic masculinity in, 142

white on arrival (WOA), 6, 65, 71

white privilege: citizenship as, 5–6; of Italian Americans, 5–6, 11–12, 15, 38, 65–66, 87, 93; of Italian Argentines 78, 79, 87; of white men, 131, 140

white supremacy: defense of white women as excuse for, 121–22; disruption of and resistance to, 109, 119, 123–24, 129, 144; fetishization of nonwhite bodies, 120–21, 146, 162, 164–65, 175; intersection of diasporas and, 119; Italian immigrants' upholding of and participation in, 8, 11, 14, 66, 78, 87, 93, 99, 109, 110, 119–23, 144, 181; Italian American writers' resistance to, 13; rage at deflected onto other diasporas, 114; rewriting of "Italian novel" and, 99

Williams, Andreá, 14

witnessing, as allyship, 78, 88–89, 101, 119, 123, 146, 167, 175, 181

Woloch, Alex, 83

women authors: feminist debates about, 27–29; United States, 19–20. *See also* Alcott, Louisa May; De Robertis, Carolina; De Rosa, Tina; Highsmith, Patricia; Wharton, Edith

Woolf, Virginia, 68, 187n13, 192n28

working class, 6, 9, 13–14, 29, 50, 88–90, 102, 123–29, 140, 163

Working Toward Whiteness (Roediger), 6

World Health Organization, 156

World War I, 36–37, 44

World War II, 8, 72, 113, 163

"The Yellow Wall-paper" (Perkins Gilman), 151

Zanoni, Elizabeth, 79

Žižek, Slavoj, 41, 185n26